Everyw
Noghwhere Bodili

JASON de HAAN

CONTRIBUTORS

Nicholas Brown
David Diviney
Ryan Doherty
Candice Hopkins
Crystal Mowry
Richard Rhodes
Gustaf Sobin

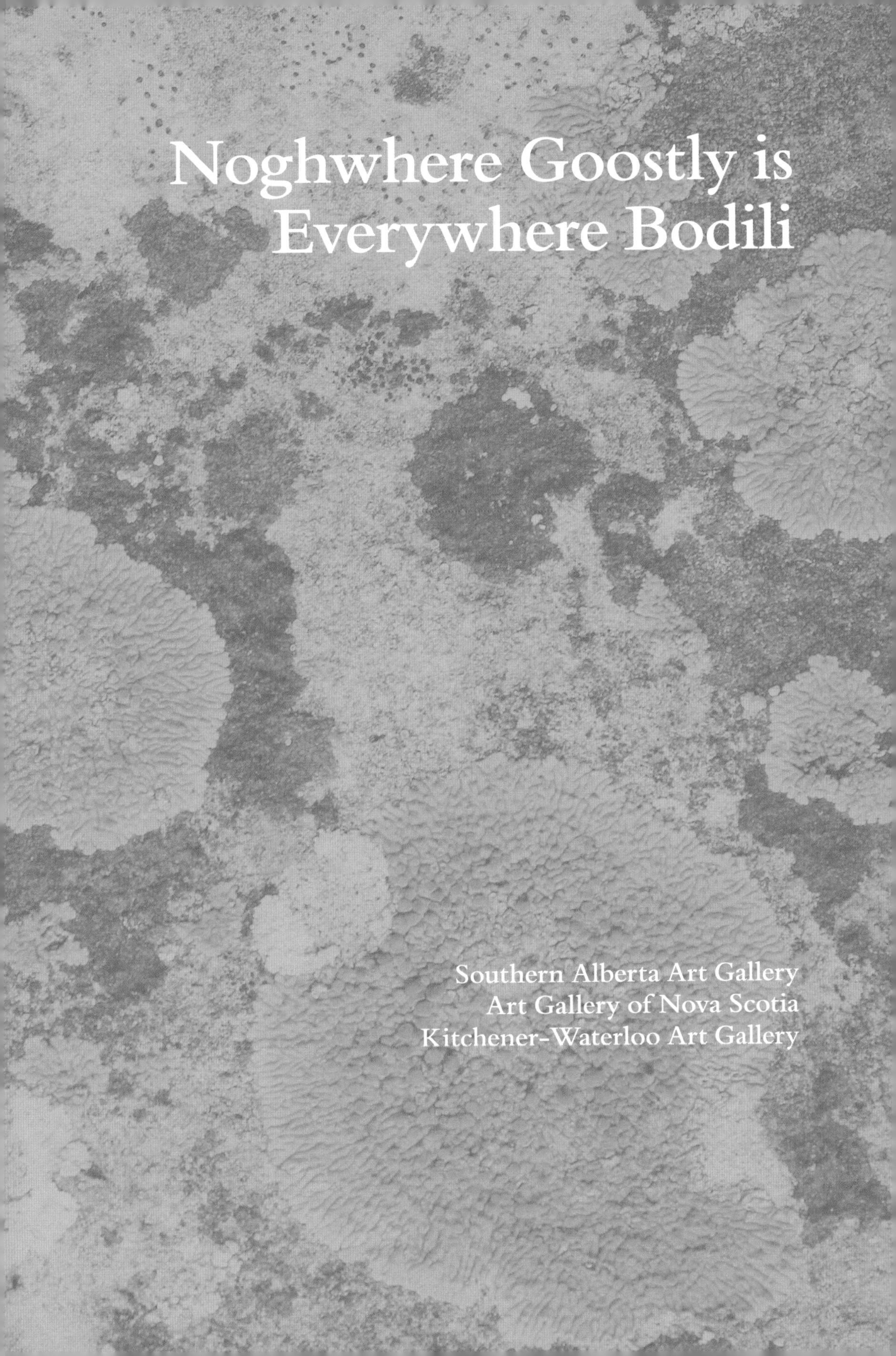

Noghwhere Goostly is Everywhere Bodili

Southern Alberta Art Gallery
Art Gallery of Nova Scotia
Kitchener-Waterloo Art Gallery

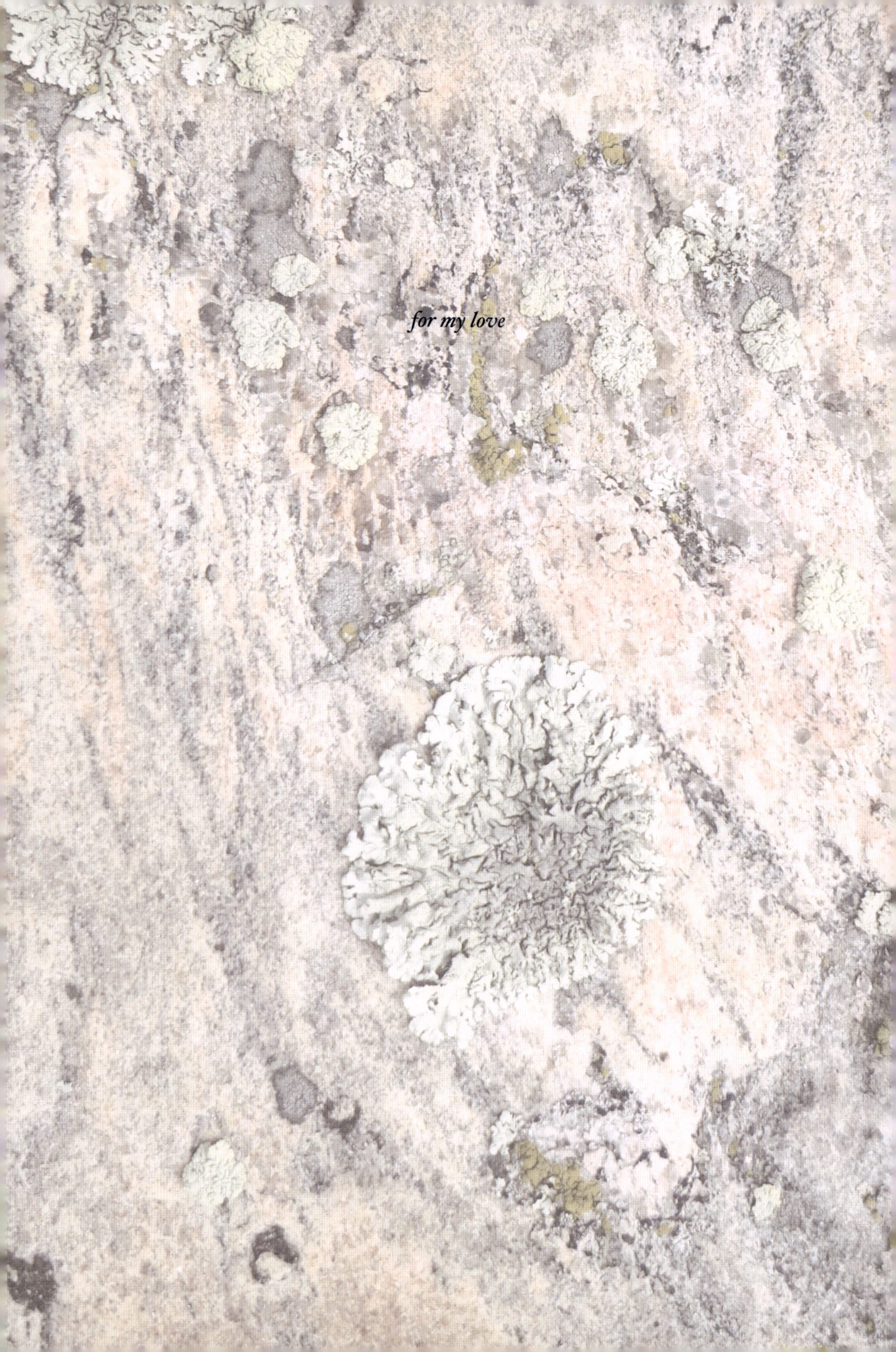

for my love

Everywhere Bodili is Noghwhere Goostly

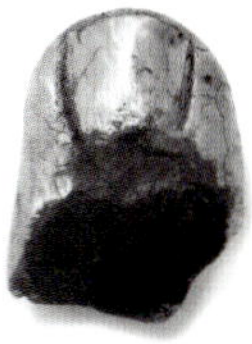

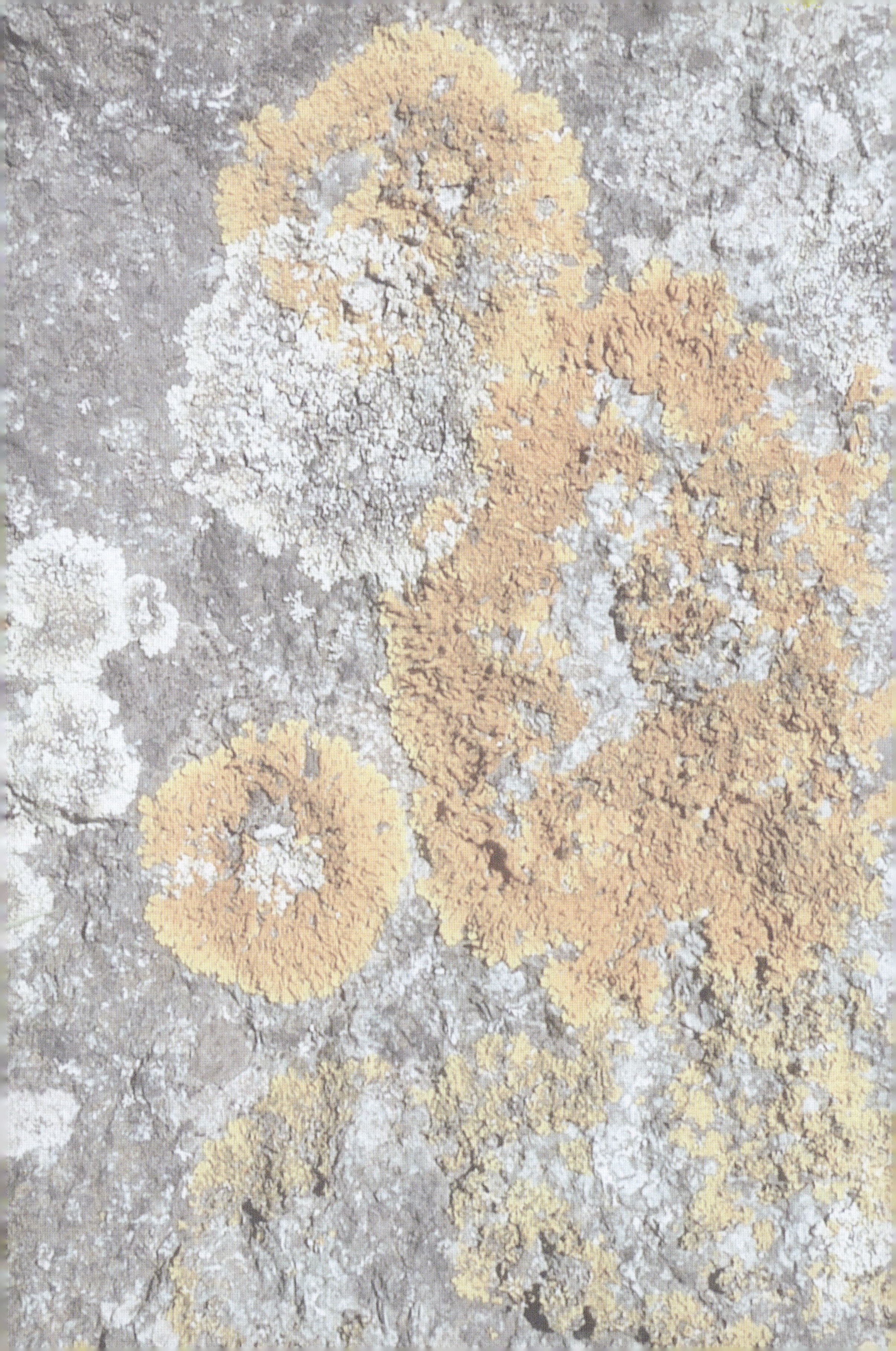

The Skull with the Seashell Ear

Gustaf Sobin

We're duly forewarned. Culture, in the eyes of archeologists, refers exclusively to material culture: to the little we can glean and, upon gleaning, interpret from those vast, subterranean warehouses of mute artifact. Long since removed from any sociocultural context whatsoever, the artifact, be it bone, flint, or the charred tube of some steatite bead, reaches us bereft of instigating factors—language, gesture, ritual. For all intents and purposes, the artifact reaches us blank. It can, of course, be dated. Thanks to thermoluminescent and radiocarbon analyses, a time frame can usually be established. Furthermore, the artifact itself can be compared, typologically speaking, to other artifacts. One bit of material evidence can be brought to substantiate, to testify for another. The artifact remains, nonetheless, an essentially mute object: a thing in a taxonomy of things, methodically numbered, classified, relegated. It belongs, ultimately, to nothing more than inventory itself.

Occasionally, though, an object seems to break free from all such relegation. From the tight circle of so many given, scientific determinants, it will assert itself at a depth, a dimension, entirely its own. Such is the case with a skull discovered in 1955 by archeologists excavating a megalithic chamber tomb at Roque d'Aille in the Var. The skull, unearthed from the lowest and consequently earliest stratigraphic layer, had quite clearly undergone cremation. Exposed to the latent heat of a pyre of less than 500 degrees centigrade, the skull, according to modern analyses, hadn't suffered the cellular decomposition that's invariably brought on by higher temperatures. Calcined, it had done little more than blacken.

But it's not the relatively commonplace discovery of a Neolithic skull, dating from the third millennium B.C., that so astonishes us today. It's not even the fact that the skull, upon examination, turned out to be trepanned. It had been carved open, apparently, with the aid of a rough flint—a primitive crown saw—and the brain had been operated on for an estimated period of three hours. The whole intervention had left a cicatrice nine centimeters long. No, it's neither the black skull nor the jagged scar that runs like some kind of virulent root about one side of the skull plate that so fascinates us today, but the ear, the artificial ear, that once locked into the left side of that hollow, black receptacle. Carved from a seashell, the spondylus Graederopus, its artisan had used the shell's thick hinge to replicate the earlobe and its shallow vault to imitate the concavity of the ear's outer whorl. Ironically enough, the external ear is also known, anatomically, as a concha.

We're left examining, finally, a delicate prosthesis, one of the earliest artificial members ever discovered. It measures sixty-five by thirty-six millimeters: approximately the measurements of an average human ear. Paleopathologists have determined that the subject of this conchate device was almost certainly a woman, a young woman. Furthermore, these specialists are convinced that the woman had not only survived that harrowing "open brain" operation, but had gone on to live for many years, for they've detected on the underside of that artificial organ tiny microscopic traces of patina due, unquestionably, to wear. Was this the result

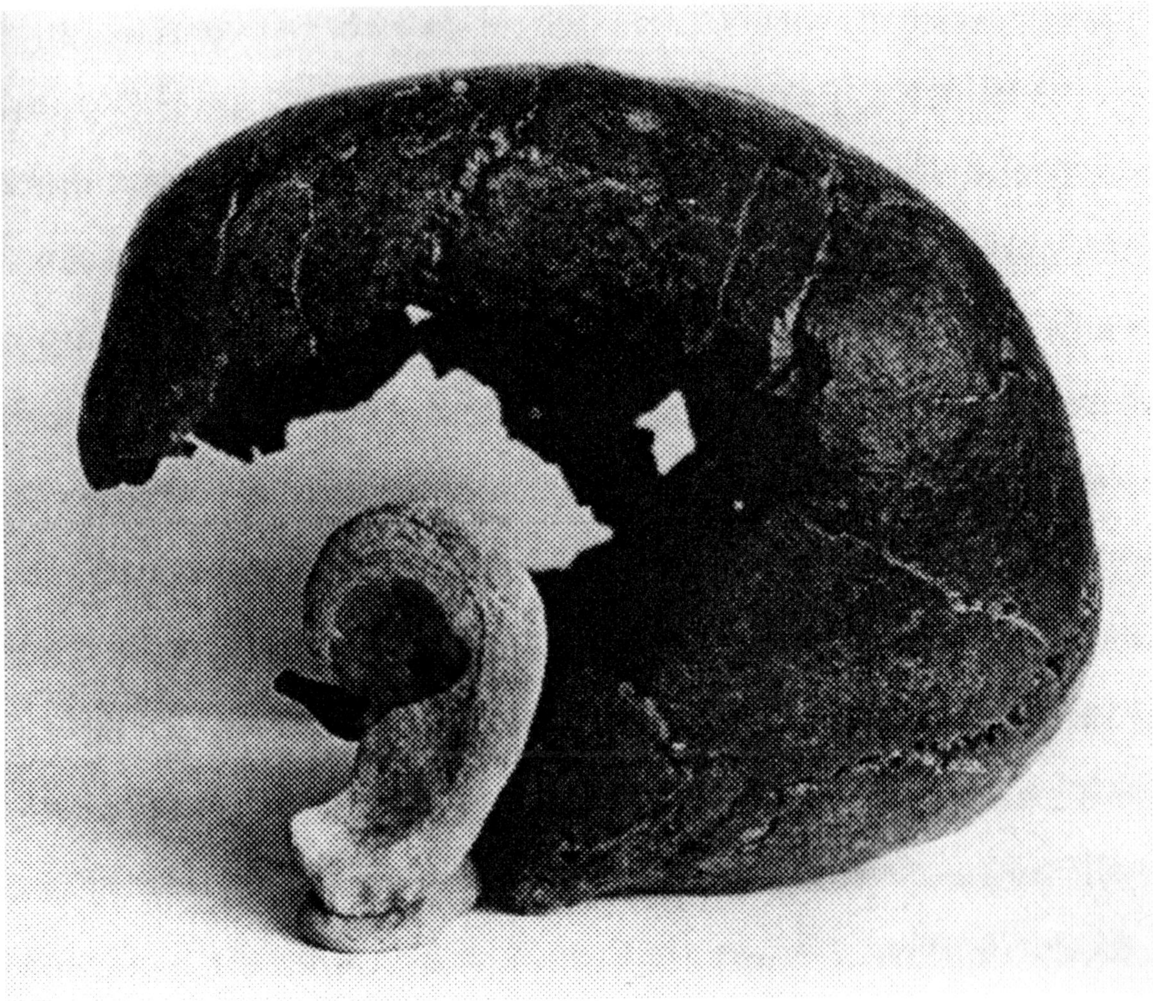

of simple abrasion (the mechanical rub of one surface against another) or the deliberate toying, on the young woman's part, with her curious appendage? Had she fondled its slick underside so often that specialists—peering through electromagnetic microscopes five thousand years later—would pick up traces of the infinitesimal luster left there by the play of her fingertips? By the roll of her thumb and forefinger over its nacreous lip?

Who was she, we might ask ourselves? Given her spectacular attribute, had she enjoyed within her given community a particular status? Was she invested, for instance, with divinatory powers? The ability to hear what others couldn't? To decipher, say, the opaque messages emanating out of rock or, even likelier, out of water, that element for which she was so expressly equipped? Yes, a medium of sorts, such as one might encounter in ethnological studies: one, that is, whose very powers had arisen out of some initial impediment.

We know, in fact, so very little. Held to a science that refuses to speculate, to consider any hypotheses whatsoever, we're left, finally, with nothing more than the burnt-out husk of a human skull and its curious, hand-carved appendage. We're left (as we're left all too often) with the illegible relic of some extinct civilization. It's as if a curtain had been resolutely drawn between the known and the unknown, between the material fact and the conditions that once generated that fact. It's as if, on methodology alone, we've been denied access to the immense fields of the possible, the probable—to an intuitive reading of a world that itself was constituted upon an uninterrupted series of intuited postulates.

We go on asking, though, don't we? Go on wondering. Was she tall, handsome? Were her eyes green, black, a deep pellucid blue? More pertinently, did she conceal the iridescent whorl of her artificial ear in a wave of hair or, to the contrary, exhibit it proudly, even vainly, under a high, piled, stick-pinned chignon? What extrasocial functions might she have performed? What shamanistic powers, exercised? Our questions, of course, can only go unanswered. But aren't the questions alone so much richer than the mean trickle of "verifiable fact" that the archeologists have offered us? Might we even come to "cherish the questions themselves," as Rilke once advised his young poet, "like closed rooms, like books written in a very strange tongue"?[1]

Might we even begin constituting, indeed, a collection, an entire library of questions? A whole, inexhaustible archive devoted exclusively to wonder, to query, to the unlimited breadth of human speculation? For the curtain that has fallen between the unknown and the known, between the magnitude of our questions and the paucity of our answers, affects not only archeology but every other field of human endeavor as well. As a result, we've grown estranged from origins, deprived of even the vaguest glimpses of those first, founding landscapes. Today, nothing can be acknowledged that hasn't first been processed, electronically channeled, compiled. We're on the far side, now, of inception. It's as if the dark, floating universe from which humankind has always drawn solace and the impalpable reflection of its own deepest identities has entirely vanished.

The issue itself is paramount. Have we been discussing the charred remnants of a prehistoric skull and its auricular prosthesis, or the relics, say, of some Neolithic medium, some priestess both consulted and revered for her extrasensory powers? Have we been discussing, in short, bones, or breath: detrital remainders, or the delicate apparatus of one who might well have been charged with the reception of the weightless, the evanescent, the impalpable? The question alone is well worth asking. It might, in turn, lead us through the drawn curtains themselves. Might bring us onto an ontological level of reasoning in which—at its very limits—we might encounter traces of our own long since absconded identity.

[1] Rainer Maria Rilke, *Letters to a Young Poet*, trans. Reginals Snell (London: Sidgwick and Jackson, 1945), 21.

The archeological materials for this essay have been drawn from Odile Roudil and Georges Bérard, *Les sépultures mégalithiques du Var* (Paris: Editions du CNRS, 1981), 102–106.

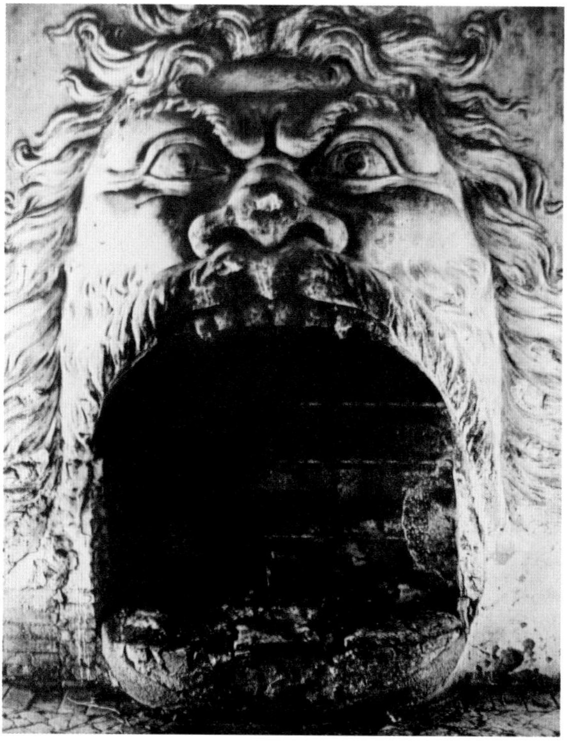

In Conversation

with
Jason de Haan, David Diviney,
Ryan Doherty and Crystal Mowry

Crystal Mowry: The subject of silence seems like an appropriate place to start a conversation about the images and strategies that have a subtle presence in your work. In the text by Gustaf Sobin there is a reference to the inherent silence of an artifact once it is categorized—I believe he refers to such objects as being "essentially mute." One gets the sense that you approach object-making in a way that engages with that notion. Your work often suggests the distillation of time, yet it resists the stasis that is associated with taxonomy. Might there be any truth to that perception?

Jason de Haan: I like very much beginning this discussion with silence and the muting of objects. I think the important distinction here is that Sobin is talking about historical objects being classified within a particular system that strips them of the power or status that they once possessed. Introducing new forms into the world as art is something different, of course, but that is not to say that silence has not been at the fore of my mind in recent making. The muteness that Sobin describes is nearly total silence, but silence is far from mute—it includes patience, duration, pause, quietness, slowness and even gentleness; these are qualities that are inherent in several of the processes that I am occupied with. My interest is in engaging these to a degree that evokes responses, speculations as sensitive as Sobin's. Take, for instance, his attention to both the overarching social and intimately personal (even erotic) in his meditation on the original owner of the prosthetic seashell ear:

Given her spectacular attribute, had she enjoyed from her community a particular status? Was she invested, for instance, with divinatory powers? The ability to hear what other people couldn't? To decipher, say, the opaque messages emanating out of rock or, even likelier, out of water, that element for which she was so expressly equipped?

Was this the result of simple abrasion (the mechanical rub of one surface against another or the deliberate toying, on the young woman's part, with her curious appendage? Had she fondled its slick underside so often that specialists—peering through electromagnetic microscopes five thousand years later- would pick up traces of the infinitesimal luster left there by the play of her fingertips? By the roll of her thumb and forefinger over its nacreous lip?

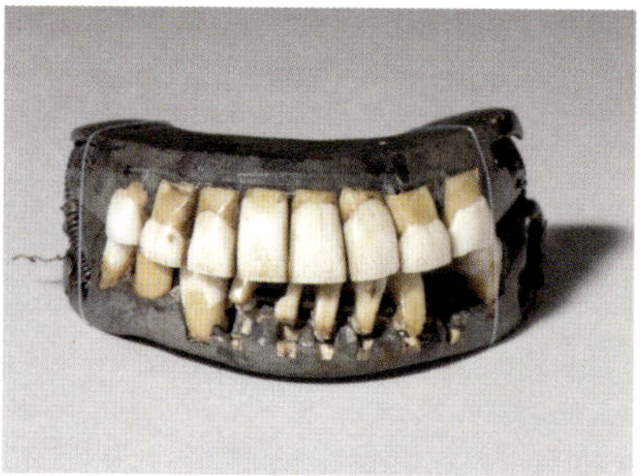

I really love how he brings that to life. This idea of the "curious appendage" is also of particular interest. I am currently in the midst of a number of small carvings, of various fingertips from meteor fragments. Obviously there is an overlap there, as well as with other historical oddities, including George Washington's wooden teeth, or even better, Tycho Brahe's golden nose.

David Diviney: As with the carvings of fingertips that are in production, previous works such as your *Salt Beards* series (2009–2013), tie into this notion of the "curious appendage." Beyond the literal read here—i.e. these particular works can be seen as merely peculiar representations of bodily extremities—these objects can also be looked at as an extension, if you will, of something that is potentially more significant and broader in parameters. Like the imagination. Fantasy. Or even wonder in the most general sense. This thought, alongside your mention of "historical oddities" and Crystal's comments pertaining to a resistance of "the stasis that is associated with taxonomy," immediately brings to mind the idea of the Wunderkammer, or cabinet of curiosities, and its contents—objects whose categorical boundaries have yet to be defined.

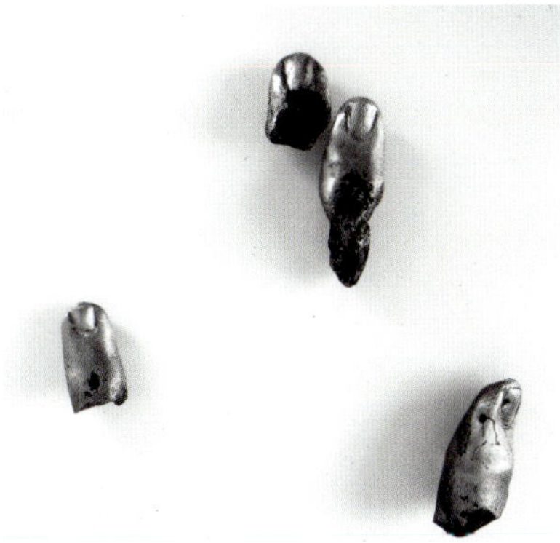

JdH: I do consider them extensions, projections, often of imaginative space—time-space for example—and yes, you are correct, in these two instances the figurative is not the primary concern, it comes after a set of associations and actions. The figurative is of interest, but only because it emerged from considerations of temporal scales and distances in both of the works you mentioned, among others [*Future Age* (2012) and *Zeus at Olympus* (2011), for example]. Those perceptual shifts allow for movement into wonder and the fantastical; this space for projection can be so vast. But fantasy also leaves room for doubt, so it is not an altogether spectacular endeavor.

I am most interested in the Wunderkammer in its reverence of material richness and in its somewhat non-hierarchical structure's allowance for lateral narrative and chronological readings. These open categorical boundaries, as you put it, and allow for questions like: what kinds of information can an object retain? Or, *when* is an object? In this respect any number of figurative busts—the potential range is compelling—and meteorite fragments that fit in the hand ask those kinds of questions. I also appreciate the inherent metaphysicist poetry of the natural world, which is so fetishized in the Wunderkammer. Acknowledgment of the unseen, the finding, the making—the circumstances—I appreciate that aspect as well. In that space objects are attached to narratives; they become specific. The task, as in art, is accessing that. I think knowing and not knowing, guessing, speculation, doubt are all part of the same oscillation—the questions that an object can ask about itself. They may lie beneath the surface but are fundamental to understand how we place ourselves, in movement, in relation. In some cases I have turned to natural phenomena and systems, transmission, or open timelines to attempt that resistance of stasis.

Ryan Doherty: In light of taxonomies, the Wunderkammer, and your interest in their non-hierarchical approach, how can I not bring up Borges's text in which he describes the Celestial Emporium of Benevolent Knowledge: that delightfully unorthodox Chinese Encyclopedia in which animals are classified into categories such as "those that belong to the Emperor," "those that tremble as if they were mad," "those that from a long ways off look like flies" and a host of others each more fabulously absurd than the next. Much of your work is similarly unbound from logic, residing instead in literary imaginations, magic realism, poetry and fantastic narratives. Borges's list (fictional or otherwise) is repeatedly cited in essays about art, but I'm pleased to see it is equally popular in disciplines from economics to neuroscience. In most instances, the conclusion is that how we perceive and organize knowledge does not always fit the mold we may think most appropriate, and that it is equally important to approach the world upside down and backwards [and here we must mention your work *Moby Dick* (2009–ongoing)].

The second thing I wanted to address was this notion of stasis, and in particular a term you used in some early conversations I had with you: potentiality. For me, the term captures notions of infinite possibility in that moment of pause—a space where imagination and narrative thrive. In many ways you've addressed this in your comments already, but is there more to potentiality for you? I'm thinking, for instance, of ideas of stored energy, which may relate to your work with crystals. Or perhaps, intertwined with the wealth of potential, is the promise of fulfillment? That within your work there is the capacity for the realization of something, good or bad, which in turn offers some sense of hope or anxiety.

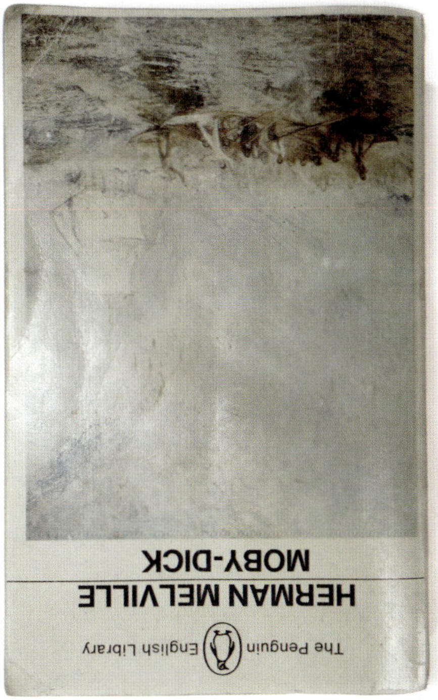

JdH: Yes, the ongoing *Moby Dick* project (I am slowly making my way backwards through the 135 chapters) is a good example of that shifted perspective; it allows for a new kind of search through the text. Of course this read is very drawn out and confusing, but also not without substance and experience. It is still the same material content, to the exact unit, after all. In his text Richard Rhodes finishes with the thoughtful acknowledgement of what will be read as the last sentence of the novel. To extend his logic, the first sentence (the last of the novel) was seen as: years ago.
and the great shroud of the sea rolled on as it rolled five thousand
sullen white surf beat against its steep sides; then all collapsed,
“Now small fowls flew screaming over the yet yawning gulf; a
but read as: .“ago years thousand five rolled it as on rolled sea the of shroud great the and ,collapsed all then ;sides steep its against beat surf white sullen a ;gulf yawning yet the over

screaming flew fowls small Now"—in retrospect it seems an appropriate warning of the magnitude of the task.

I've found that unconventional processes and categorizations can be useful tools for a kind of slow unpacking, not only in that perspectival shift, but more broadly as an elaboration on how those systems are so easily stymied—anything and everything becomes a viable condition. Approaching an object from this direction, it is appropriate to come back to the moment of pause, as you put it, as a space to consider (to give pause) and to look at the world imaginatively, at which Borges is the master. He reaffirms that the world confuses itself constantly, via humankind and otherwise—so we are not talking about something that is out of the ordinary, but part of it.

I get excited by these kinds of hybrid spaces and am attracted to these kinds of compounded circumstances; they allow for so many nuanced states, my mind goes in several directions. I am planning to visit such a site in the near future: *The Great Stalacpipe Organ*, within the cave system of Luray Caverns, Virginia. There, mineral formations have been fitted with small hammers under the control of what looks like a conventional organist's keyboard, becoming a functioning musical instrument. Recently, I visited the Royal Tyrrell Museum in Drumheller, Alberta—site of one of the world's richest fossil beds. Among the eon-spanning remains, and at the tail end of the exhibitions, lives a mature soft-shell turtle, its tank wall mounted and visible from both sides. At night, save several tanks of cockroaches, the turtle is the only living being in what is otherwise a mausoleum of the ages. I continue to think about the odd circumstance of a living species, virtually unchanged for close to 200 million years, inhabiting a building which describes its own development, on an unfathomable timescale, with the long-dead, petrified remains of that which has come before as company. Two very different remains of the past manifest in the present.

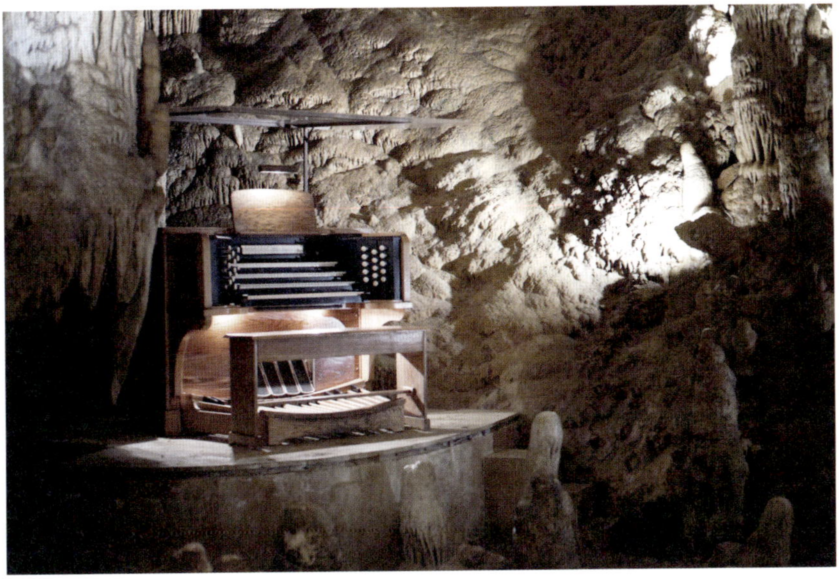

So yes, you have the stored energy in crystals but other kinds of charges can also be found in materials and conditions that are somehow able to store them, and are defined by their own specific existences. This leads to further questions about how material can take on qualities beyond the material. This is part of how I think about potentiality.

DD: Whether by way of an uncharted path through a classic text such as *Moby Dick* or in the reading of "lateral narratives" that rest latent within certain objects, a (re)examination of language and its structures, written and otherwise, seems to be a prevalent area of inquiry for you with respect to this notion of potentiality, the unknown, etc. Take the title of this publication and its source, for instance.

JdH: The title of this publication is *Noghwhere Bodili is Everywhere Goostly*. It is also one of the variations on the titles of the exhibitions that this publication accompanies. It is a Middle English phrase taken from *The Cloude of Unknowyng,* an anonymous 14th century text of theological mysticism. Miruna Dragan introduced the text to me and we have worked collaboratively from it in the past. Its main proposition is to take the courage to surrender your mind to a realm of "unknowingness." The text often compels the reader to consider positions above and below "the cloud." It is obviously concerned with presence, non-presence and the presence of non-presence—they are considered as equal, sometimes simultaneous states; *something* can be the same as *nothing* and, naturally, vice versa. In a sense the text requires the negotiation of a neither/nor space. It also unhinges objects from perception to a degree, the thing apart from sight, which comes back to potentiality. So I am taking *Noghwhere Bodili is Everywhere Goostly* as a rubric for my work. For the last few years it has functioned as a productive space to think about objects and being as a process of space. I also think that this kind of in-between space calls for, and nurtures, ingenuity, an answer to Sobin's appeal: *Might we even begin constituting, indeed, a collection, an entire library of questions? A whole, inexhaustible archive devoted exclusively to wonder, to query, to the unlimited breadth of human speculation?*

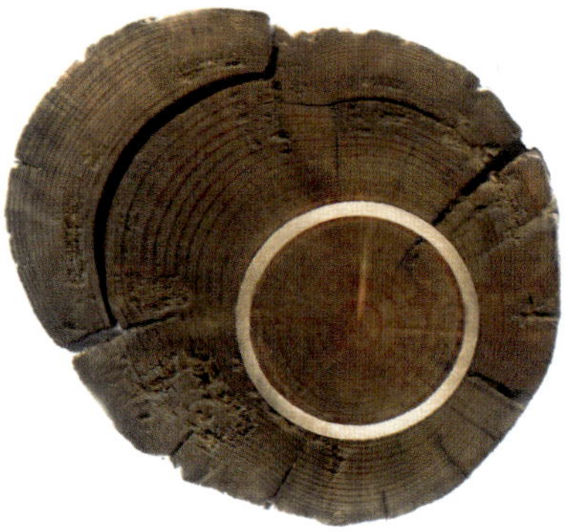

RD: There is a lot to go on there, but I'm drawn to that idea of the unknown, or unknownness. Given your poetic tendencies, I'll mention that this notion has come up with regard to the poet Rimbaud, who wrote: "Les inventions d'inconnu reclament des formes nouvelles." That is to say, for Rimbaud unknownness is not inherently present, but invented or created. And moreover, that to do so, new forms or structures for language would be necessary. Much like the surrealists who would apply automatic writing and other strategies to construct a sense of unknownness, you seem to have approaches—using found objects for instance—that serve you in a similar fashion.

But perhaps your practice lies somewhere "in between" as you state. One could argue that whether second-hand books, busts, pianos, organ pipes, gravestones or mirrors, you both "discover" and "invent" a quality of unknownness within them. Discovery, in these terms, seems to be more about unearthing something already there, something quantifiable; whereas with invention, the sum is greater than its parts. It is more akin to alchemy, or at least the illusion of it (which is just as effective to a captive audience), where one and one is three and lead transforms into gold. Invention is asking the questions many wouldn't dream to ask (and here I think Sobin's library of questions would be of great value). Would you agree that your work is balanced somewhere between discovery and invention, and in doing so resonates with that unknownness you refer to?

JdH: I do agree, I think that is a helpful way to think about the work in general. The discovery element comes from the belief that my encounters with objects, materials and situations should not be forced and that I can react to these as I encounter them in life—so that there is also an ethic established about how to live creatively; how to flexibly respond, connect to place and transform. This is also the reason that I am nearly always project-based, working in diverse materials, under various conditions. I like to be able, as much as possible, to open up what I think is already there. Histories are part of the active quality of much of my work and should be acknowledged, as should ongoing processes. In this conviction, objects should be dealt with not only by the imagination; experience is also essential. I much prefer presenting an object in which the process of its development is evident, integral. Discovery is present in both finding and contending with them.

Invention is also a useful term, though I don't have much interest in the development of imaginary narratives, at least to the degree that they have no consequences. I like that you equate invention to asking questions—a number of my works have come from speculation on a set of already specific conditions: what if this stone that I picked up off the beach was once a well-defined portion of ancient statuary? Or, is it possible to determine the specific atmospheric conditions that exist above a given geyser and select a group of non-indigenous tropical plants that could thrive within this bubble?

Maybe the balance that you talk about has something to do with the continually unfolding. One of my current favorite works of art is one of the last of Alighiero e Boetti's life, *Self Portrait* (1993). The work is a bronze statue, slightly scaled down, in the artist's image. It holds a garden hose in its raised arm, the water spouts out, up and arcs down onto the top of the sculpture's head, where it turns to steam. The work is heated from the inside. The year after he made this work Boetti died of brain cancer; an incredible late work, both a portend of his demise and an affirmation that energy persists in his ideas. Some of my recent activity has also considered the remains of the body and of ideas. *Petrify Me* (2013) is a series of impressions on paper executed in various graveyards (Annandale-on-Hudson, New York; Wall Badlands, South Dakota; Crow Agency/Little Bighorn, Montana; Corbin, British Columbia; Frank Slide/ Turtle Mountain, Alberta; etc.). Each letter of the text is taken from an individual headstone in a particular graveyard, almost as a sort of letterpress reserve. Each embossing spells out *Petrify Me*. It is the desire for a physically (mineral) preserved form, the struggle to maintain an experience via memory and language, a stoppage of time, frozenness, fossilization and loneliness. In these I am thinking of a longing to be immortalized by the mammoth forces of nature, but also purely by chance; to be freed from the expected continuum, while the important question remains: what carries on?

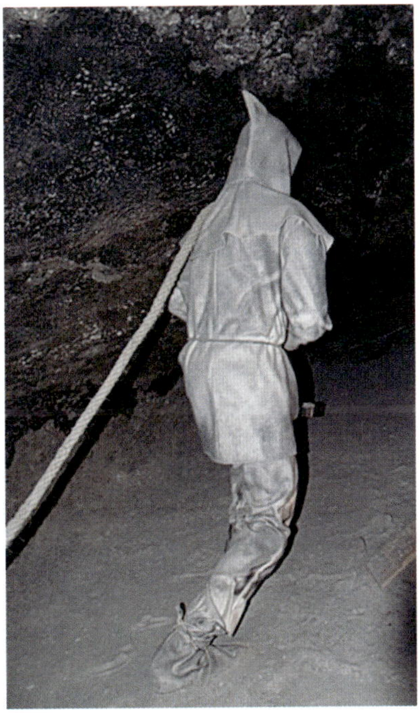

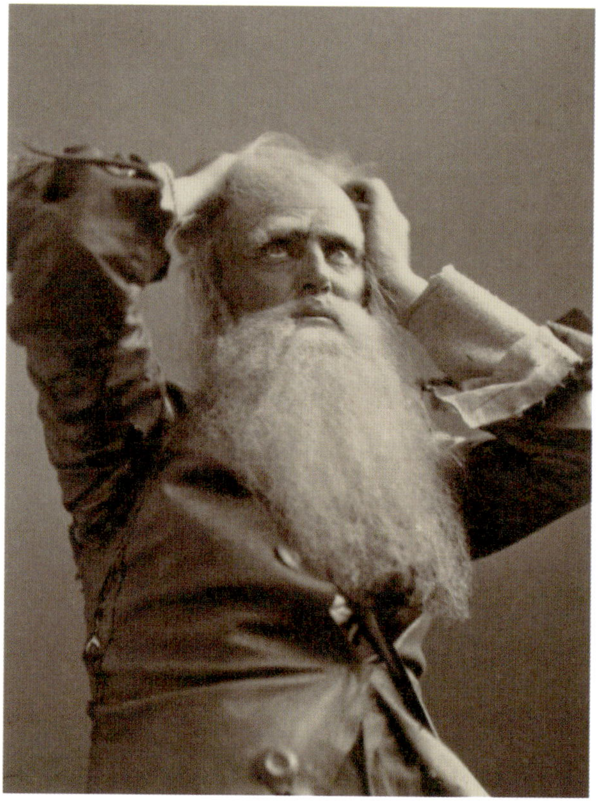

The Reader

Richard Rhodes

On the homepage of Jason de Haan's website (www.jasondehaan.net) a costumed man with long white hair and beard is asleep against a tree. It is Rip Van Winkle. He is the character of the Washington Irving short story who nods off in the woods under the rule of the British king George III and then wakes up 20 years later with George Washington as president of the United States of America. Rip is a sleeper-through-history, the quintessential Catskill Mountains slackard, who left life behind to disappear into a land of dreams. If he is de Haan's homepage proxy, it is not for the sleeping through history, but for the dreaming. This is a Rip who has slept into art.

de Haan has made a name for himself in the past half dozen years with sculptures, collages, installations and public projects that engage time, especially the long-scale perception of time, seriously. From his first exhibitions in Calgary—a city where concentrated conceptual attitude and aptitude has been expressed by artists such as Eric Cameron, Chris Cran and John Will for decades—de Haan has staked out a position in which his art functions as a type of retrieval mechanism to resuscitate lost time and stimulate the imagination. His art is about displacement and simultaneity. The now sits atop an unfaded then in a reversal of the progressive model of time that once defined modernism and established the perpetual cutting-edge GPS of the avant garde. For de Haan, time does not push into the future, it loops. It is the great glue that binds objects and images with human experience. When on his website we see Van Winkle with his gun across his lap and his head against the tree, he might look the picture of rest and relaxation, but the gun also suggests something like an interrupted readiness—a guy protecting his headspace.

Such expansive headspace is what drives de Haan's art. His work pulls at the boundaries of how we look at things by actively provoking us, with titles and project descriptions, to think beyond what we see. The art object is usually just the tip of the mental arena fleshed out by the work; it is often only an entry point that requires us to think back into process and the conceptual terrain of inception. Take *Pie Powder* (2008 – 2010). It is perhaps the most extreme example of an artwork that is, in effect, mostly a door onto process and history. When it showed at the Southern Alberta Art Gallery in fall 2012, viewers might have been forgiven for wondering what a beat-up old piano was doing in the gallery. The object, a much-weathered, much-distressed stand-up piano, stood in a sorry kind of silence in the gallery until you learned that it was in fact an assisted readymade created by a herd of Alberta horses.

De Haan's project description reads: "From a corruption of the French 'Pied Poudre' (dusty feet), Pie Powder suggests a form of wandering. A stand-up piano was placed in a nondescript plot of land with a number of horses for 763 days. The project became dependent upon the animals' curiosity to determine its course. The Piano remains as evidence." What that evidence showed were hungry horses. They had gnawed at the keys and the wooden cabinetry of the piano over two years of wide-ranging Canadian weather. Photos on de Haan's website show them treating it like a musical salt lick and eventually they topple it so that it lies flat near a picturesque watering hole shown in winter and spring.

All of this is gone in the gallery. The piano is mute; its present state is a metaphor for its missing prior life, its musicality, its history with horses. When the information comes, however, the piece takes on an uncanny figurative life. The ivory keys are not unlike horses's teeth, the piano wires not unlike their sinewy tendons. The whittled legs of the piano are closest to an actual match—doubling for a horse's delicate, tapering forelegs. This game of projection, of feeding information into the object and having it mirrored back as an evolving set of associate images is what I take de Haan to mean when he says the piece is "a form of wandering." It wanders in time, in our perception, in our different avenues of apprehension as an object, as a history, as a text image.

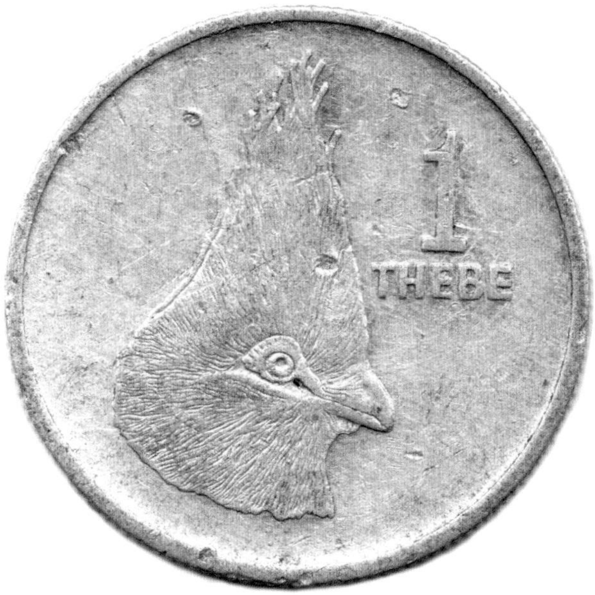

Or, consider *Cannon Ball* (2012), a three-inch sphere of metal that sits (or at least did in Lethbridge) on a waist-high white plinth. You can look and notice the density of the thing, the imprint of the circumference seam left from the mould, the gleam of the hard, variegated surface with its craters and tapering curls of different metallic colours. A cannon ball? Sure, but it is also a globe, a planet, an asteroid, or, maybe, a baseball—something to be handheld. This listing of evolving kinships is how we work through what we see when we look. Imagination comes into play to shape what we see. In de Haanian terms, it is how we "wander" through what we see.

The project text is more definitive. It tells us that the work is: "One coin from each of the World's actively circulating currencies. 3" Sphere. Edition of 3." But while this might seem like the definitive description of the work, it is really just a foil that allows us to compare these objective facts with what can be imagined otherwise. In other words, we weren't far off in having seen a kinship to a globe, or a planet—every nation is present and accounted for. Nor were we far off in registering that a connection with hands falls within orbit—dig into your pocket to find your own circular coin. From its title, de Haan delivers us a weapon. The words—cannon ball—are a way to channel thoughts to consider the connections between money and military history, money and blunt force destruction, money and power, money and dominance, money as a vestige of the pre-modern era. The title is a conduit into that history. We see an object that is round and gleaming and hard with a past of liquidity worn on its surface. We register it as an artifact. It seems more than a cannon ball. It is something archaic, resurrected from the beginning of history.

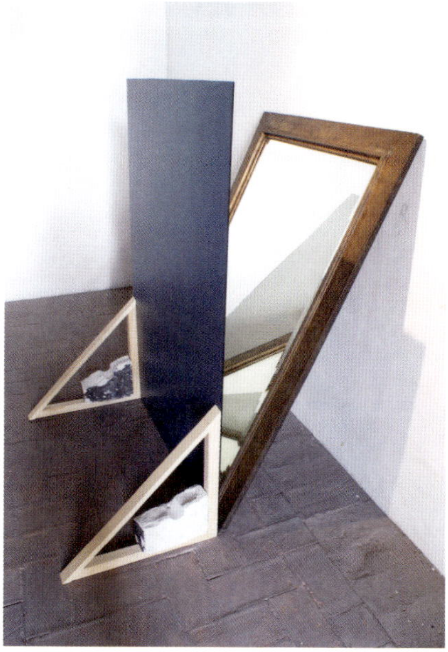

This associative depth is the compelling aspect of de Haan's work. He invites us to wander with what we see, to see more than what is in front of us. His art begins with a Duchampian interest to make an art that is more than retinal, more than present in three measurable dimensions. At times, he has had fun with this, like with *Spirits Looking Up at Themselves* (2009) and *Spirits Looking at Themselves* (2010). Both works involve mirrors that reflect one another. The 2009 work was an installation at the Museo de la Ciudad in Querétaro, Mexico, a city with a history of glass production and a museum with a mandate to interest children in the arts. The latter fact is relevant in that the mirror that leans against the wall in the piece is said to be a "mirror haunted by children," and indeed there is an adult/child relationship in the angle at which the haunted mirror "looks up" to the standing mirror across from it. For the viewer, there is an unequal infinity of reflection to see, rising on one side, falling on the other. A year later, in Toronto, at the Clint Roenisch Gallery, two "haunted" upright mirrors were stood apart at conversation distance with equal matching infinities of reflection that created a deep space of engagement between them which the viewer could peer into from the outside.

These exclusive conversations between ghosts invited some literal wandering by the viewer, as well as more than a little speculation about what might manifest ghosthood. The works revolve on a kind of magical thinking in which de Haan uses language to reinvent the purpose of the objects and to ease their attachment to a state of being in which we understand an aspiration to see them as being more than what they are. Vision is always augmented in de Haan's work. Words and information extend what we see. This is the legacy of conceptualism in his art, its precept that sets ambitions beyond objecthood and aesthetics, into a terrain where ideas and culture and possibilities of otherness collide.

Behind this conceptualist attitude, however, is a deeper legacy that is rooted in the act of reading. What distinguishes de Haan's art is how, while resolutely object based, it again and again relies on reading as its model of relational experience and imaginative engagement. The work takes us inside the process of reading as a stage for imagination. It hovers over the transformation where letters on a page turn into mental images with an independent durational life, images that move in double time with the real world, a time apart, yet softly integrated. You can read a Tolstoy short story in July—*Master and Man*, say—and find yourself lost in an obliterating nighttime snow storm in Russia, all the while hearing summer sounds on the street outside through the imaginary howling of the wind. *Cannon Ball* presents the same kind of simultaneity as it mixes its density of melted coin with the density of words that tell us it encapsulates every nation on Earth. *Cannon Ball* is a linguistic object as much as a military and monetary one. We read through it and measure its weight in allusions to other places and other times alongside its literal measure in grams and kilos.

This is the double nature of reading. With our eyes, our ears and our minds, from a text held in our hands, we create an imaginative scrim built on written words. When the transformation process flows, it becomes a space we can inhabit, a space to treasure and remember: the foggy London of Dickens, the blustery heath of *Wuthering Heights*, the reeking sewers of *Les Misérables*—and on and on and on. De Haan's website Rip Van Winkle is a testament to the word constructions that enthrall us, to the literary characters that become family. The ground zero of his art practice is to return us to that imaginative magic.

Once on a studio visit with him in Calgary, I listened as he showed me photographs taken on camping trips that are part of an ongoing project. In them he's reading a book—Melville's *Moby Dick*—and the idea is that he will struggle to read the book, upside down and backwards, near bodies of water. It's an absurdist project that reverses the narrative flow of the book, if flow is something that can ever be had under the circumstances.

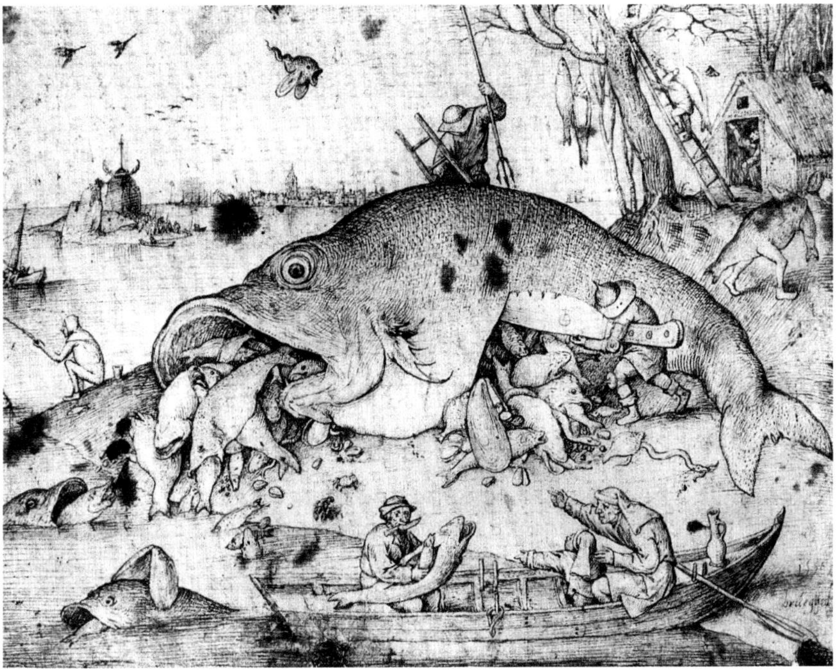

Yet for those who know the book, they know where de Haan is headed. Wherever he is reading, he's headed in the direction of the famously poetic beginning of Melville's novel where all meditation finds its way to water: "What do you see? —Posted like silent sentinels all around the town, stand thousand upon thousands of men fixed in ocean reveries."

De Haan is one of those men—he once built a boat in the basement of Calgary's Stride Gallery for a 2007 show called *Where the Ocean Meets This Guy*. Only the mast appeared in the gallery—an allusion to shipwreck. One promotional image for the exhibition showed him in the bathtub reading a book called *Survive the Savage Sea*. He's safely in the tub but you can picture the waves crashing around him from the riveted look on his face. We are meant to feel the waves too. They are part of the show, part of what de Haan provokes us to imagine.

".Ishmael me Call" is what he will read when he comes to the end of *Moby Dick*. It is an ancient name from one of the first stories, a story that made the world that has come down to us. De Haan's art tries to retrieve that beginning so that we remember where we are and where we come from. It is from somewhere fluid and inside our heads.

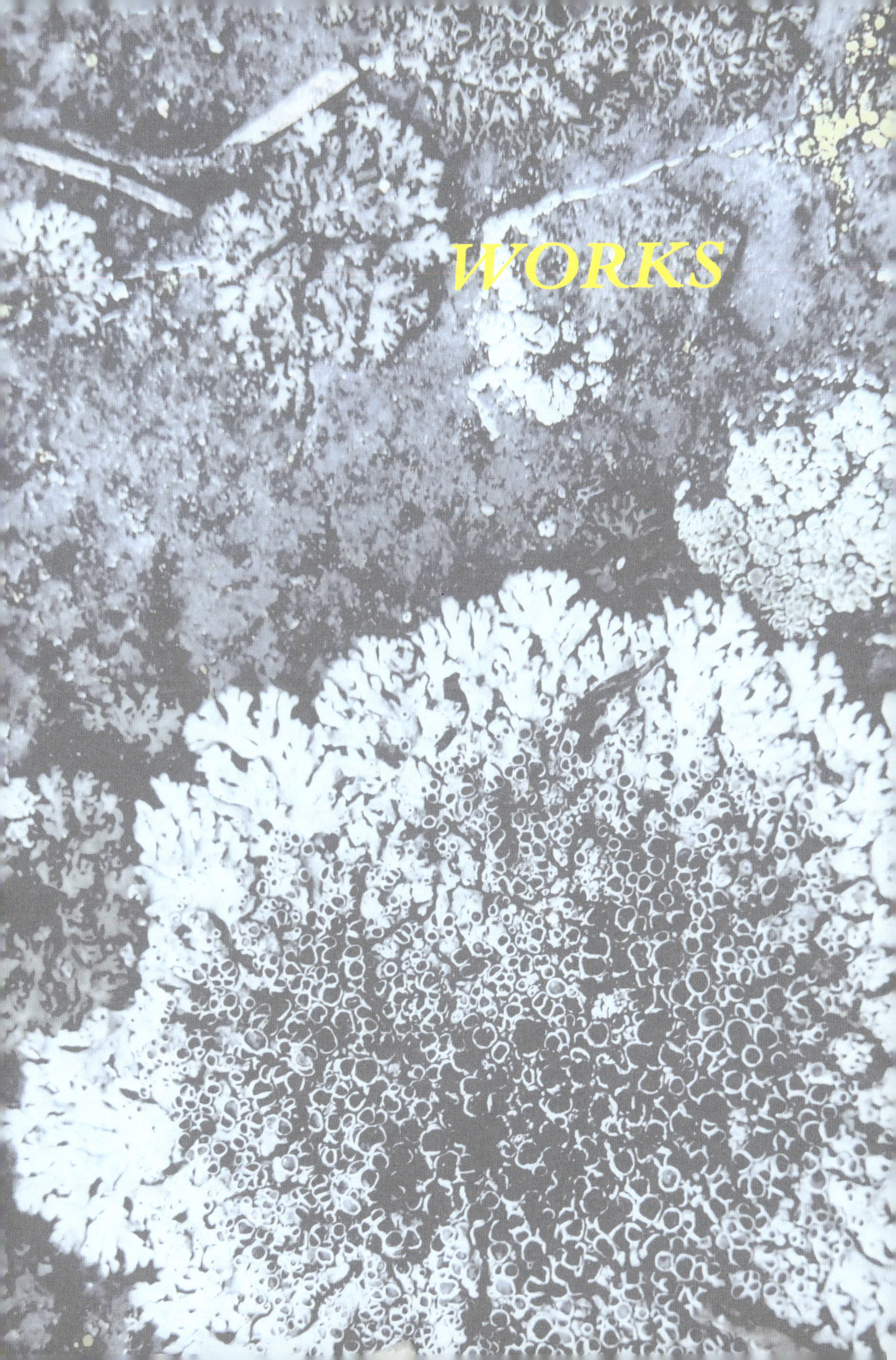
WORKS

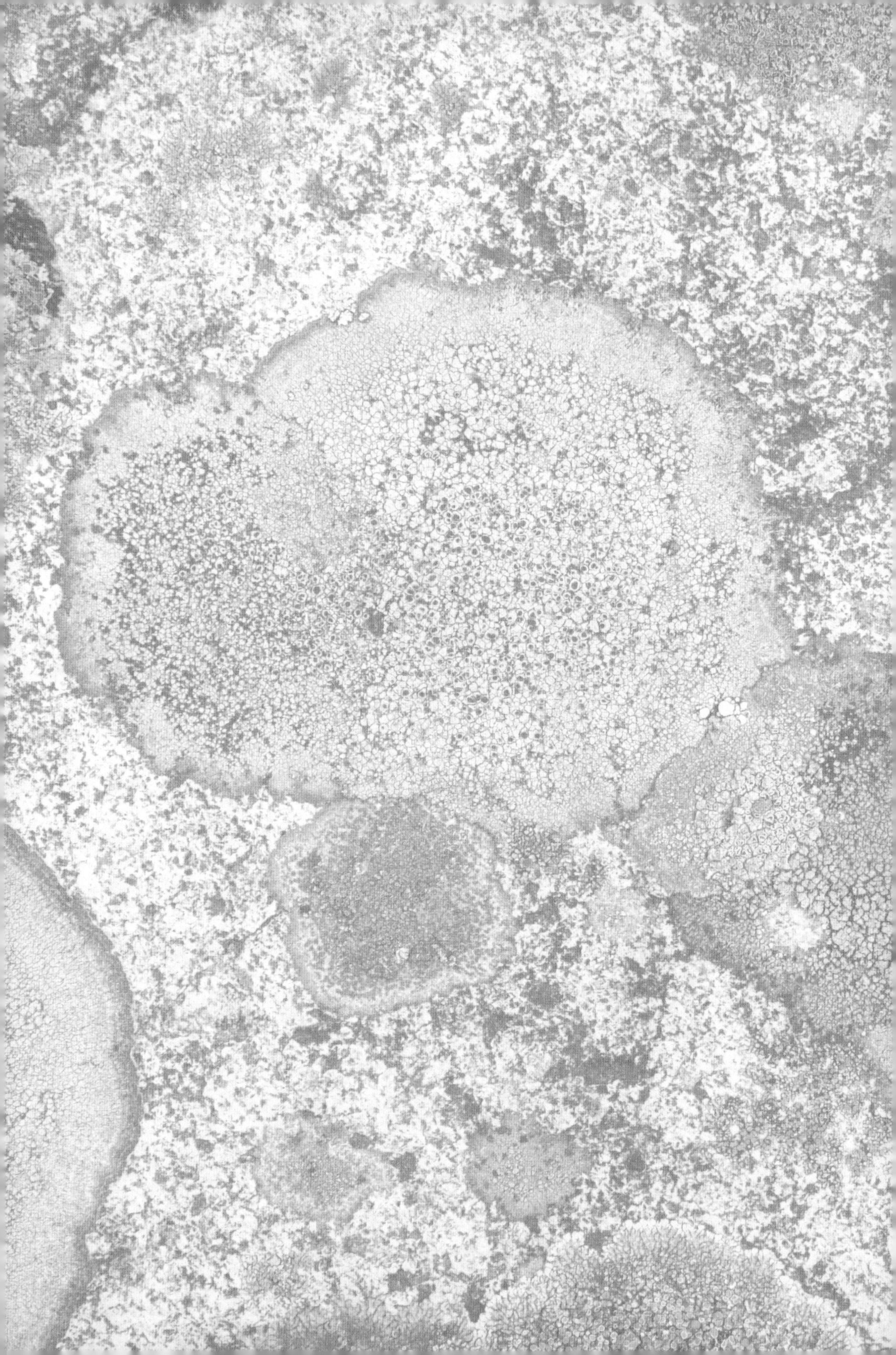

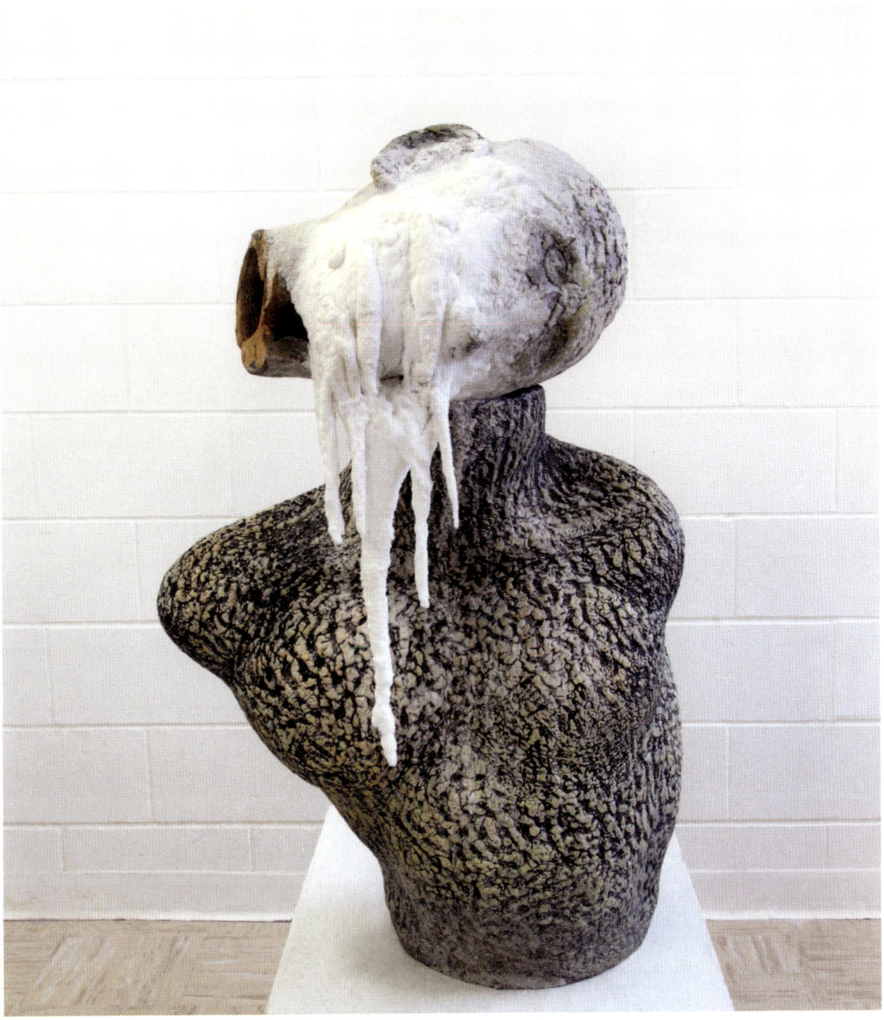

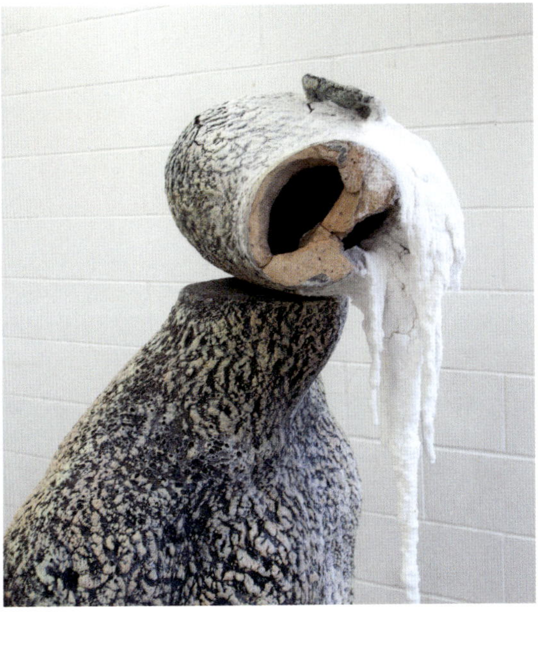

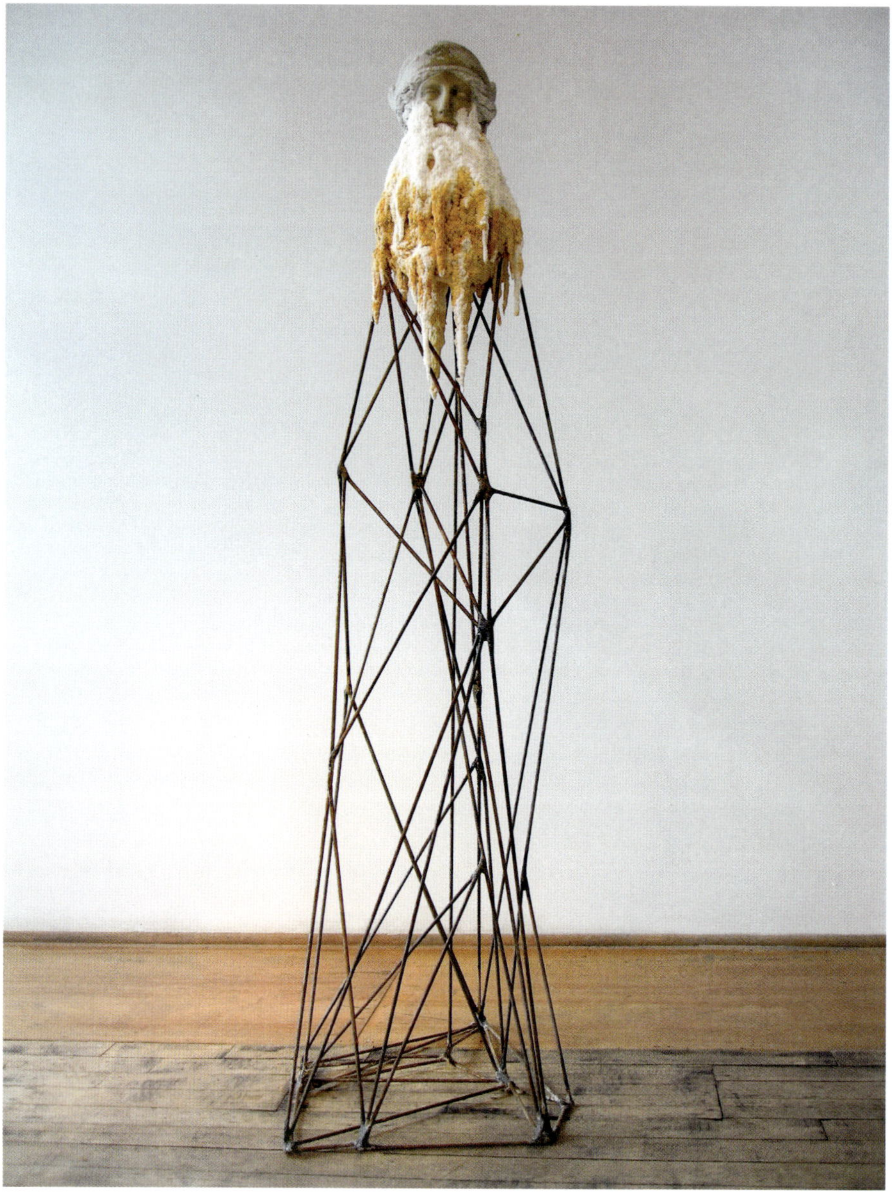

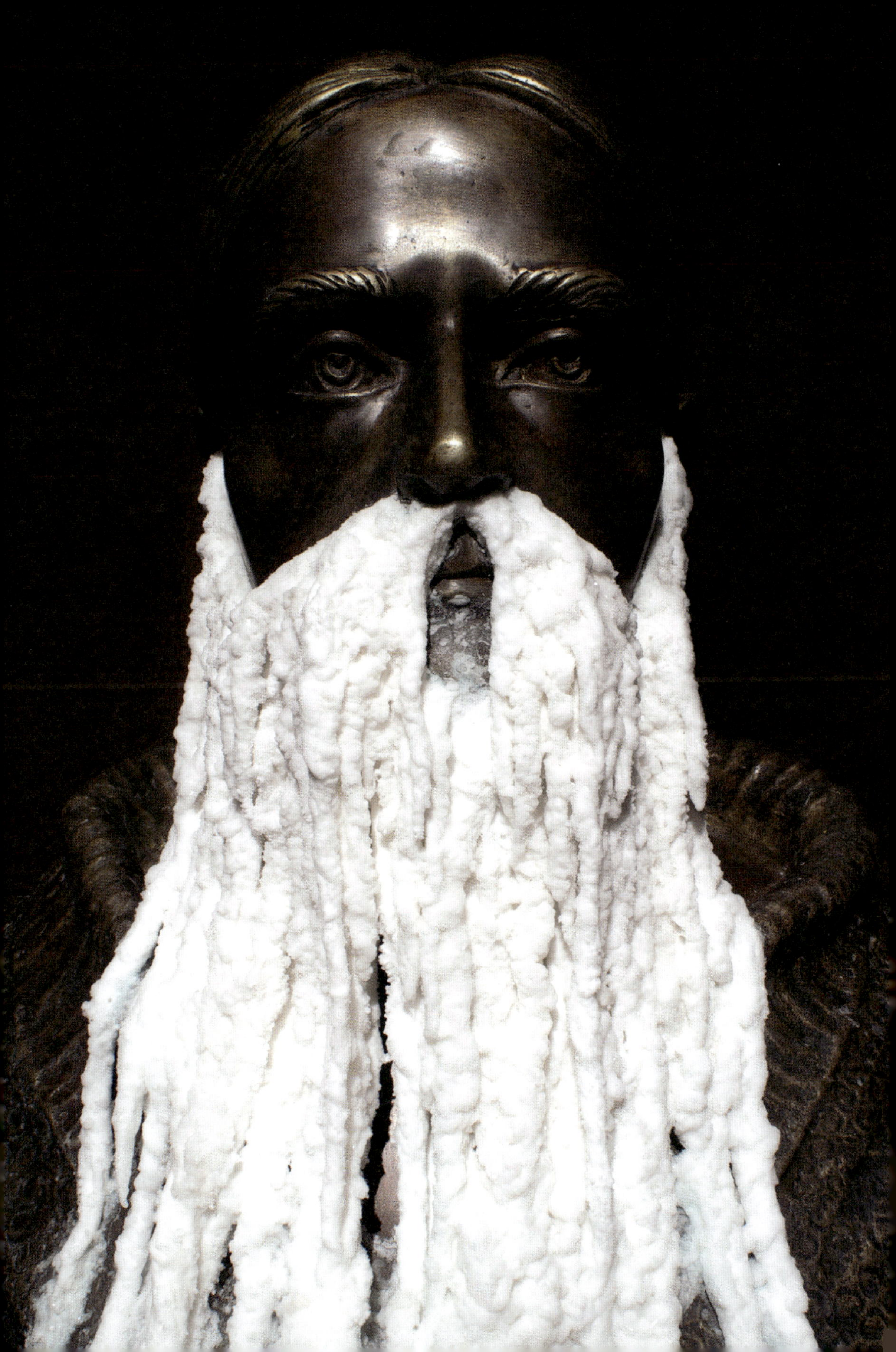

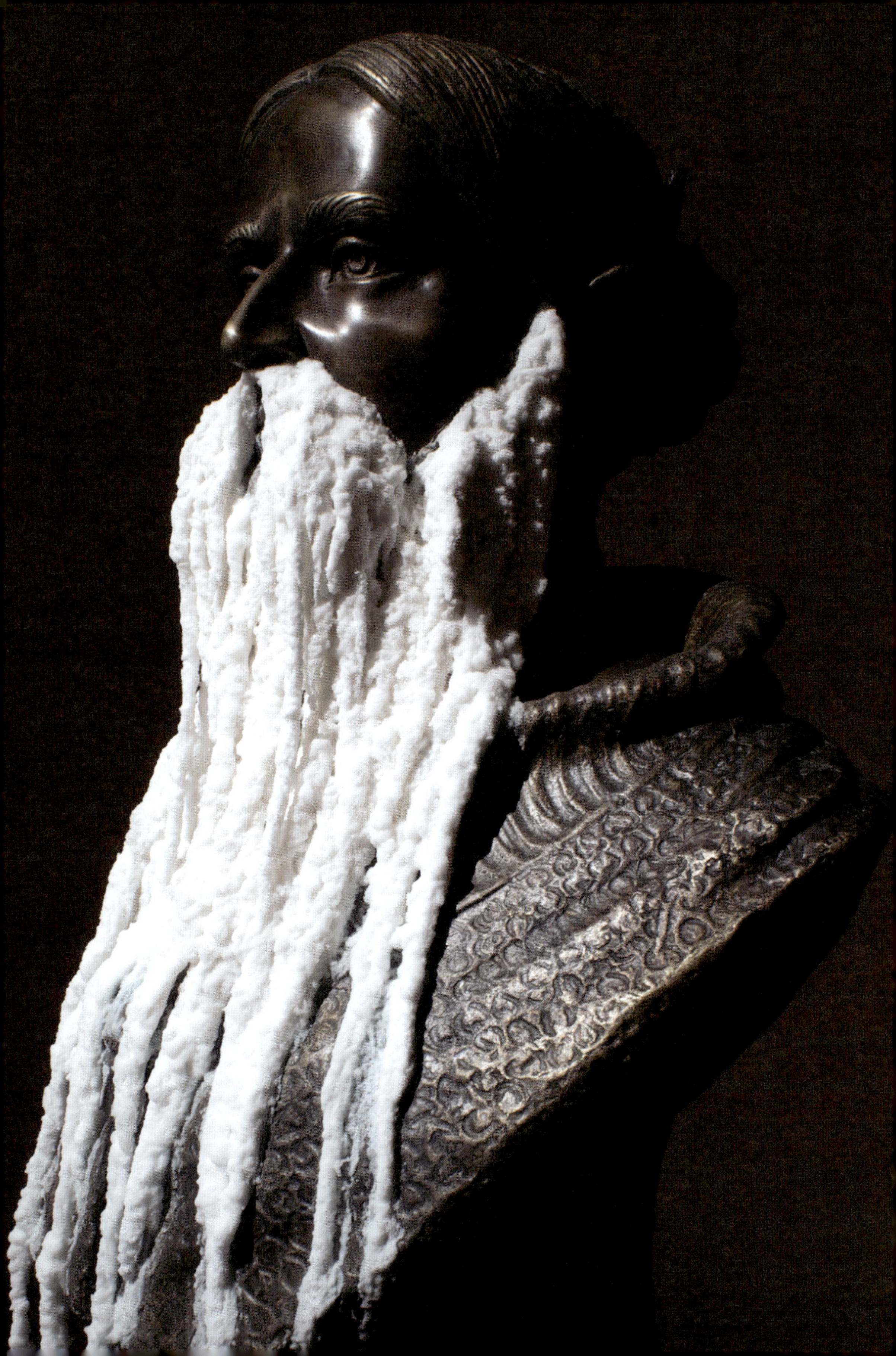

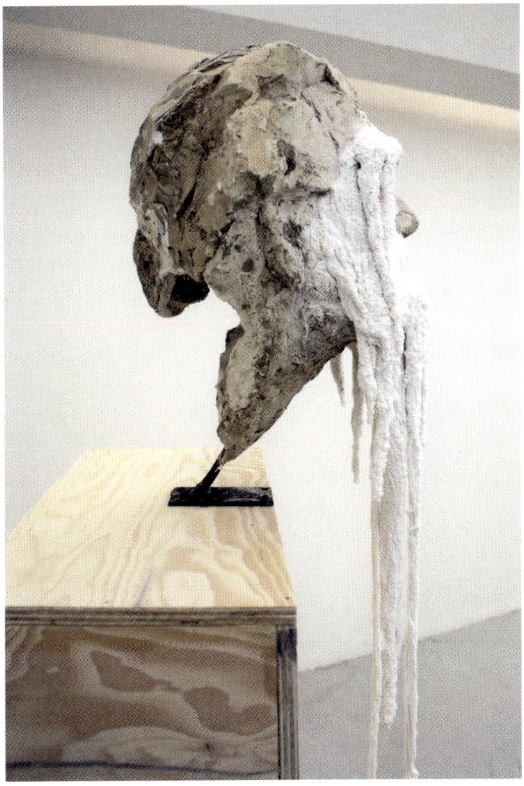

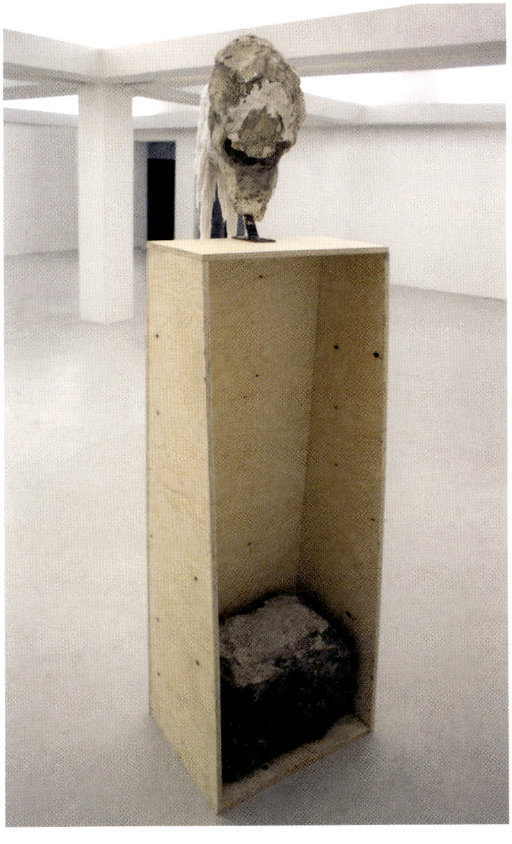

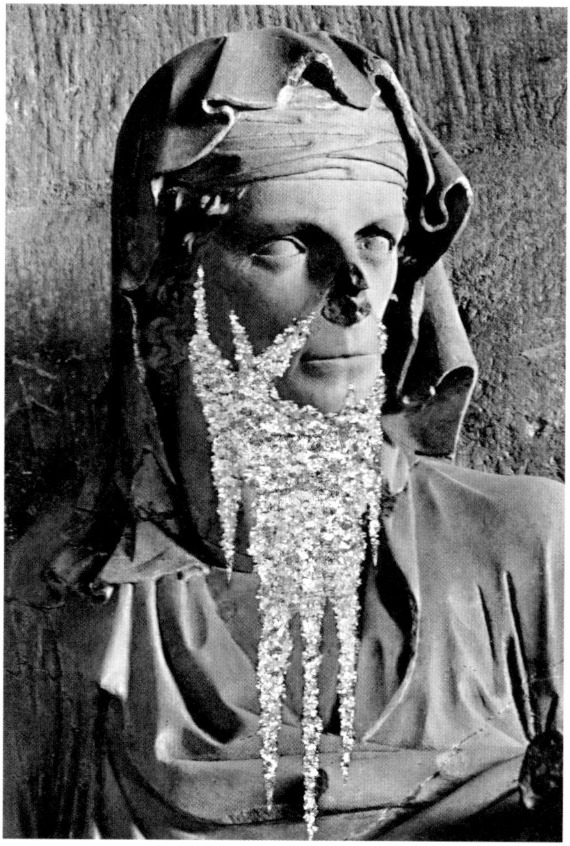

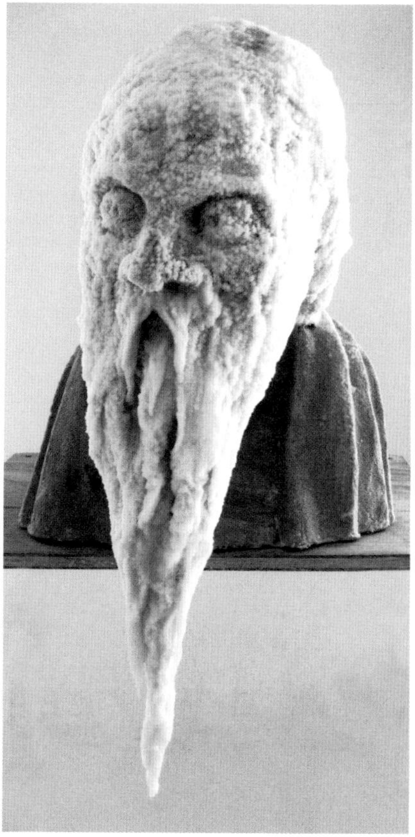

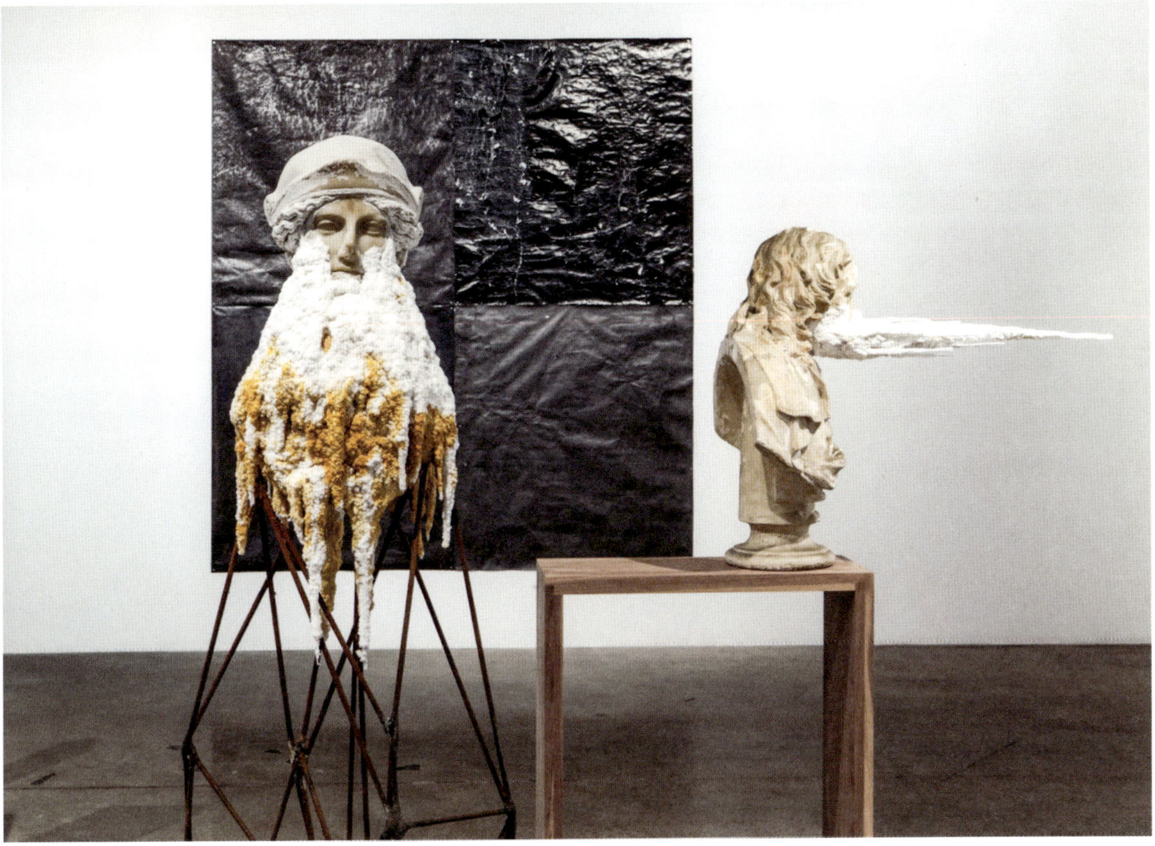

SALT BEARDS

A series of mineral growths on found and borrowed busts.
2009-2013

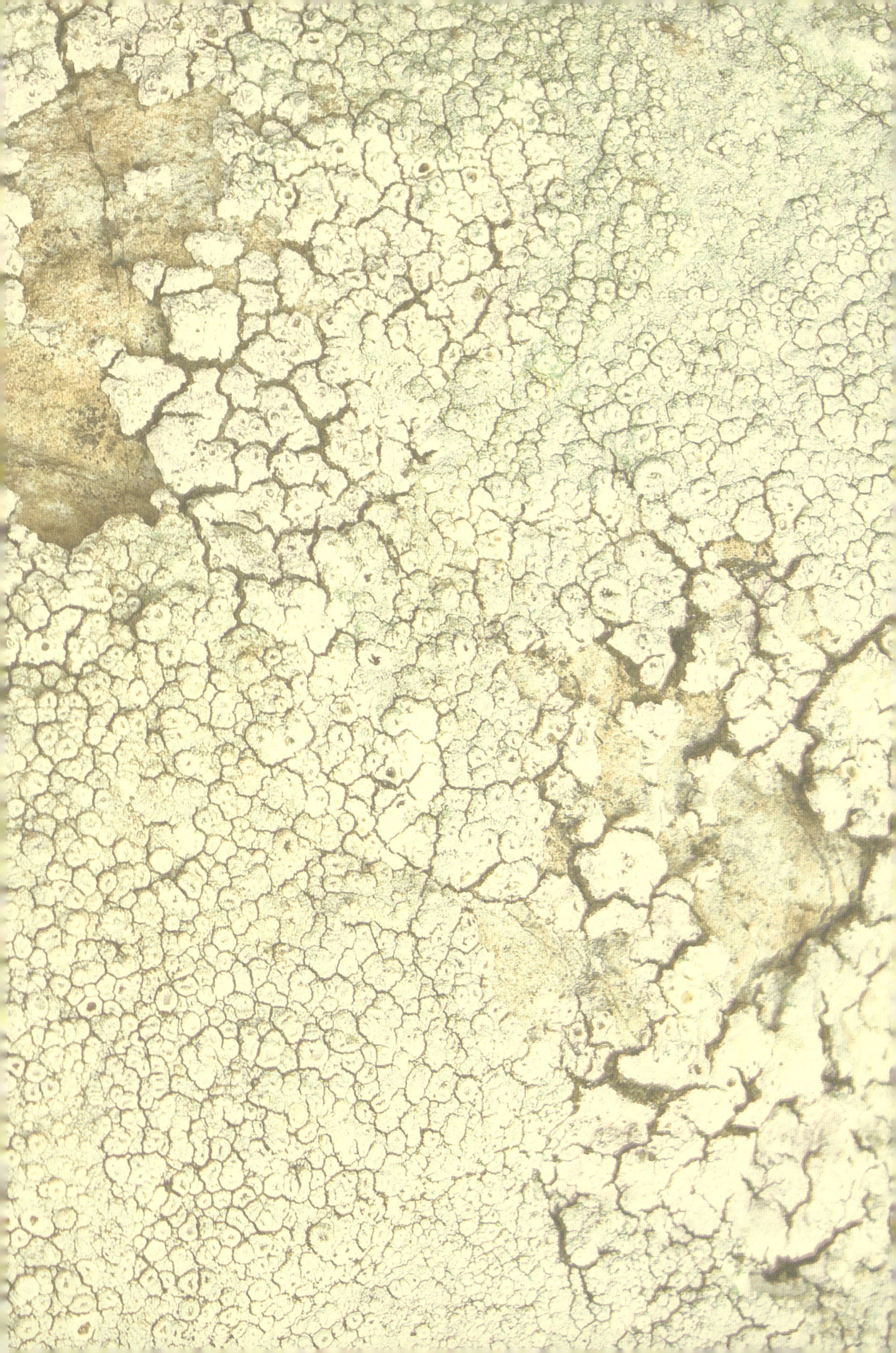

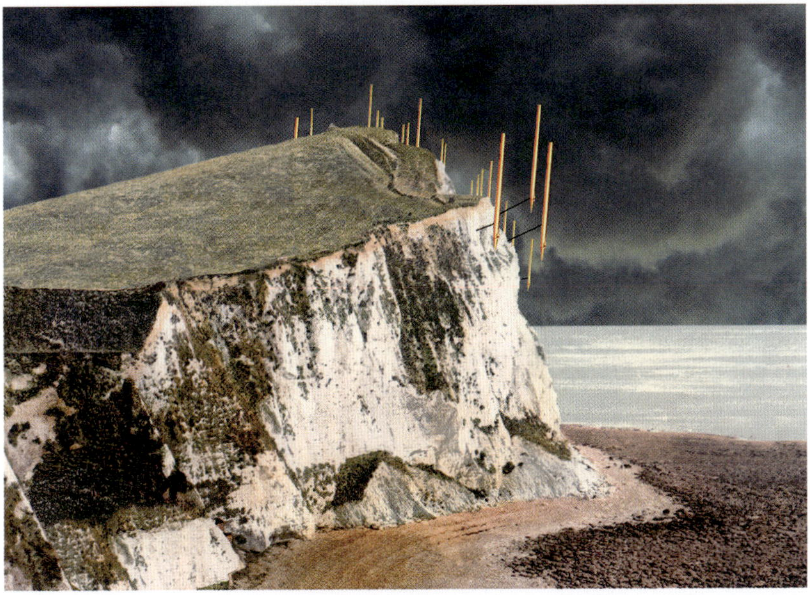

A proposal for a set of organ pipes to be installed on an oceanic cliff face. The pipes are to be mounted vertically via steel rods and secured strategically in order to translate strong updrafts into individual notes. The necessary environmental conditions include: strong and regular wind, heavy rain, waves and fog, a foreboding atmosphere, an ancient and deserved mythology, and a reputation among seafarers. These are the White Cliffs of Dover, Kent County, UK, of which the poet Matthew Arnold wrote in 1849: "*…Where the sea meets the moon-blanch'd land, / Listen! You hear the grating roar, / Of pebbles, which the waves draw back, and fling, / At their return, up the high strand, / Begin, and cease, and then again begin, / With tremulous cadence slow, and bring / The eternal note of sadness in …*"

ETERNAL NOTE OF SADNESS (previous)
2013

SET OF TEN BOOKS, EACH CONTAINING NOTATION OF EACH SECOND OF EACH MINUTE OF EACH HOUR OF EACH DAY OF EACH WEEK OF EACH MONTH OF EACH YEAR, FOR THE NEXT CENTURY, THE COUNTDOWN BEGINS WHEN YOU READ THIS
2010

PROPOSAL FOR THE CASTING OF A GOTHIC CATHEDRAL IN A CEMENT CUBE, THE STRUCTURE IS REMOVED AND THE FORM IS ENTERABLE
2010

PREPARING TO RELEASE A DEVICE THAT WILL INSTANTLY FREEZE A THUNDERHEAD, BRINGING IT CRASHING TO EARTH
2010

OBJECT TO SEND INTO ORBIT, TWO MIRRORED SURVEILLENCE DOMES ATTACHED TO FORM A SPHERE
2010

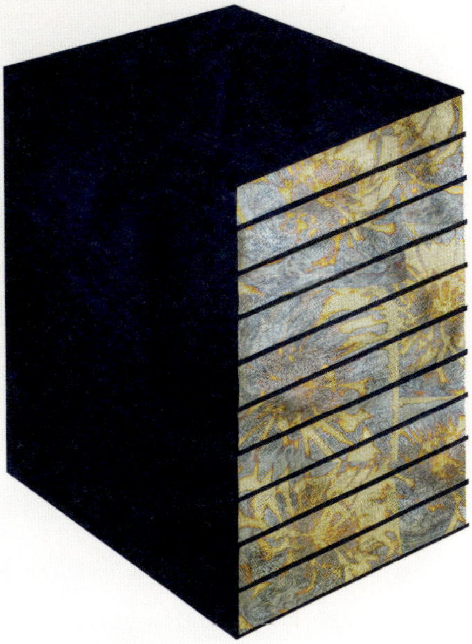
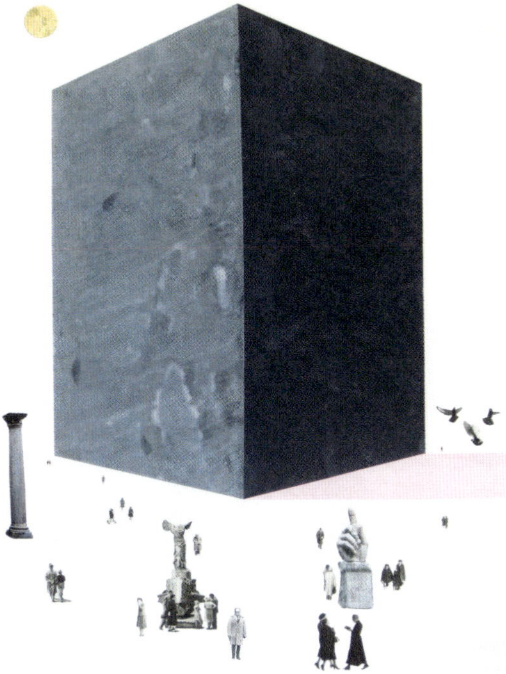
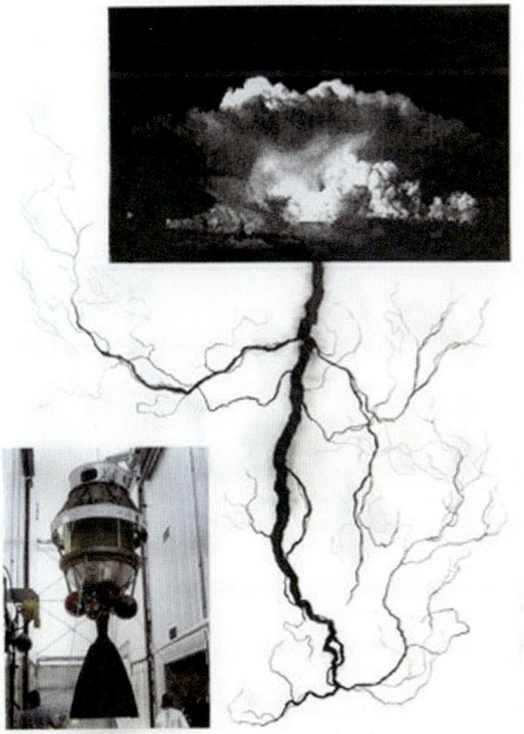
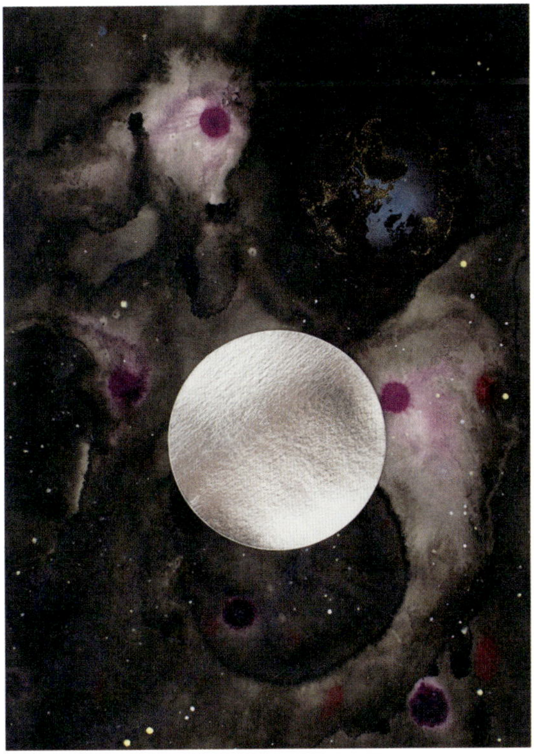

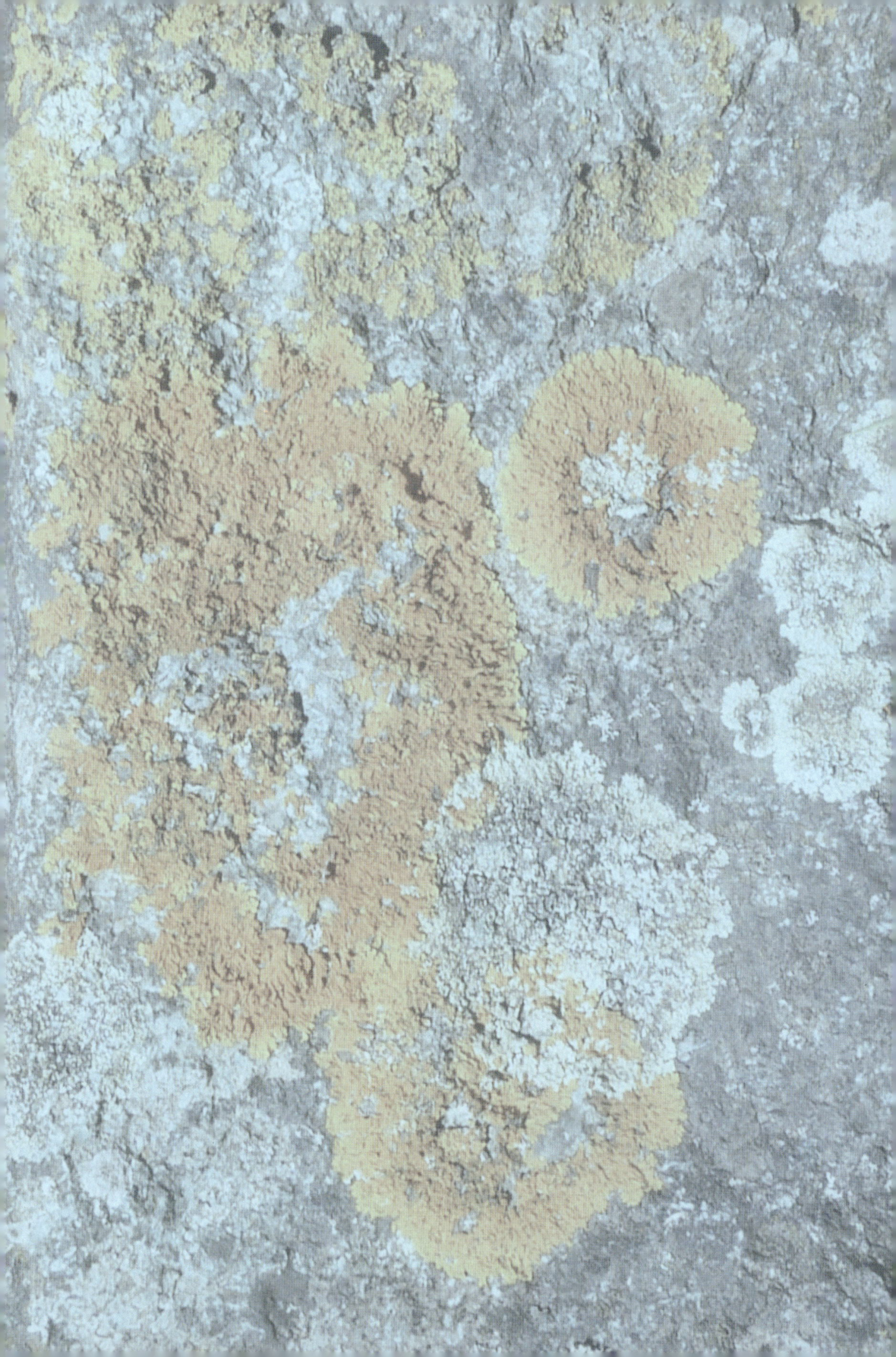

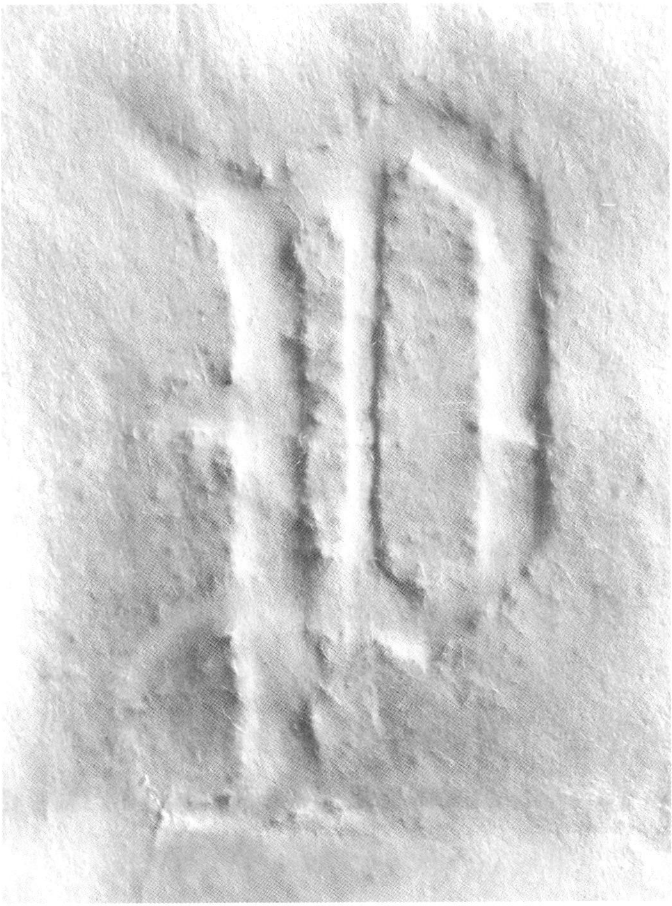

PETR

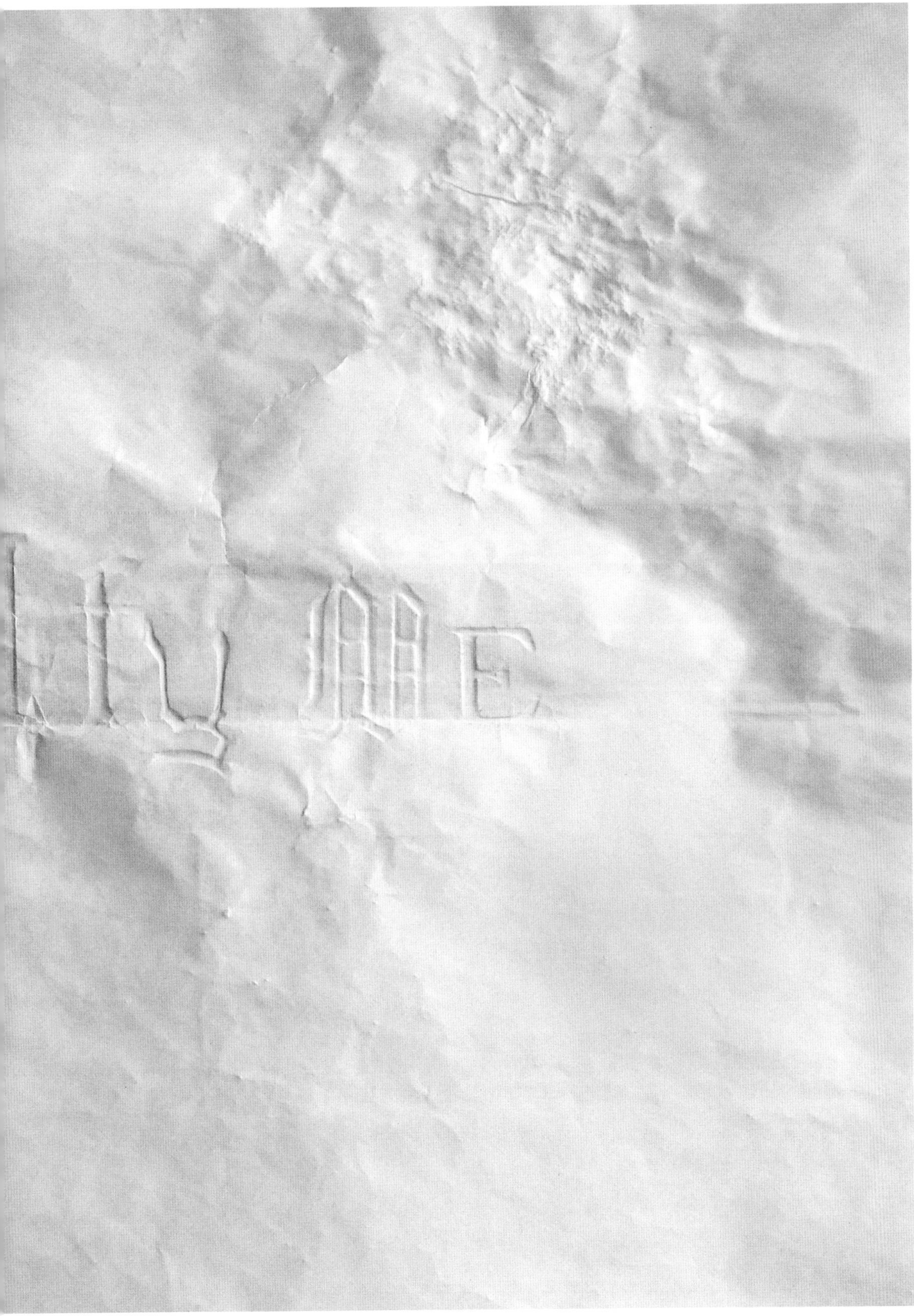
ly Me

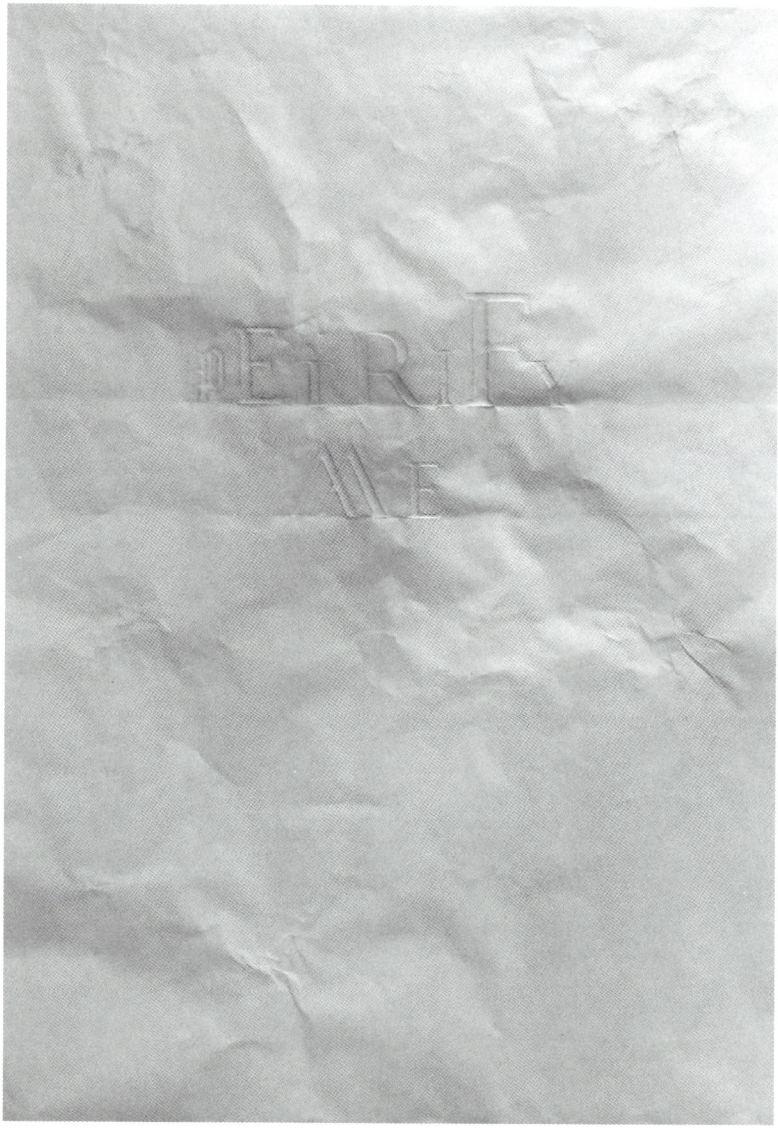

PETRI*f*Y *M*E

An ongoing series of embossed texts gathered from various headstones in a number of graveyards.

2013 –

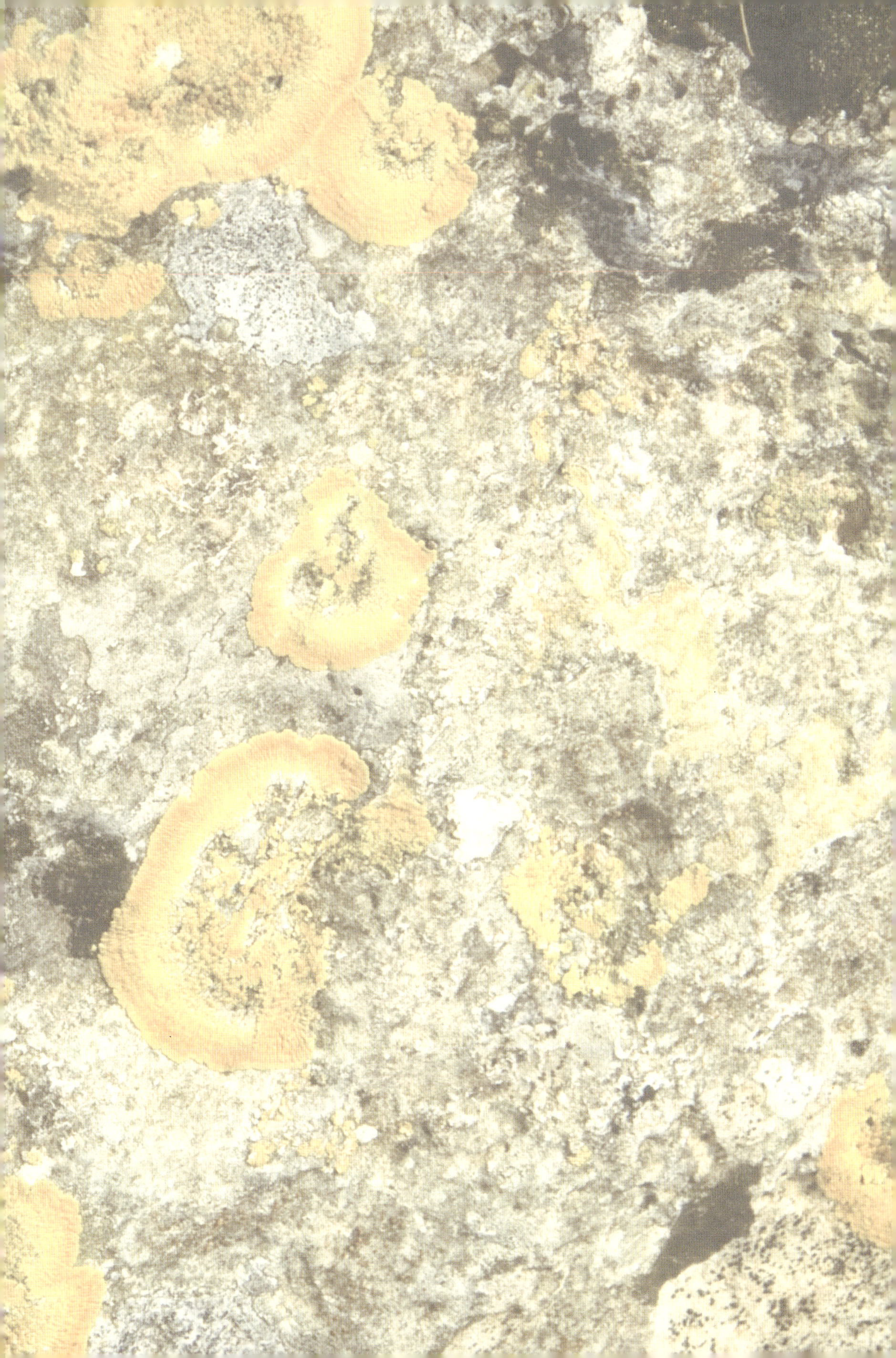

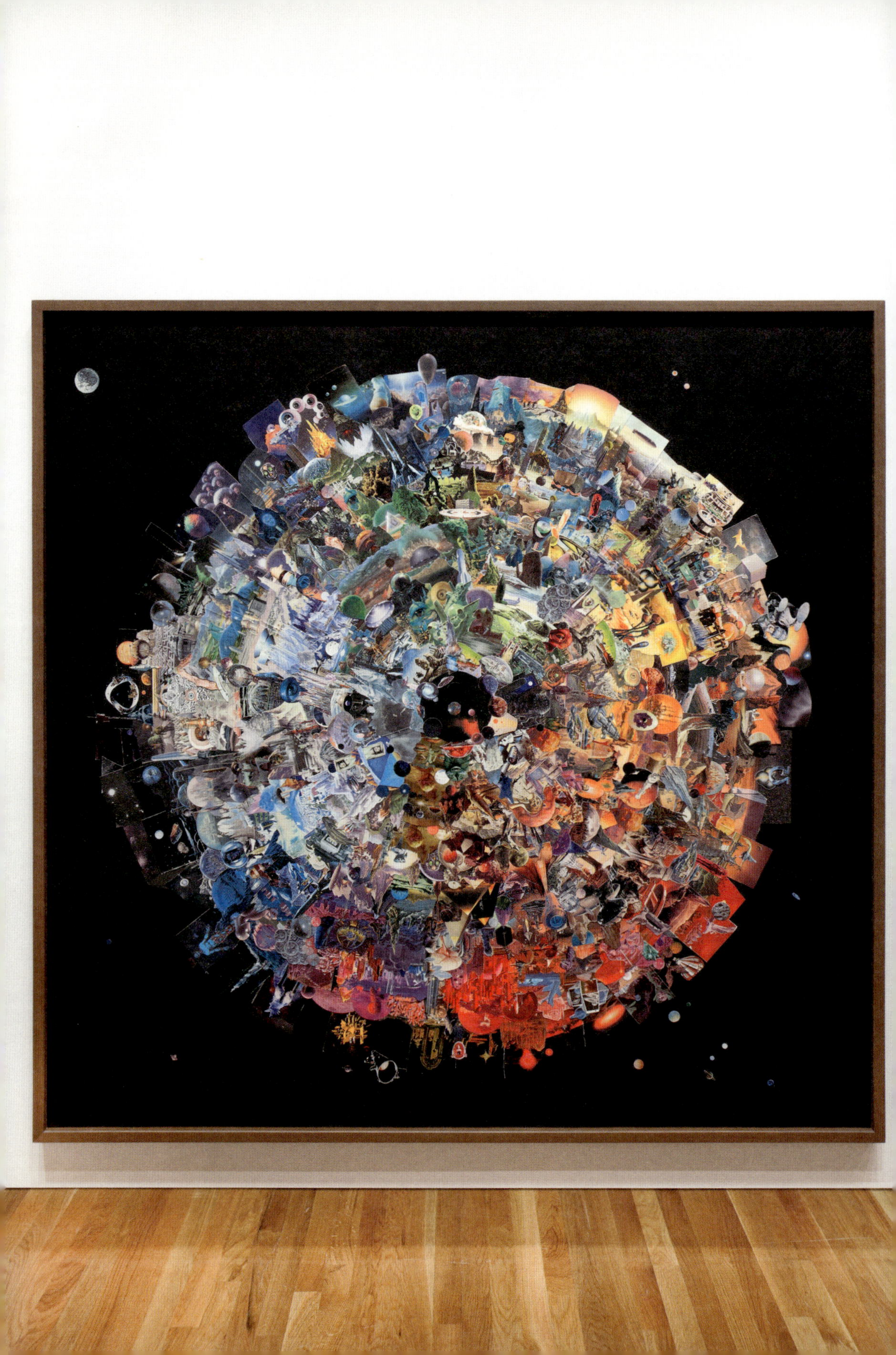

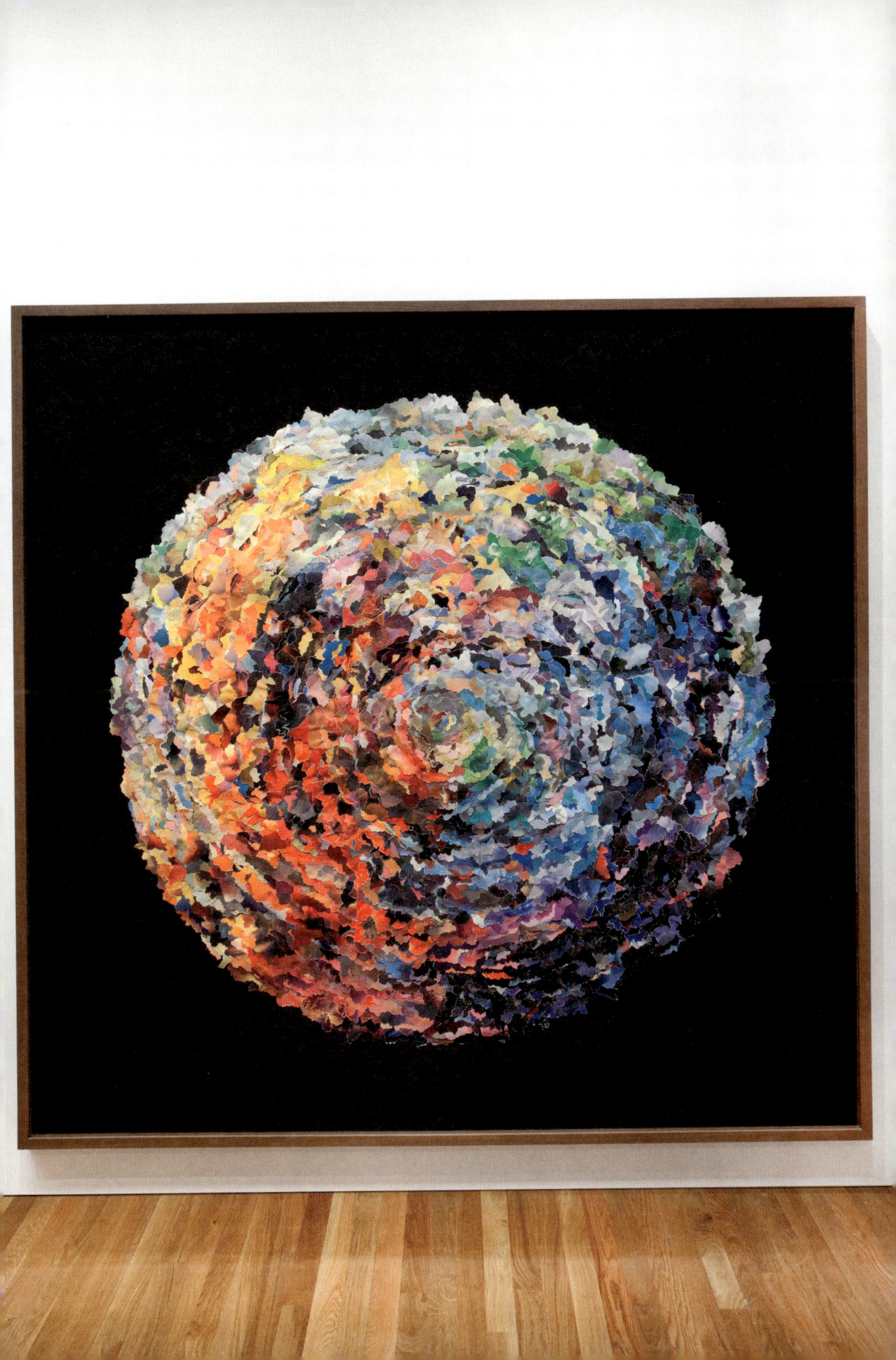

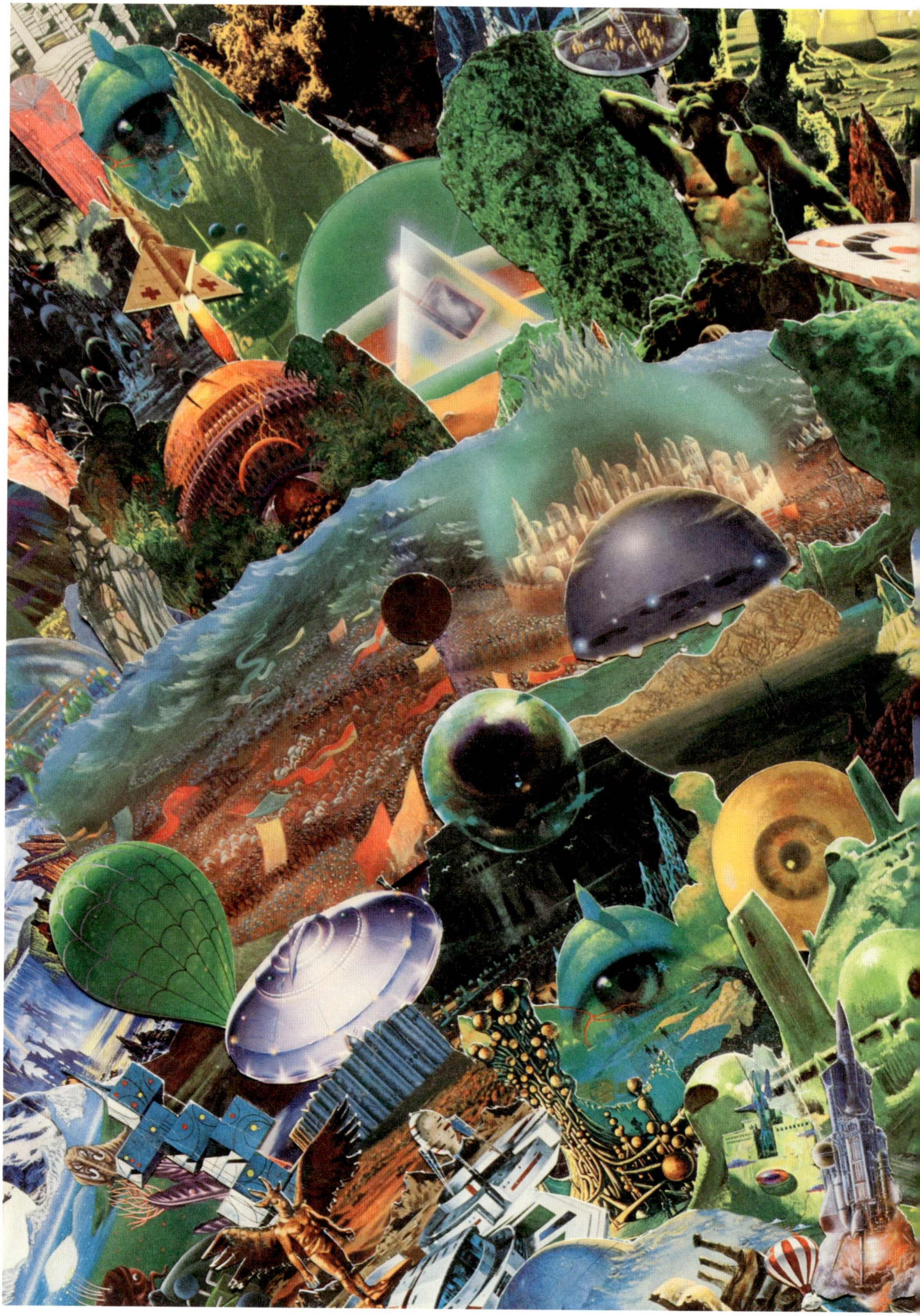

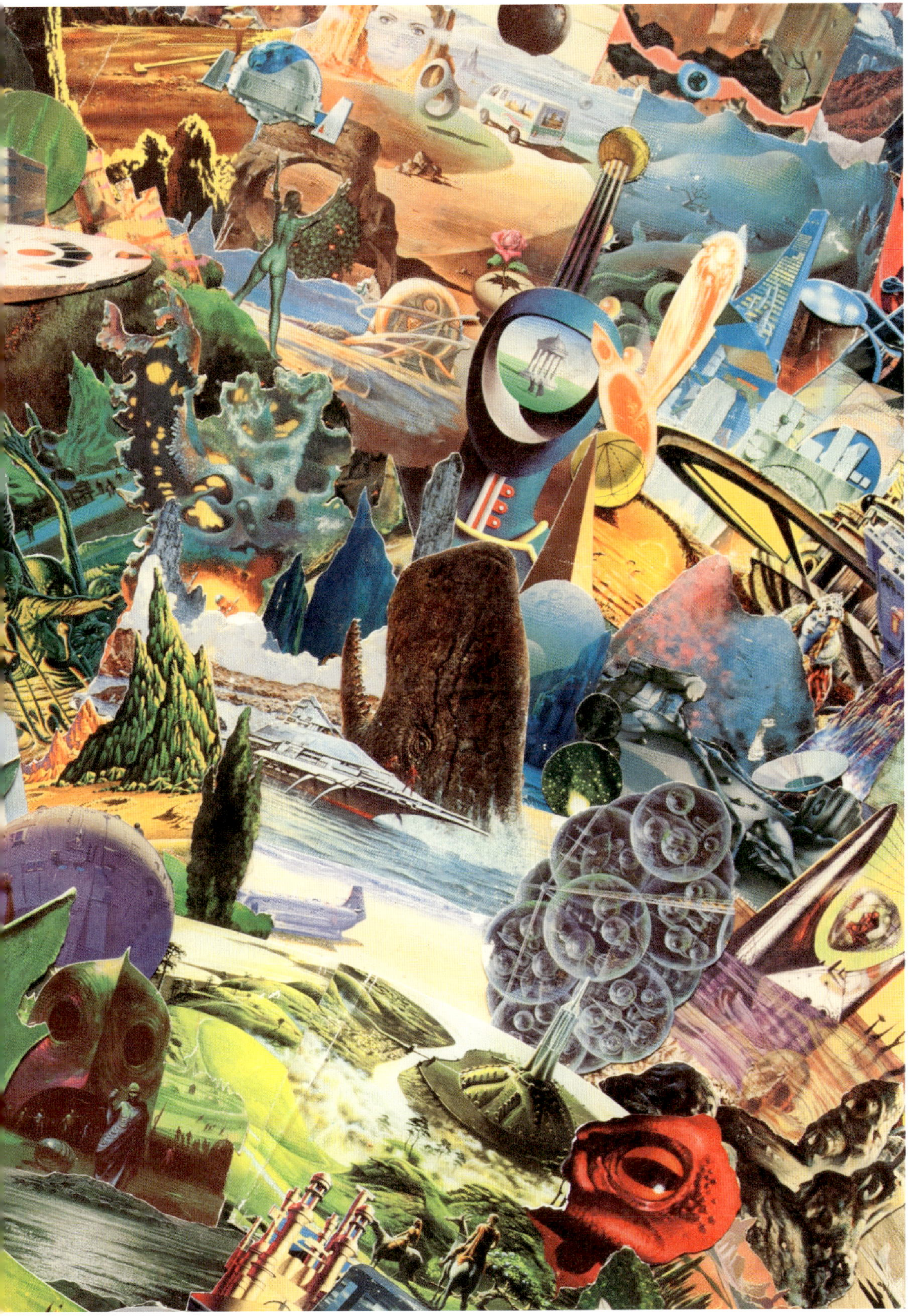

NEW JERUSALEM

A floating planetscape collaged from the deconstructed covers of science-fiction paperbacks. Named for the Biblical city of God that, according to the Book of Revelation, descends from the heavens at the end of time.

2010

NEW JERUSALEM, CLOUD-SHROUDED

2012

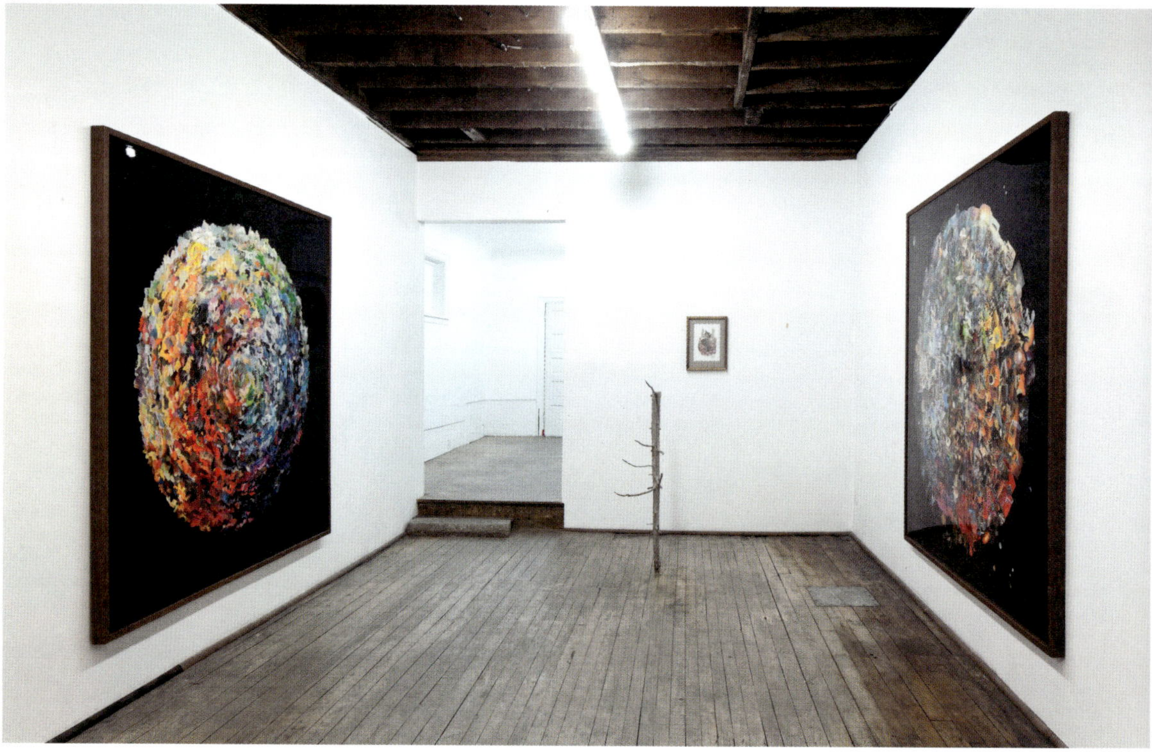

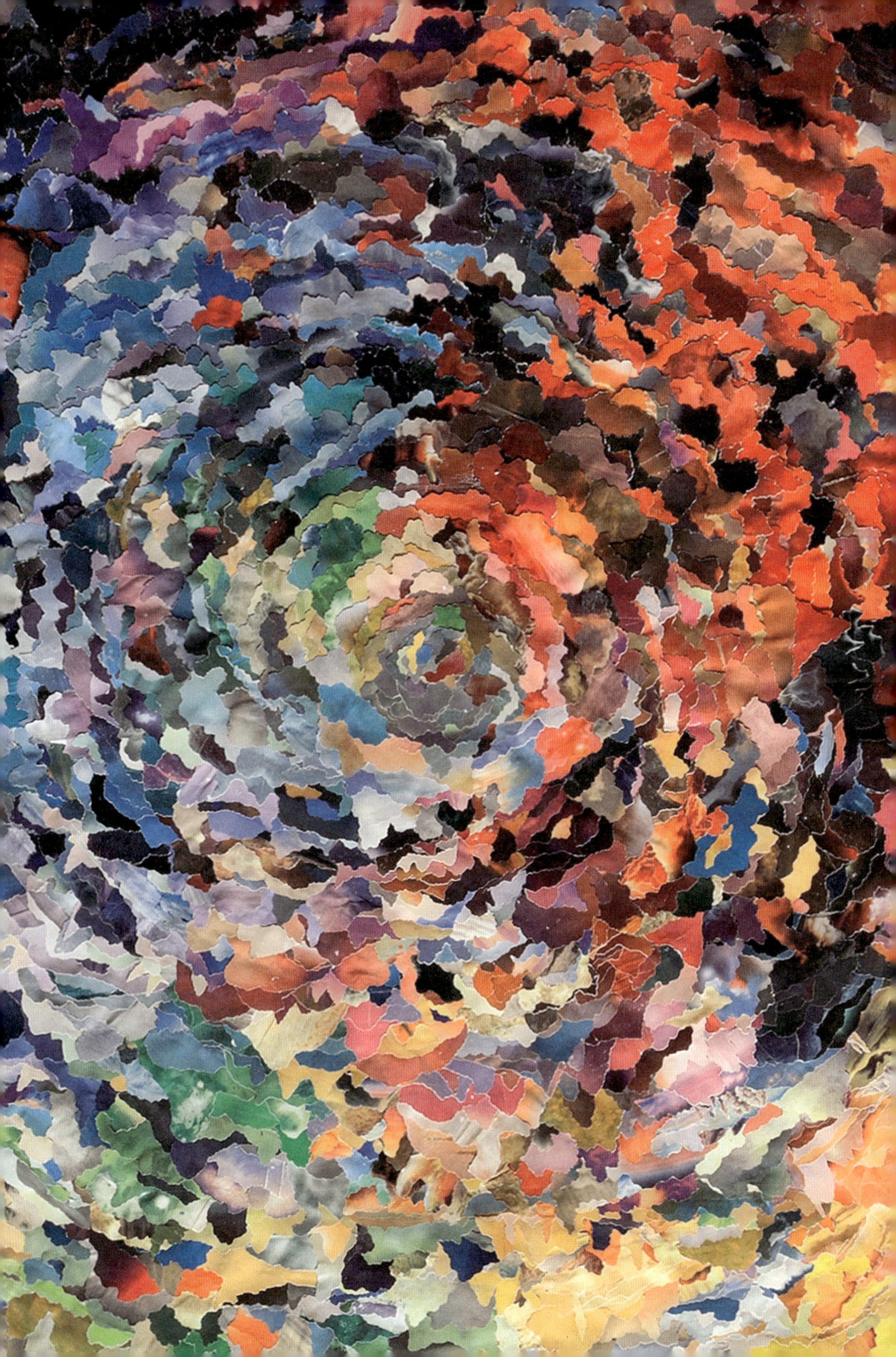

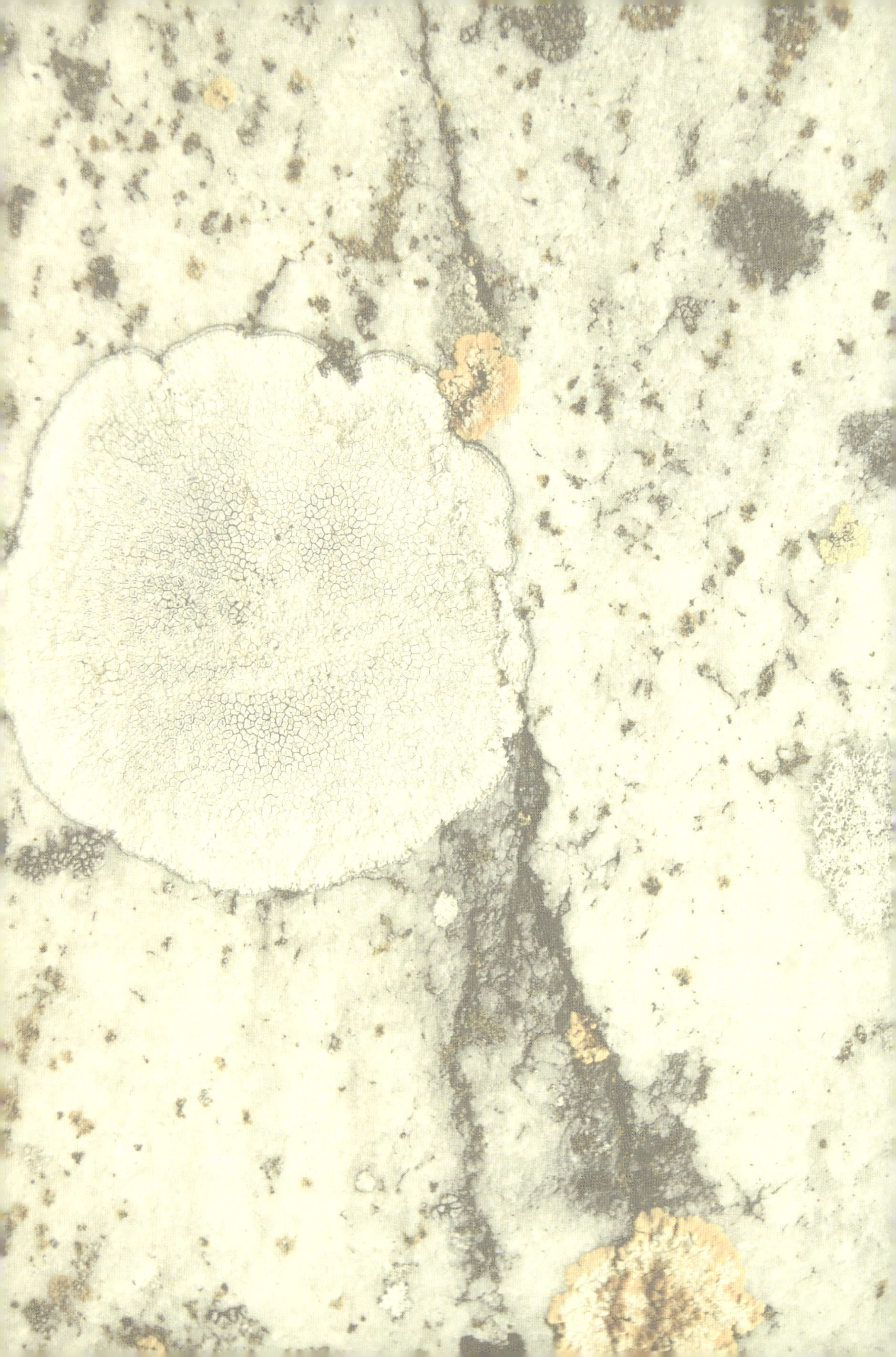

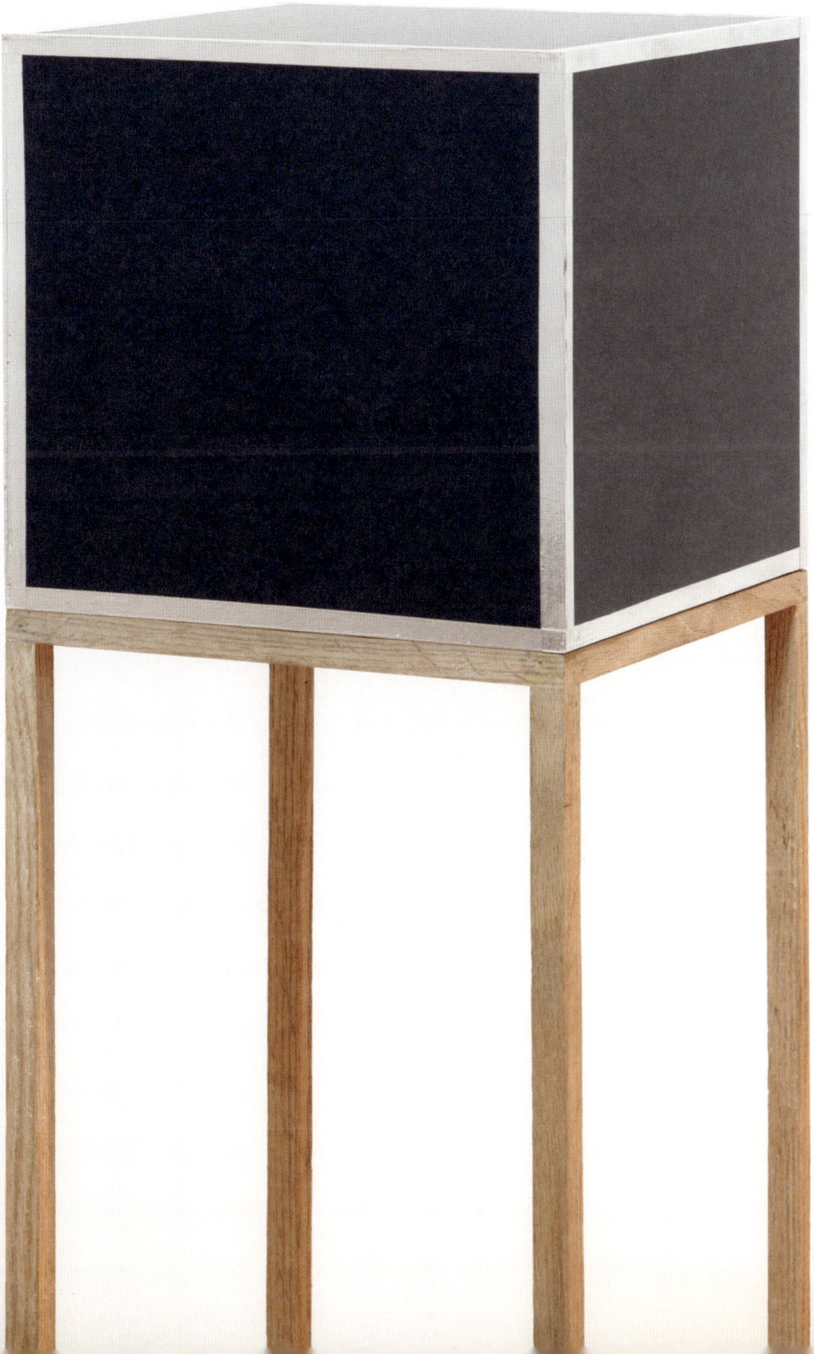

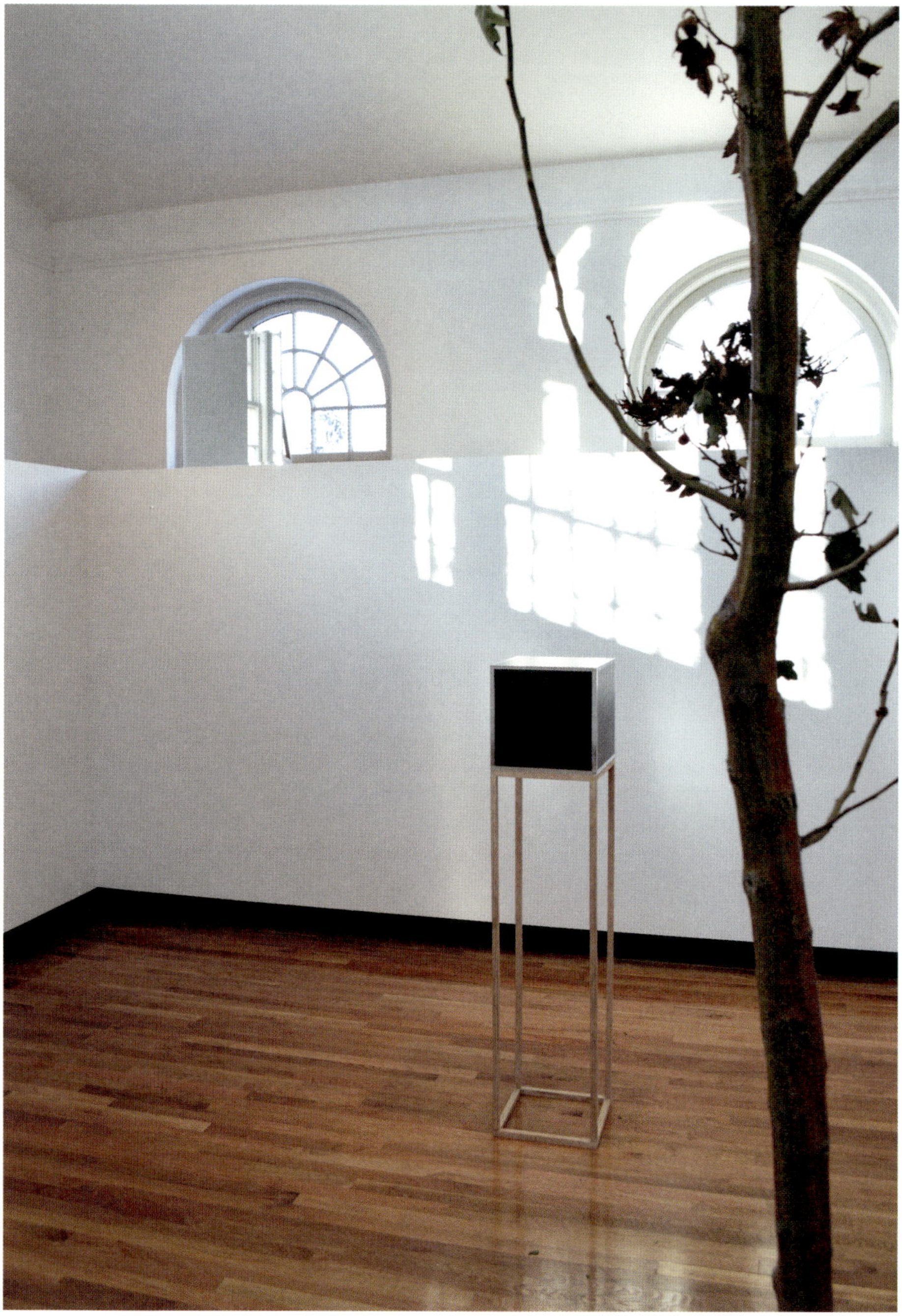

UNTITLED CUBE

Mirrored tiles containing the Northern Lights.

2008

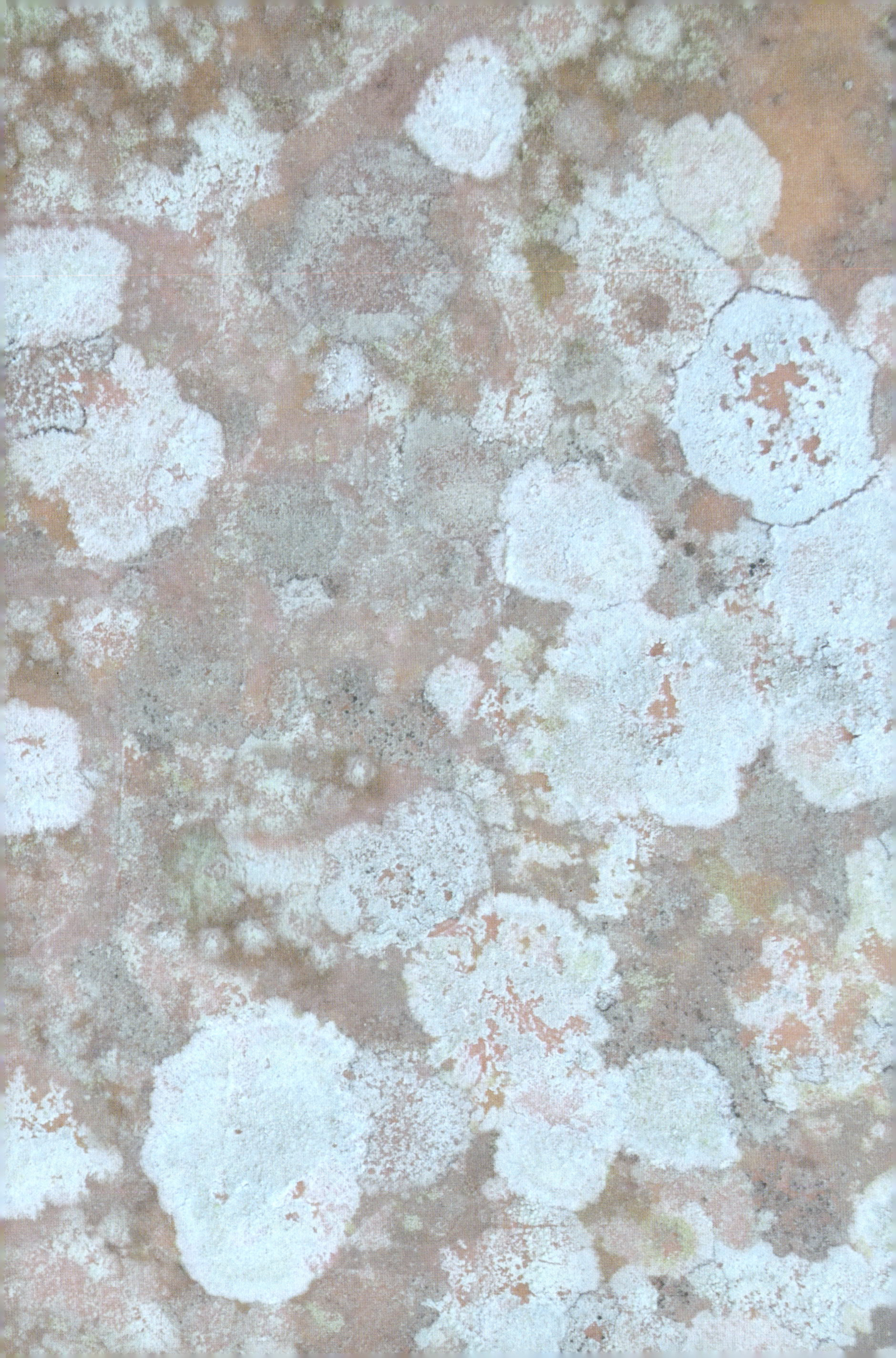

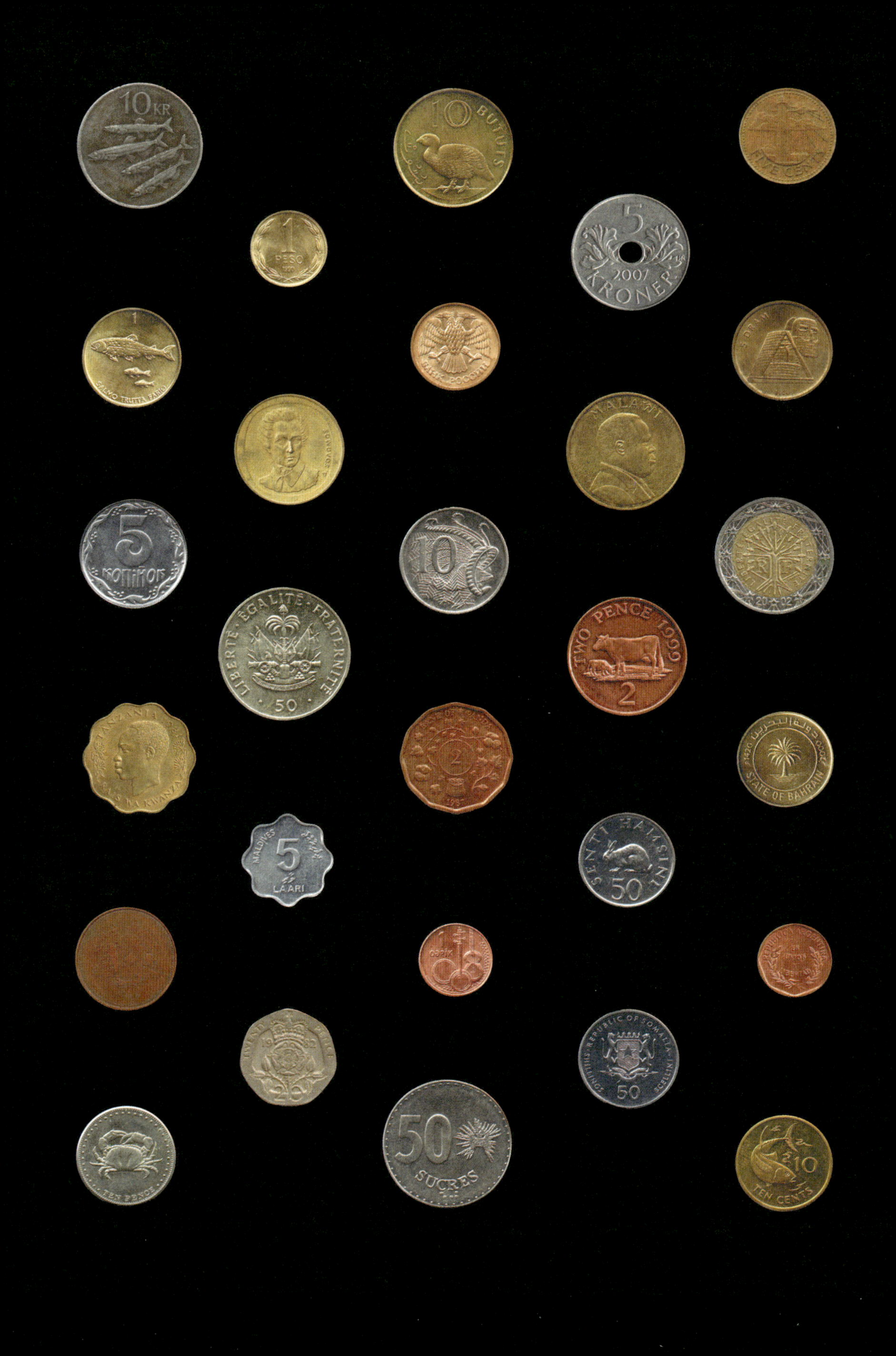
10 KR
10 BUTUTS
FIVE CENTS
1 PESO
5
2007
KRONER
SALMO TRUTTA FARIO
MALAWI
5
КОПІЙОК
10
LIBERTÉ · ÉGALITÉ · FRATERNITÉ
50
TWO PENCE 1999
2
TANZANIA
STATE OF BAHRAIN
MALDIVES
5
LAARI
SENTI HAMSINI
50
REPUBLIC OF SOMALIA
50
50
SUCRES
TEN PENCE
10
TEN CENTS

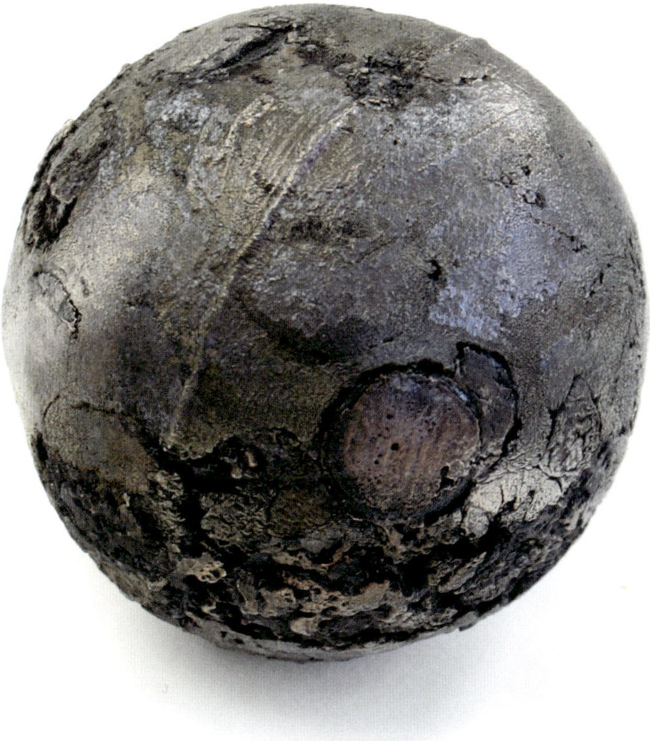

CANNON BALL

A sphere formed of one coin from
each of the World's active currencies.

2012

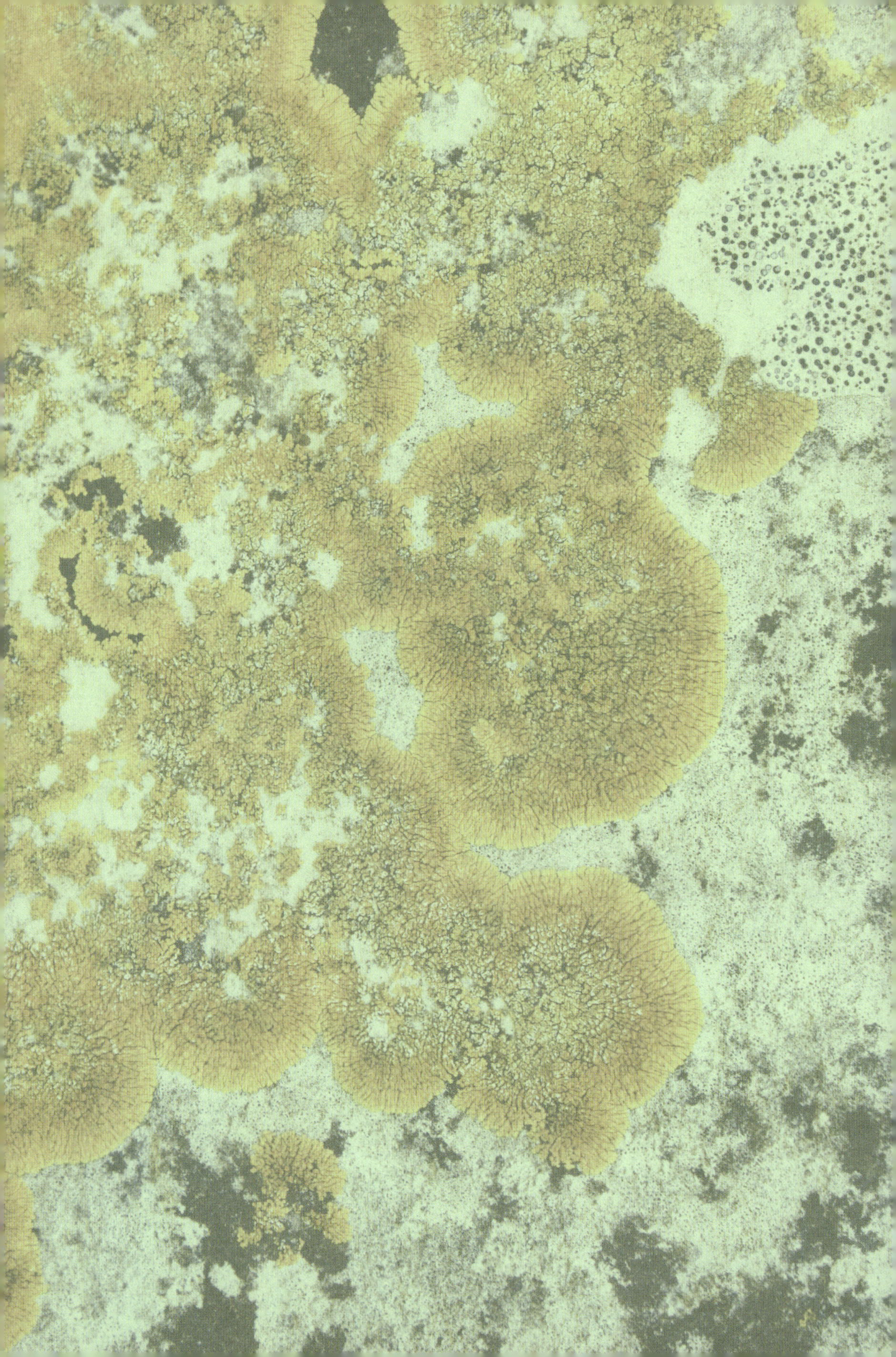

LIFE AFTER
DOOMSDAY

LIFE AFTER DOOMSDAY

Two open editions, each of 5000 to date, of beer coasters bearing the text LIFE AFTER DOOMSDAY. Distributed in bars, pubs and clubs in various cities internationally, including The Hermit's Cave, London; The Pit, Dawson City; Evergreen, Beirut.

2008, 2010

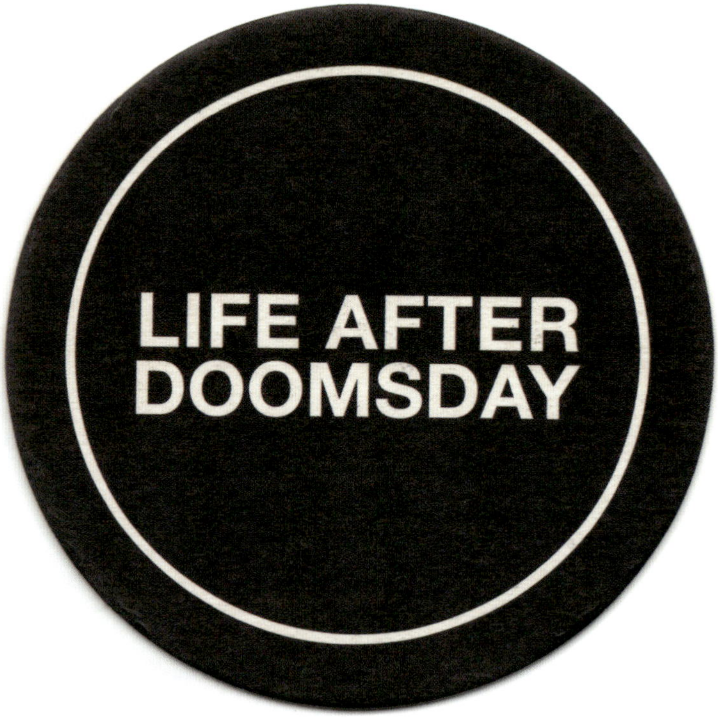

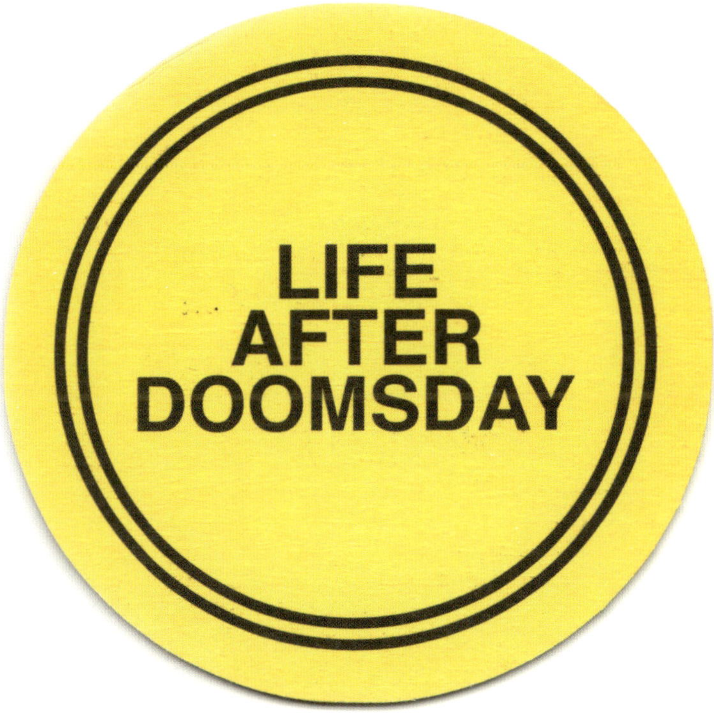
LIFE
AFTER
DOOMSDAY

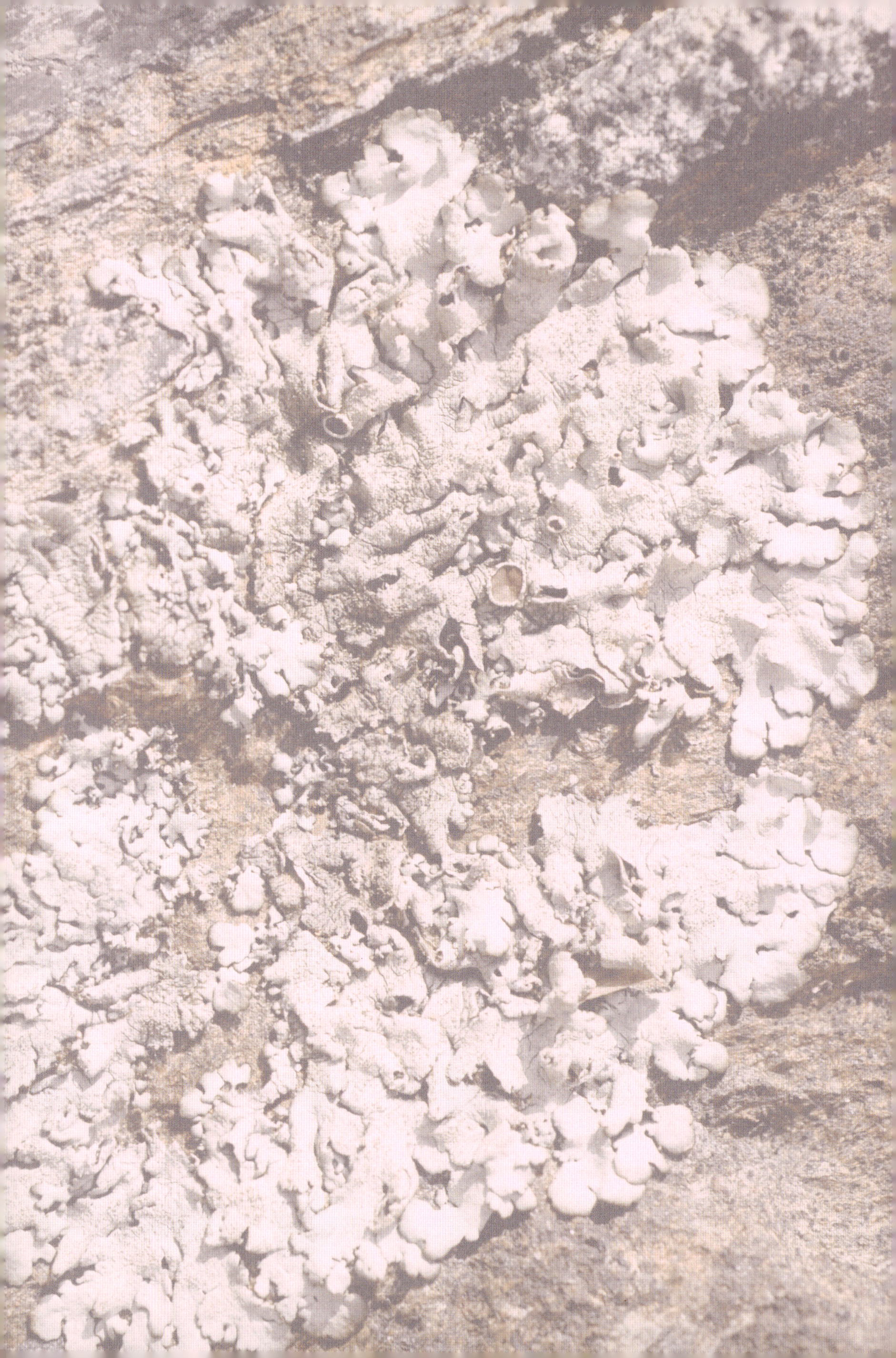

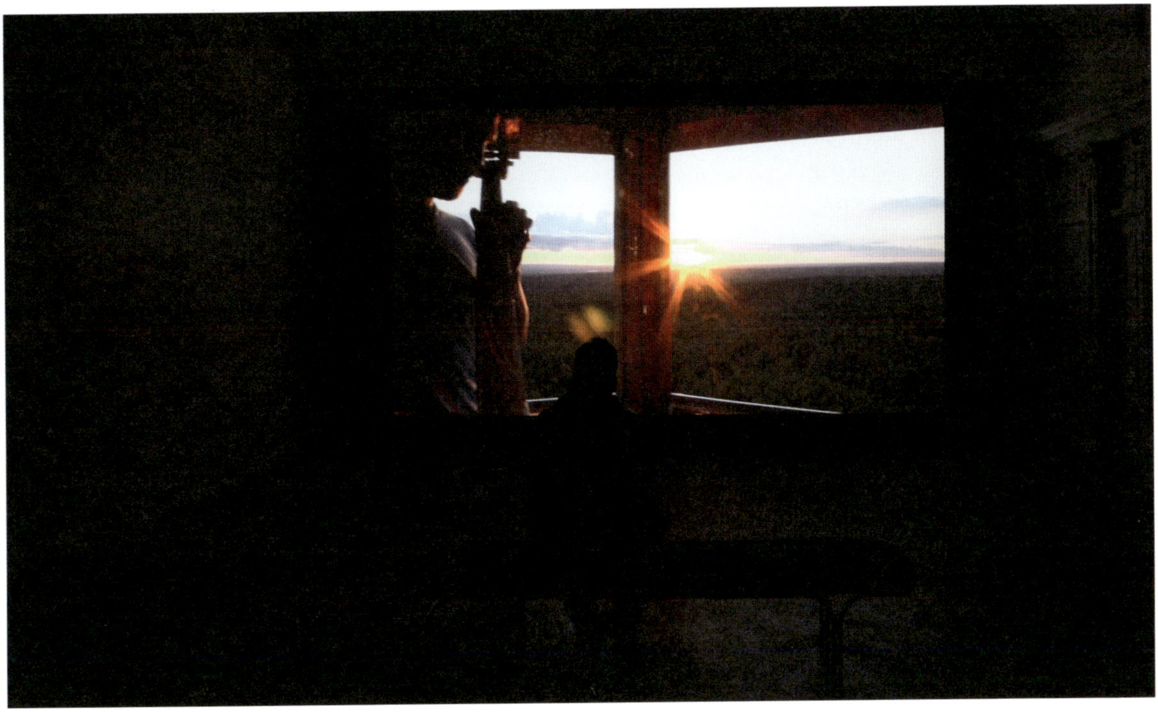

THE WOOD AND WAVE EACH OTHER KNOW
with Miruna Dragan

Daniel Bosch is a wildfire lookout in Northern Alberta, Canada. Every day, from April to October, he looks out upon the treetops from the eight by eight foot cabin of the tallest tower in the province. Dan is also a self-taught musician. While living in the woods, he crafted a cello from a solid block of spruce and then taught himself to play it. Because the cello was too big to fit in the cage of the tower's one hundred and twenty vertical steps, Dan made a body-less version, allowing him to practice during his many hours inside the tower's cabin. By wedging the practice cello between the edge of a small worktable and the cabin's fiberglass octagonal cupola, Dan discovered that he could more than compensate for the instrument's lack of a body. The cabin itself becomes the resonant chamber and the tower becomes the instrument within which the cellist plays. Now, the lookout tower broadcasts Dan's music into the immensity of the landscape and the trees become his audience. *The Wood and Wave Each Other Know* is a video work documenting this activity; the camera constantly pans 360 degrees out of the cupola's windows, while Dan plays a number of improvised compositions. A bookwork containing peripheral images accompanies the thirty-eight minute video.

2011

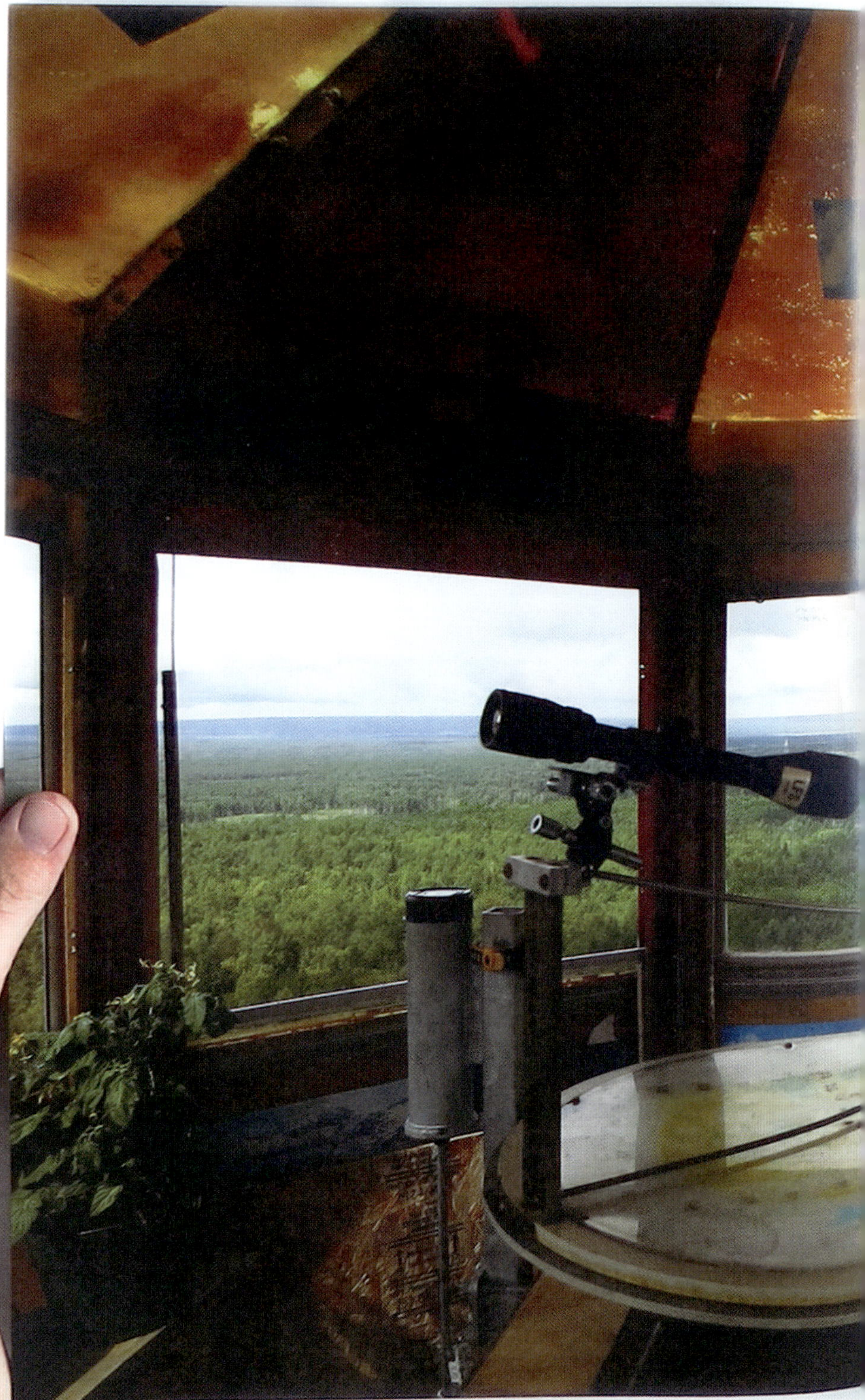

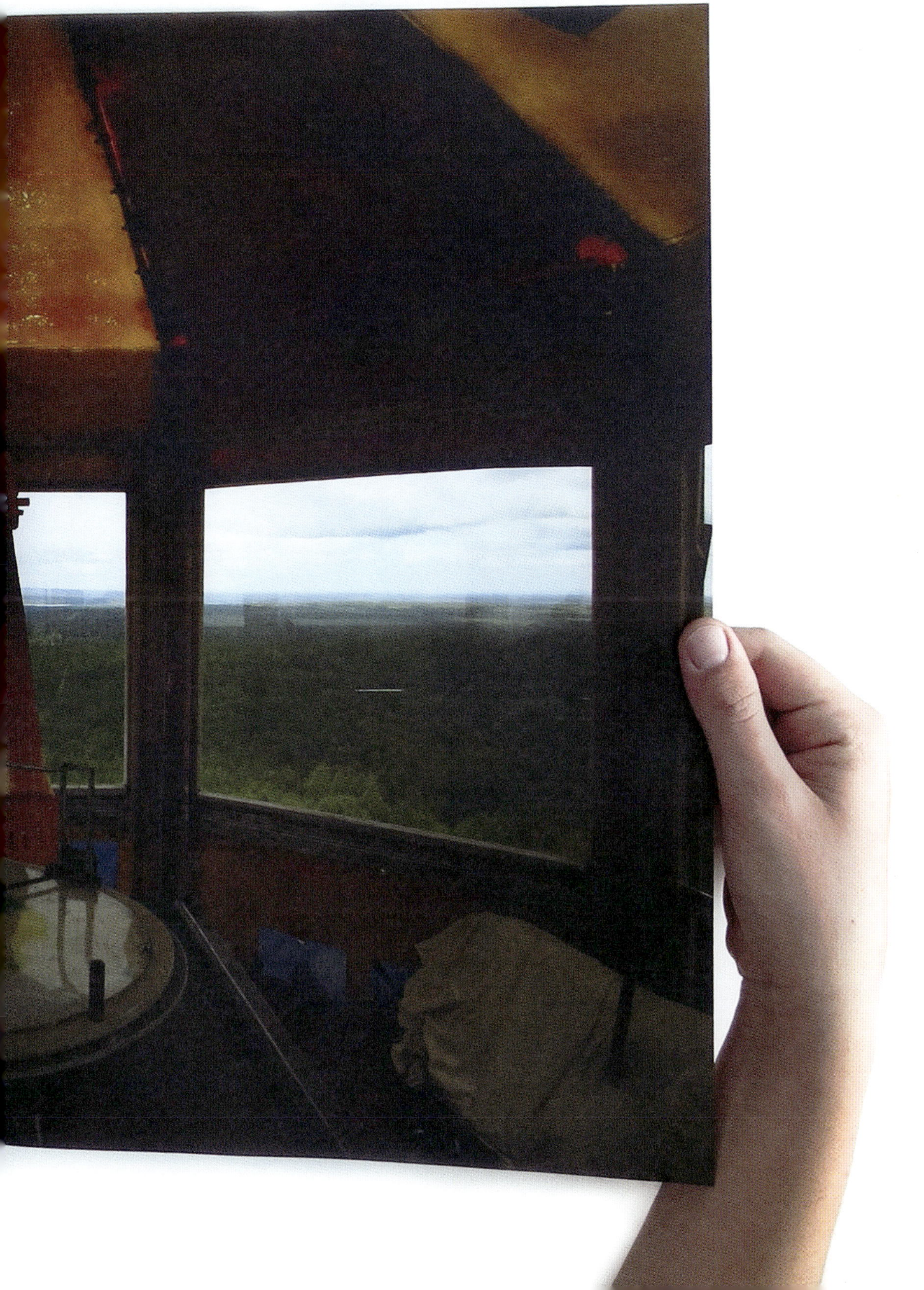

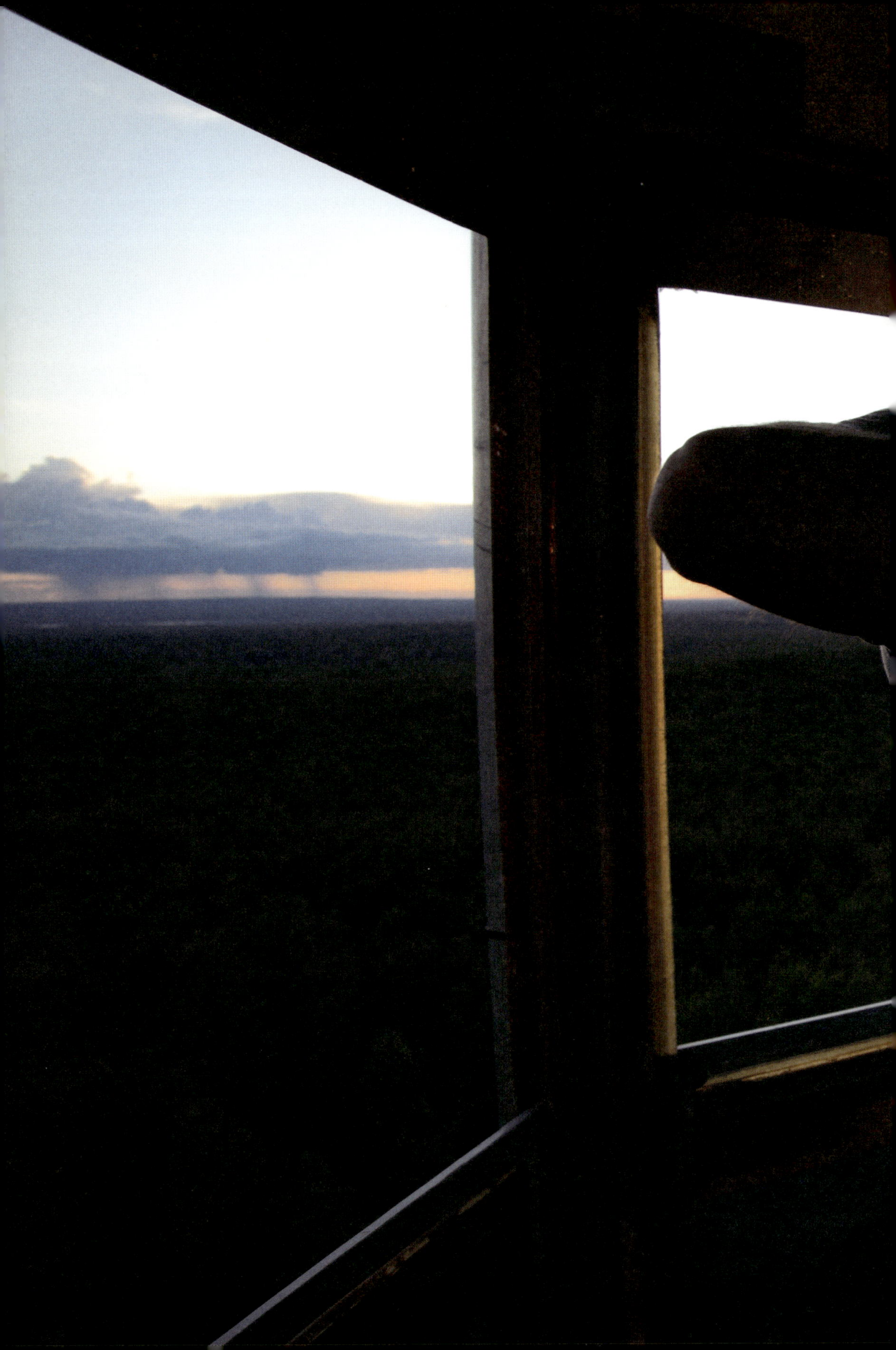

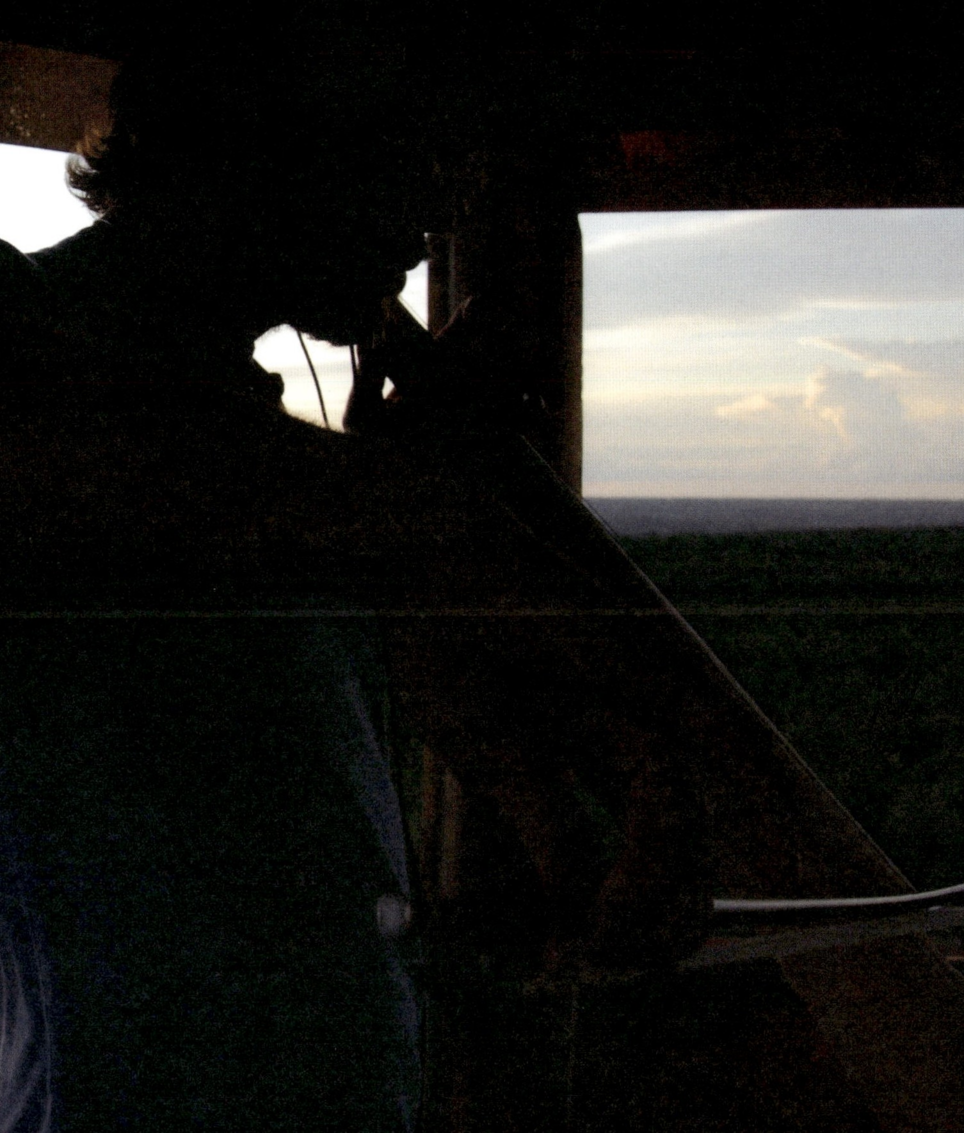

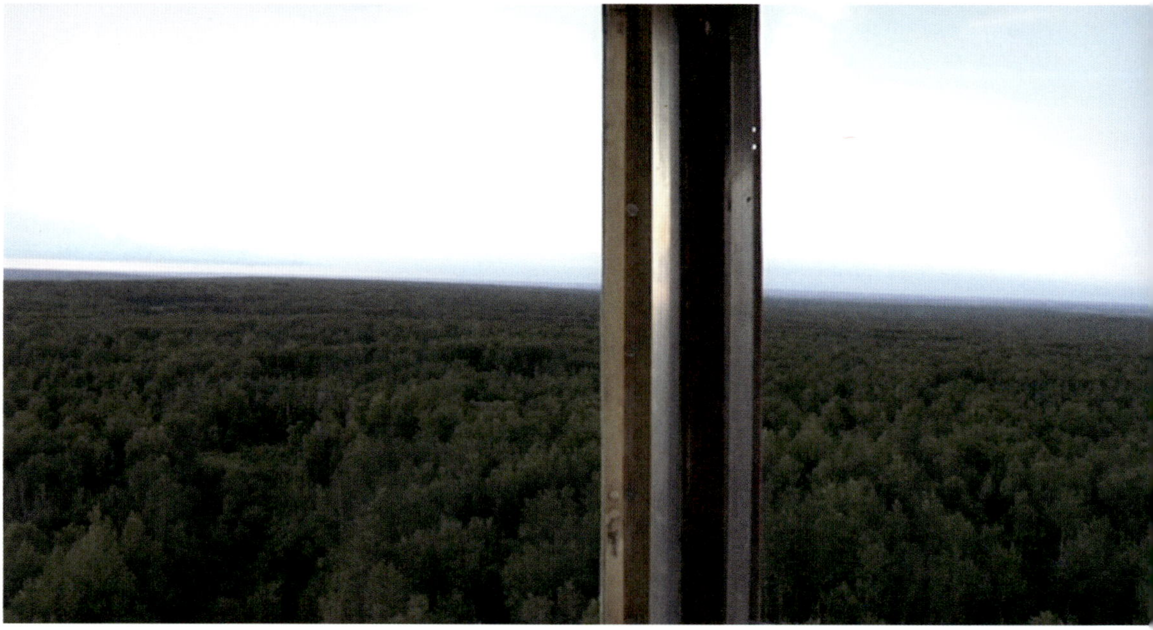

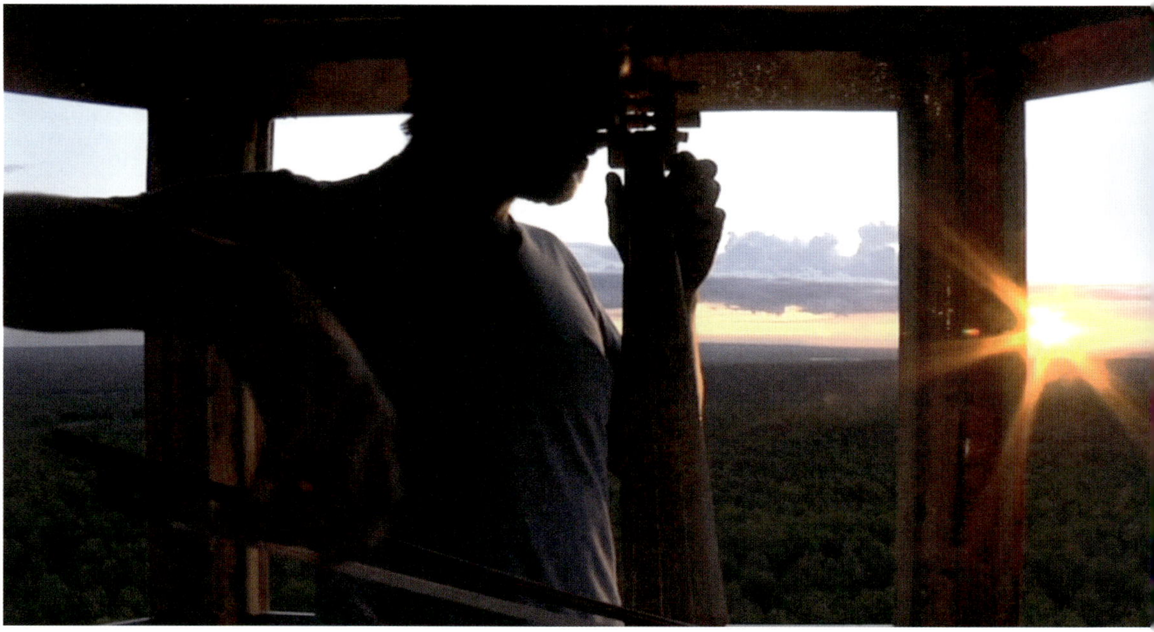

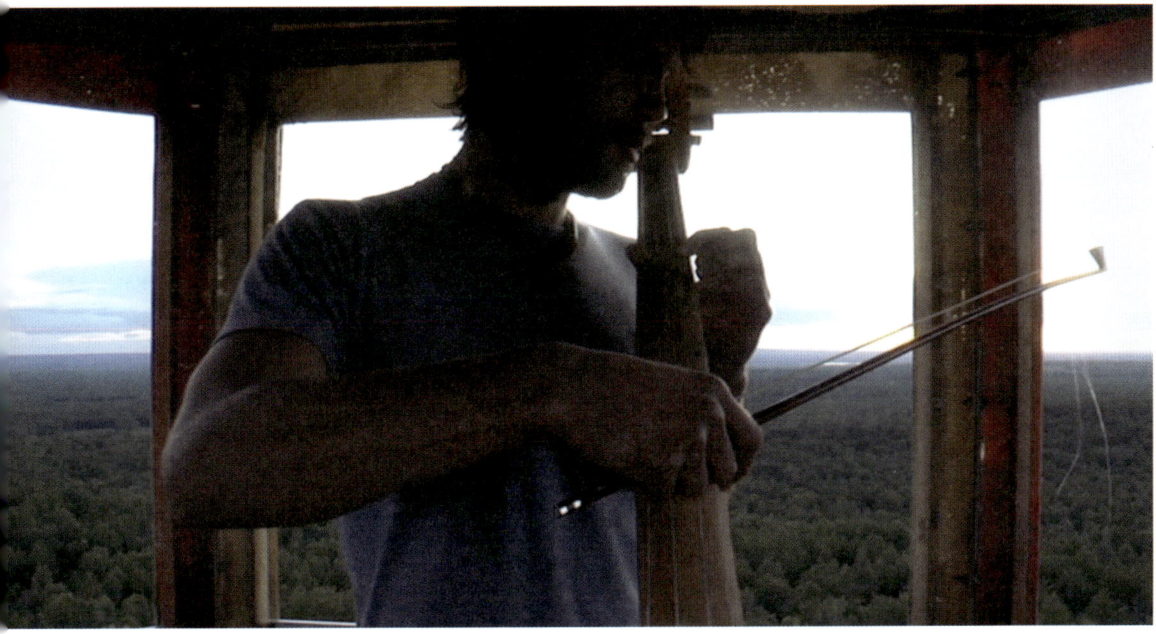

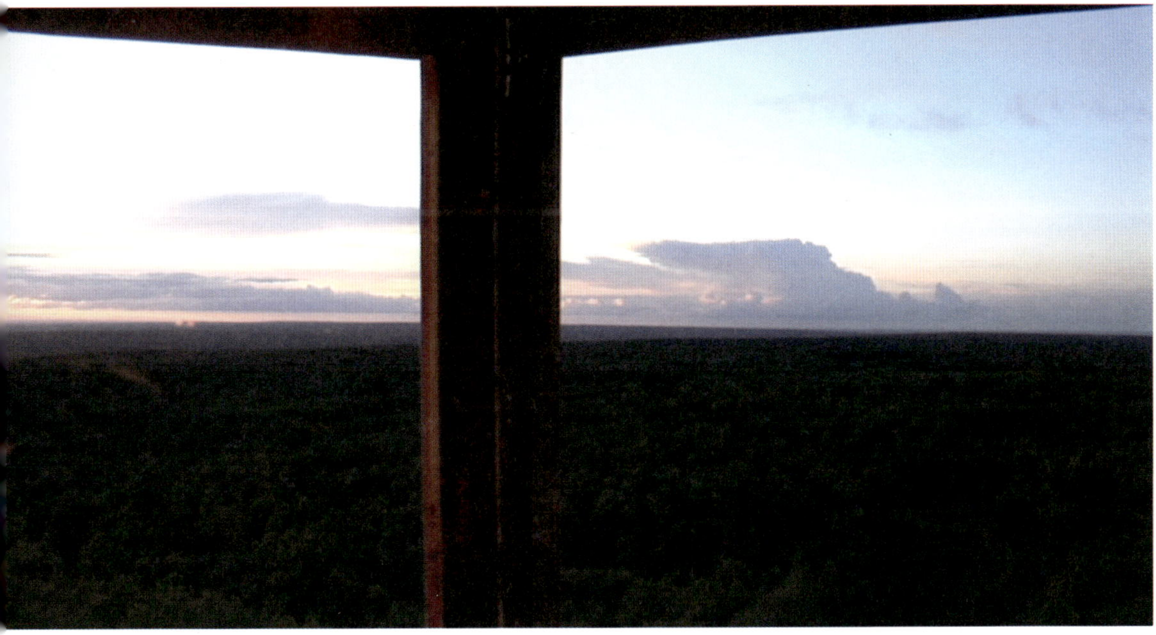

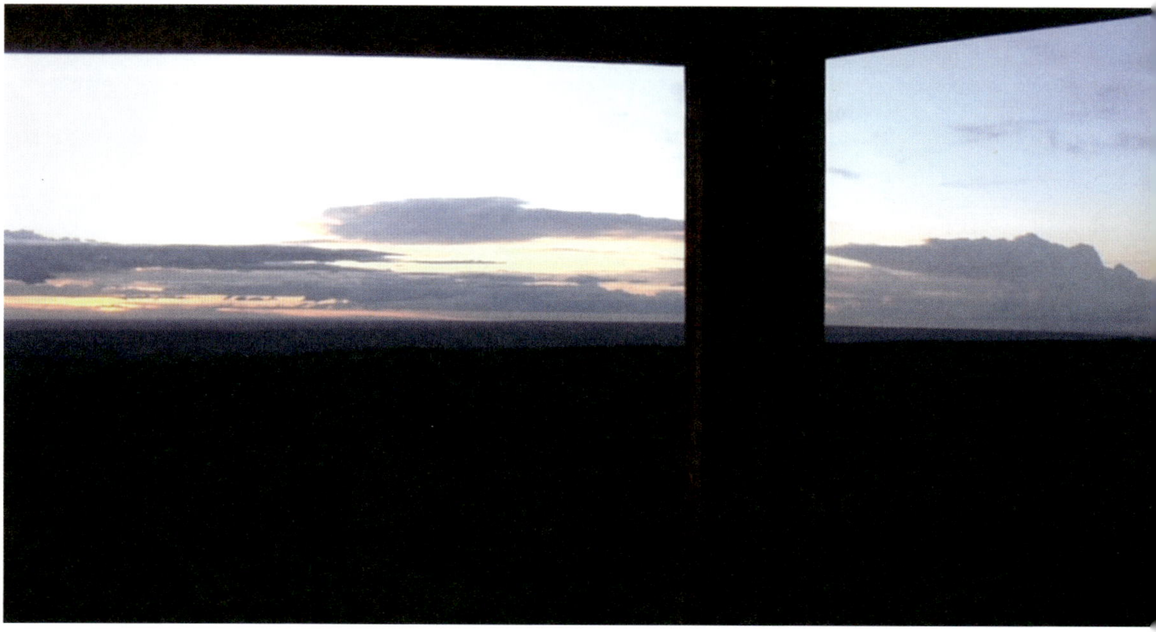

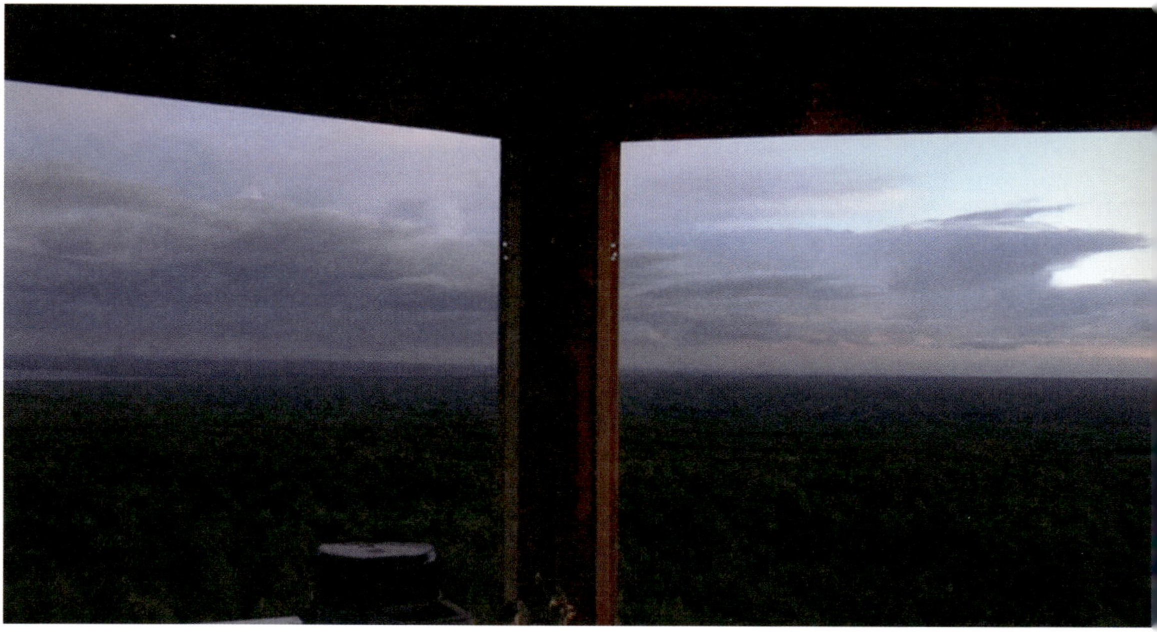

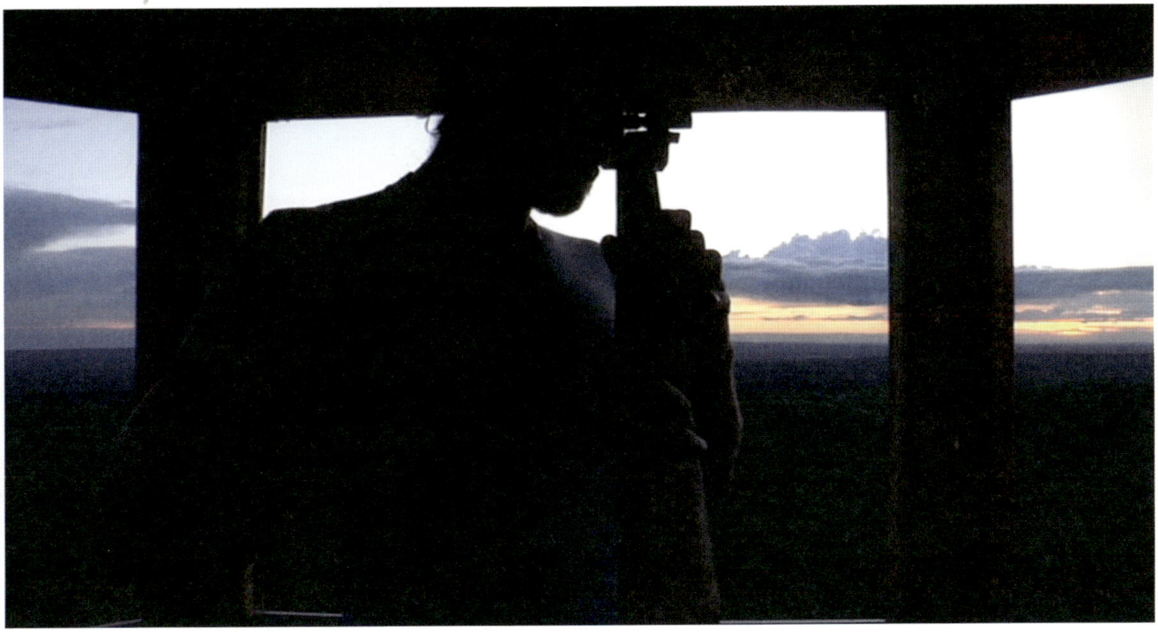

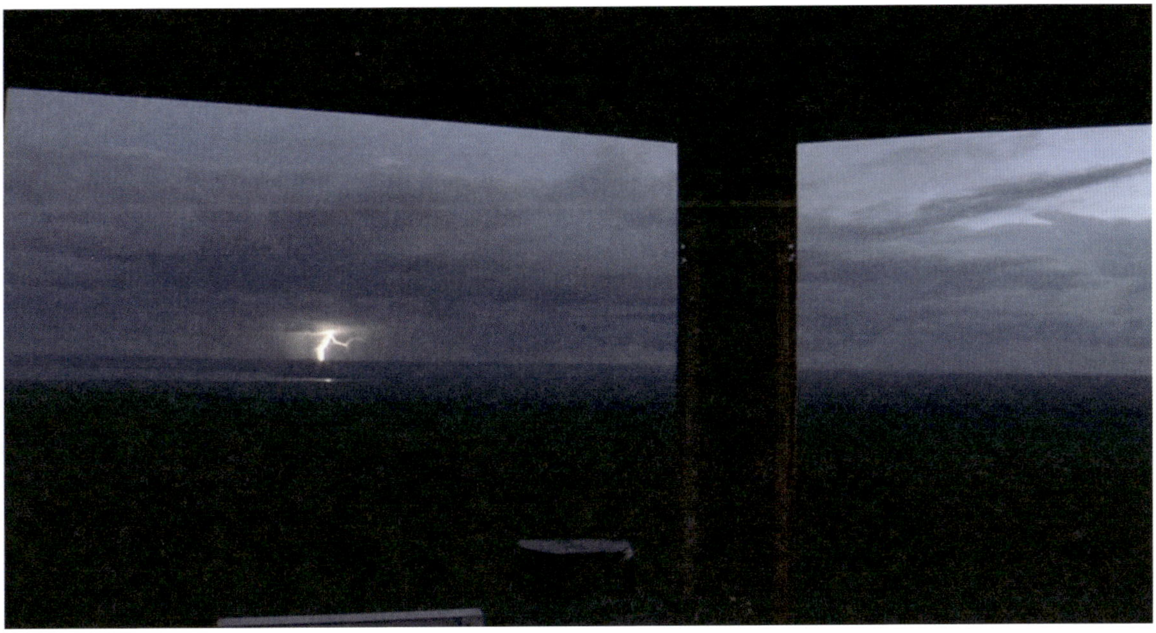

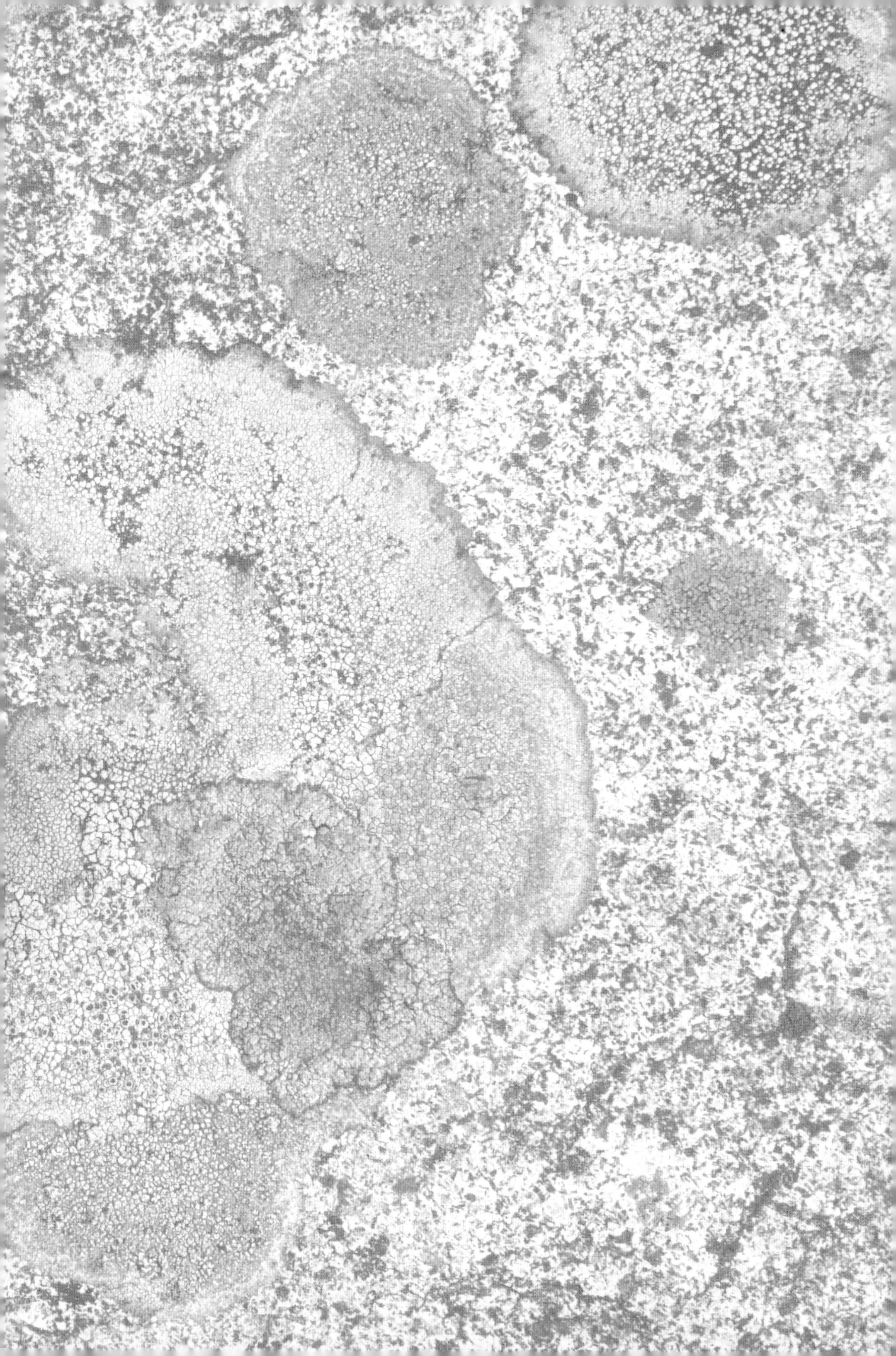

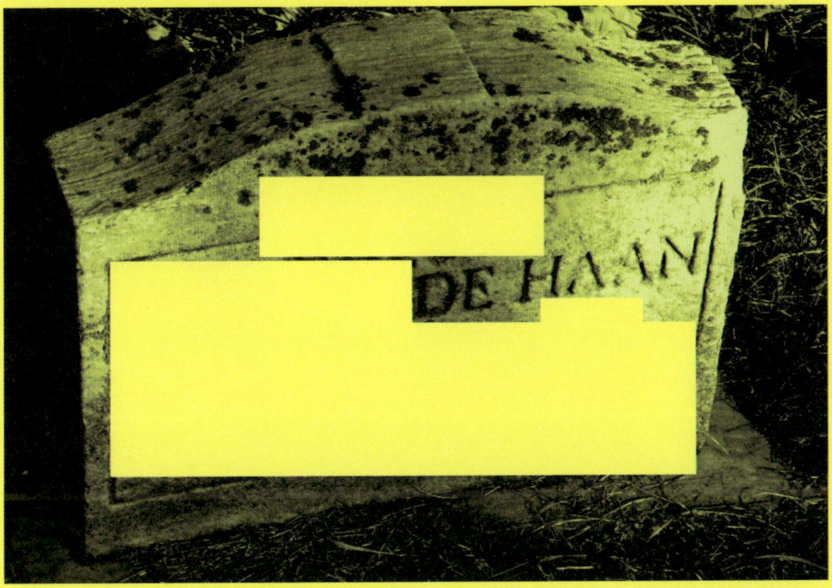
DE HAAN

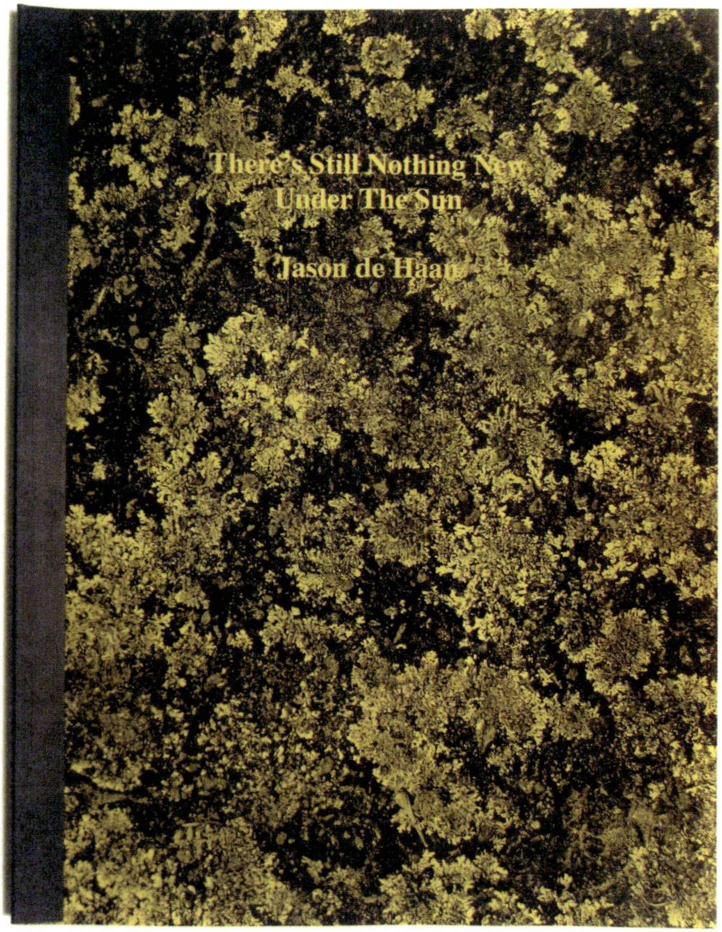

THERE'S STILL NOTHING NEW UNDER THE SUN

An image collection of de Haan family gravestones, published as a 32 page bookwork.

2011

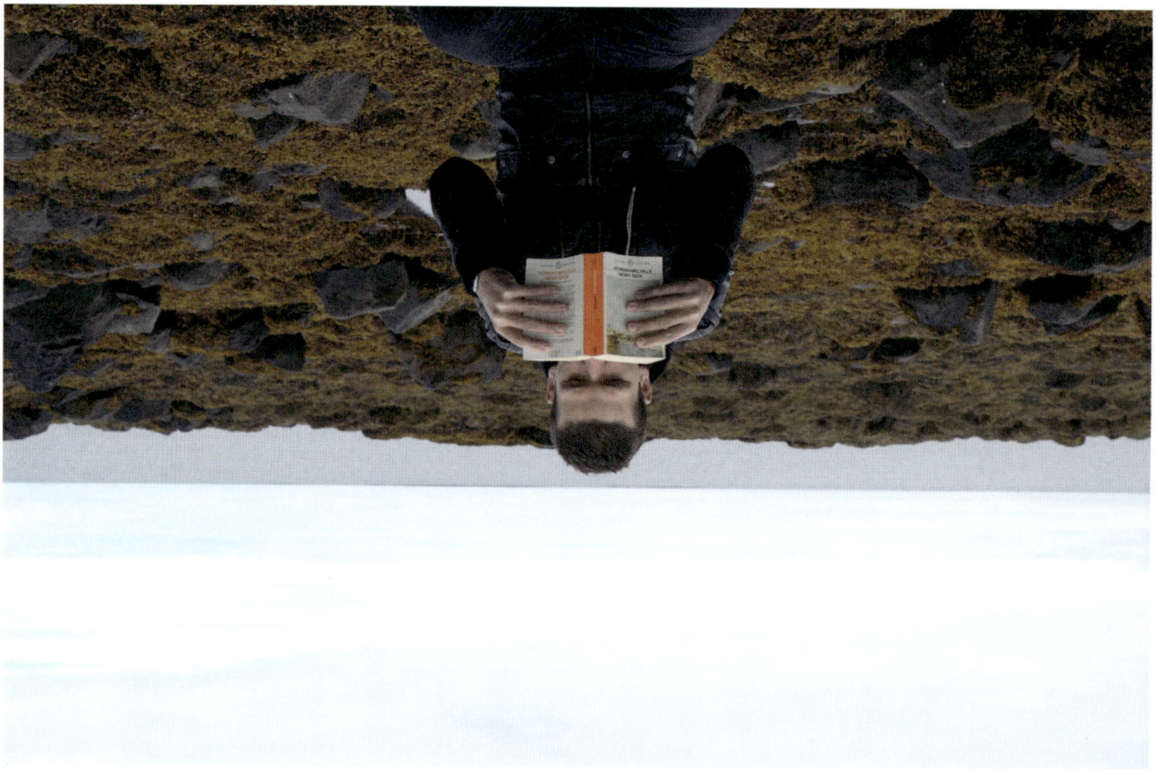

18

MOBY DICK

Mellville's *Moby Dick* is read upside down and backwards near bodies of water.

2009 –

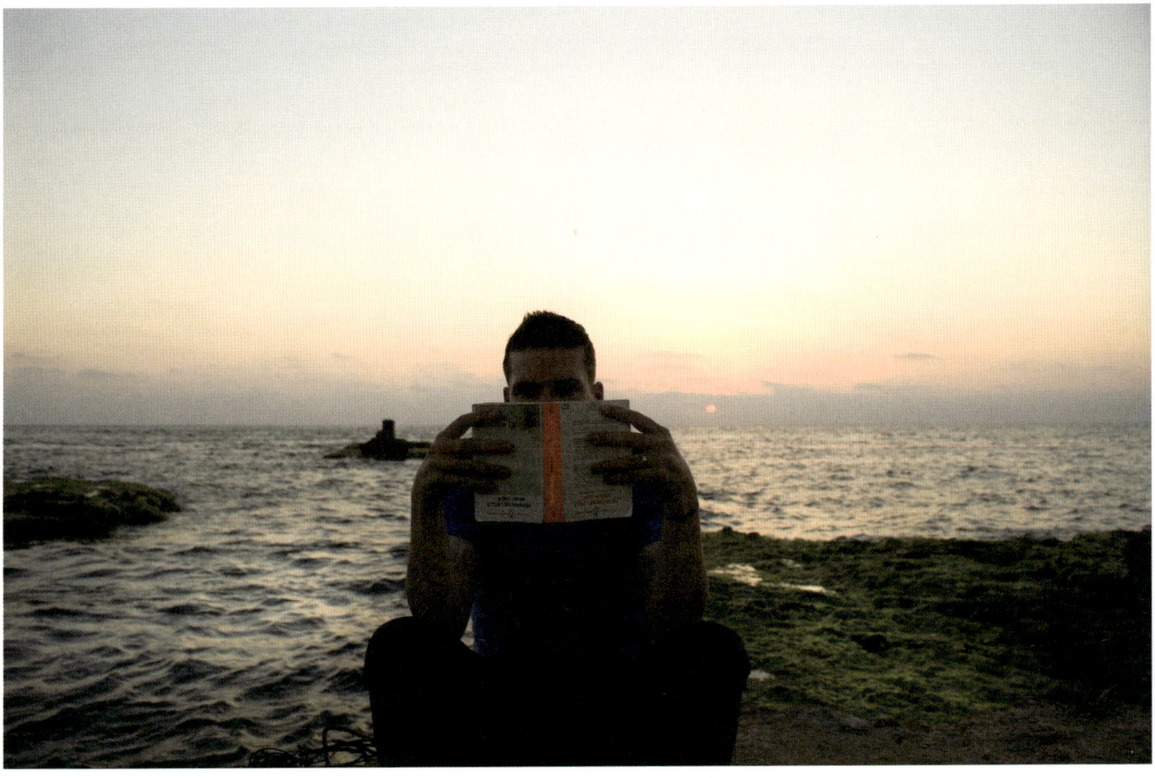

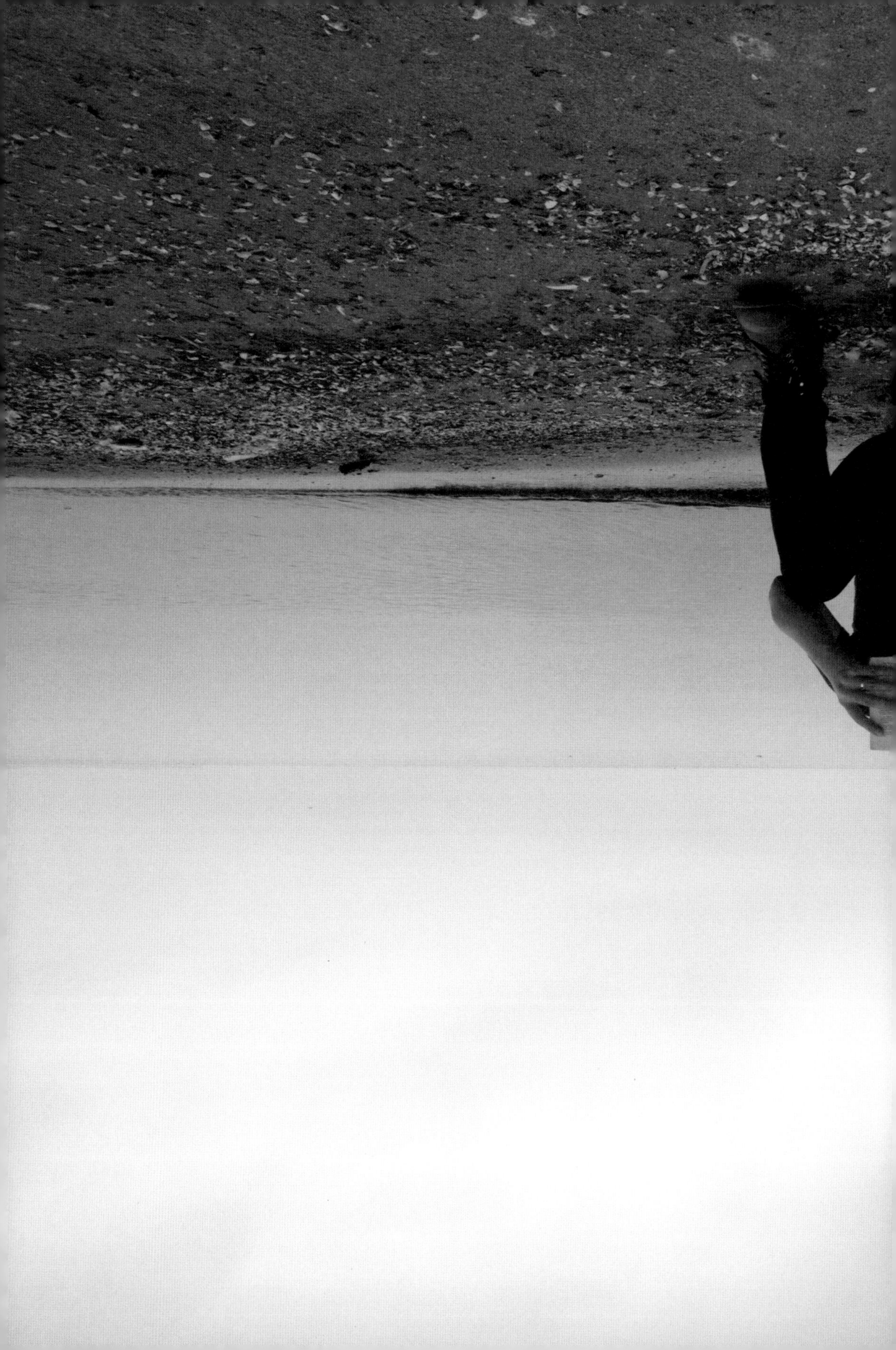

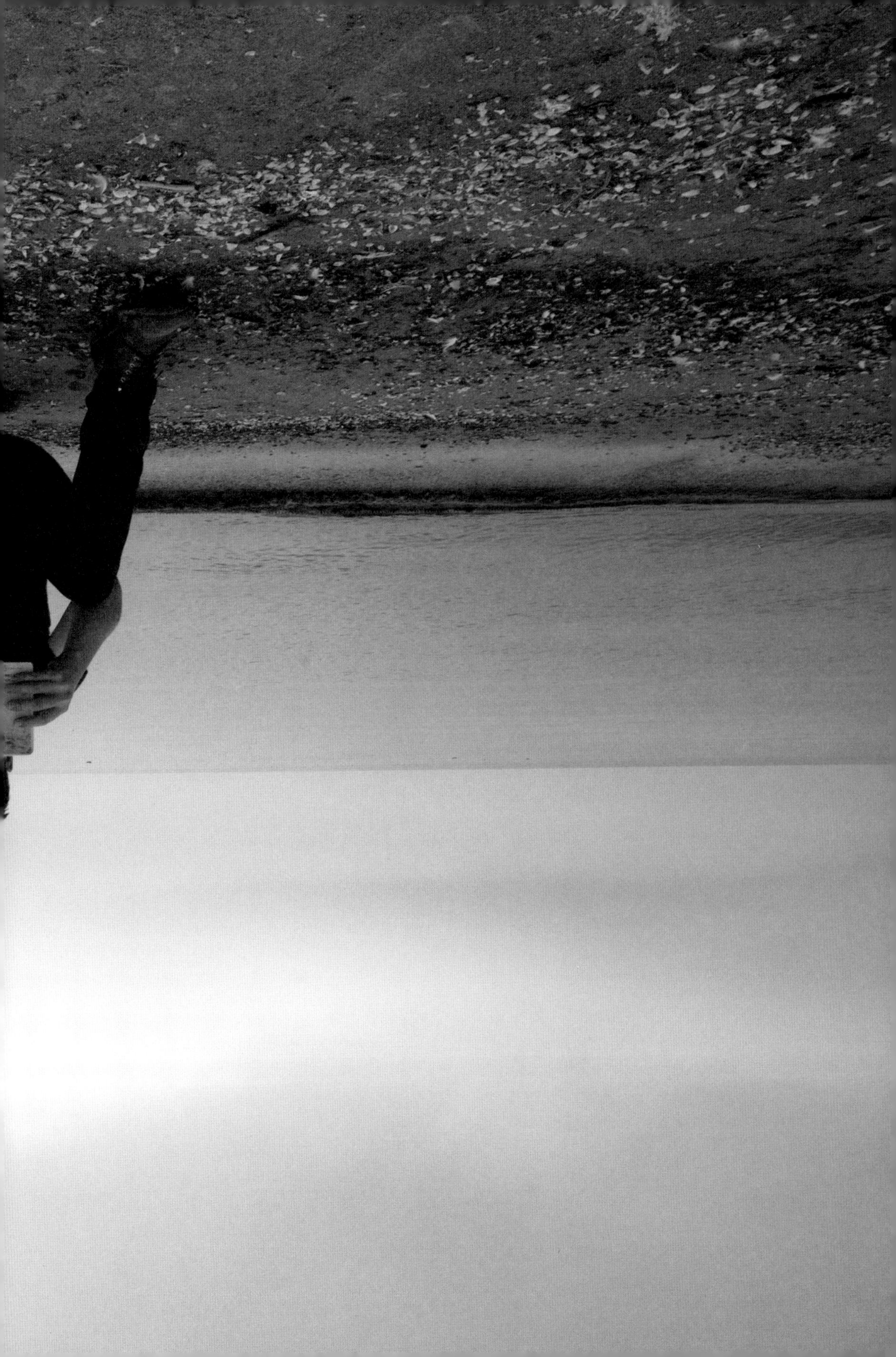

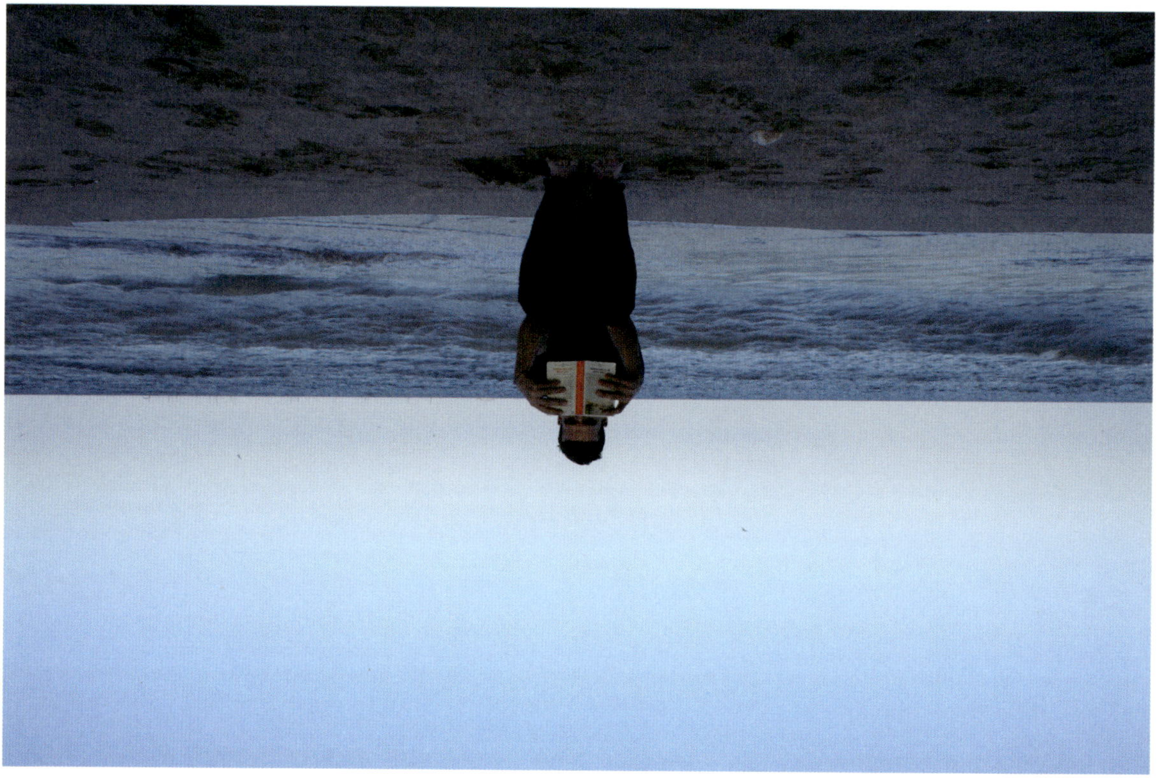

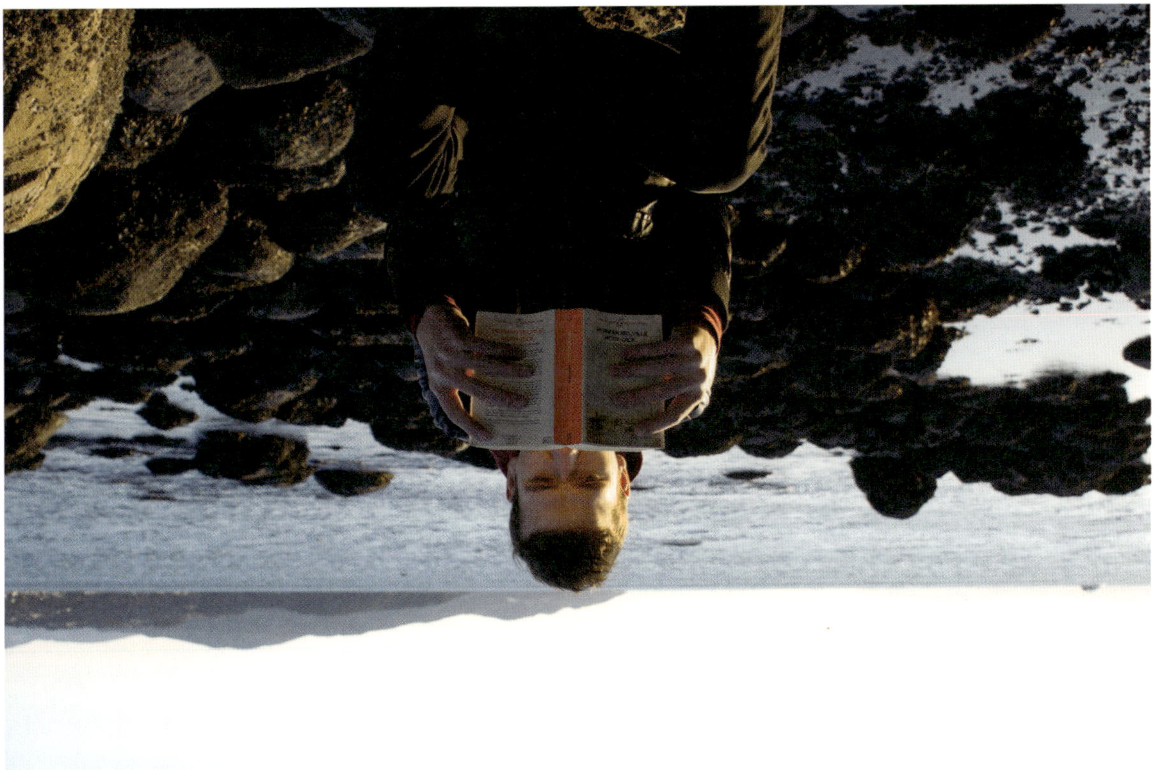

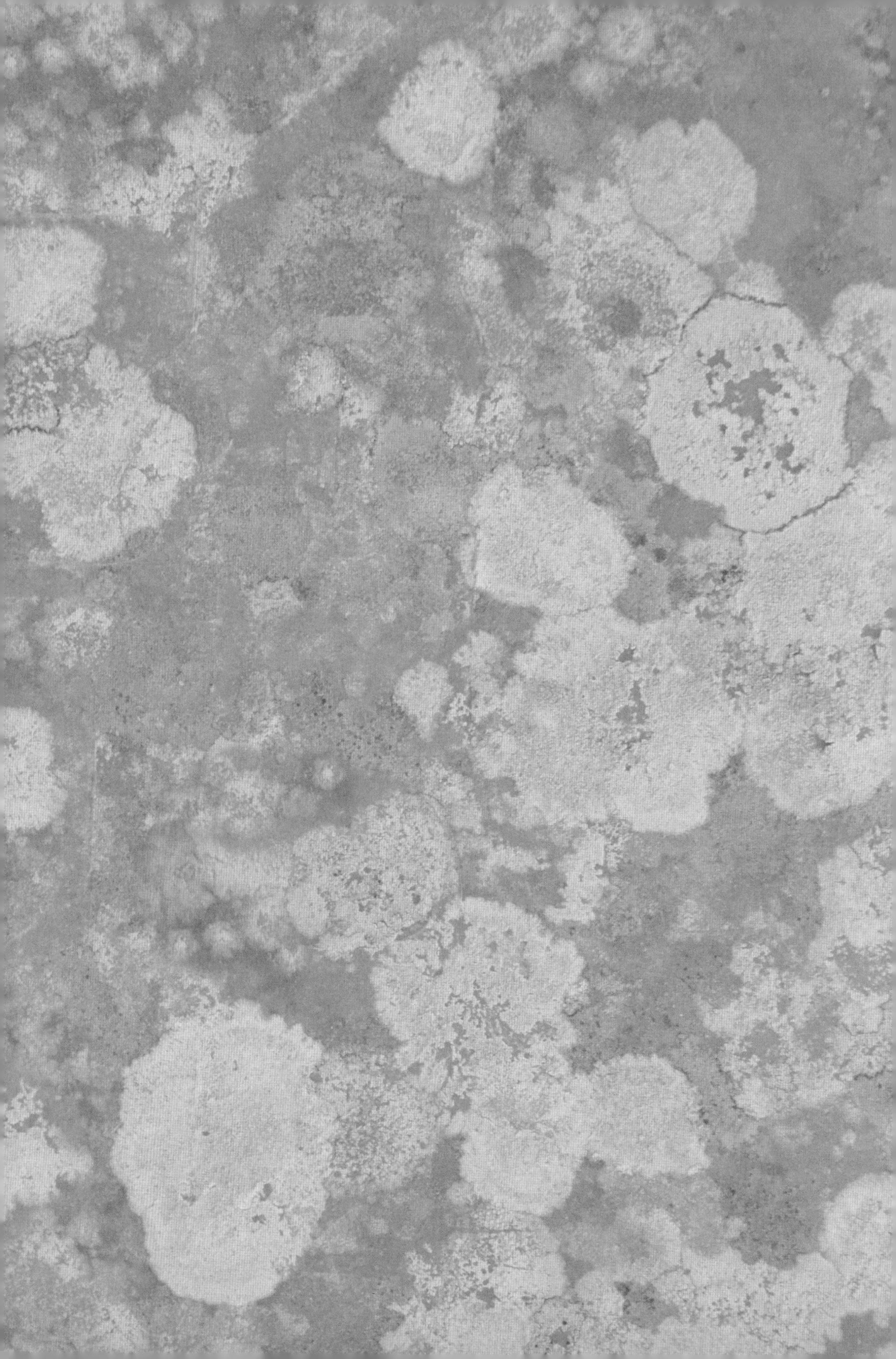

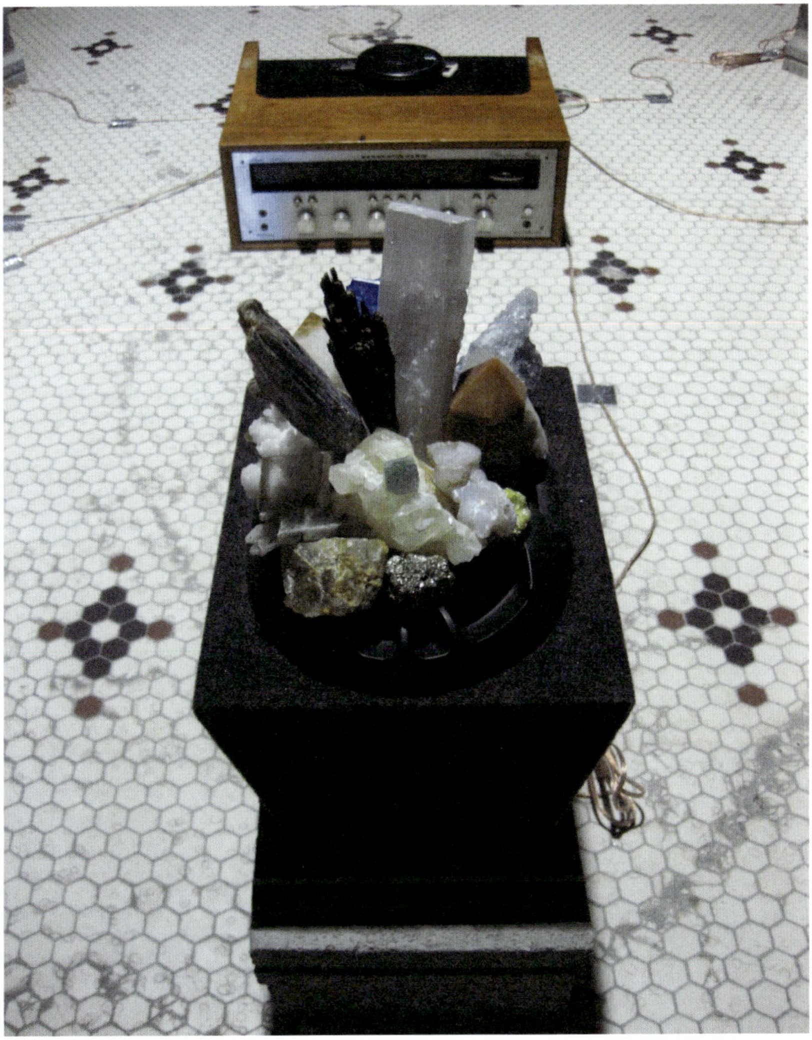

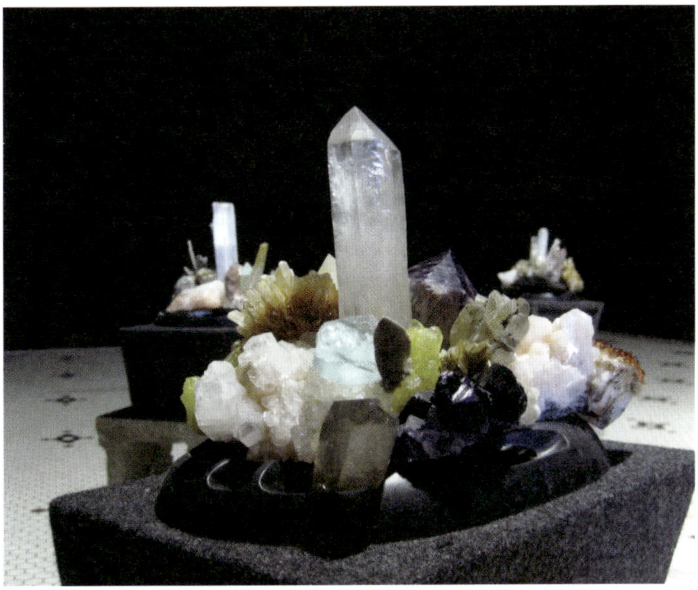

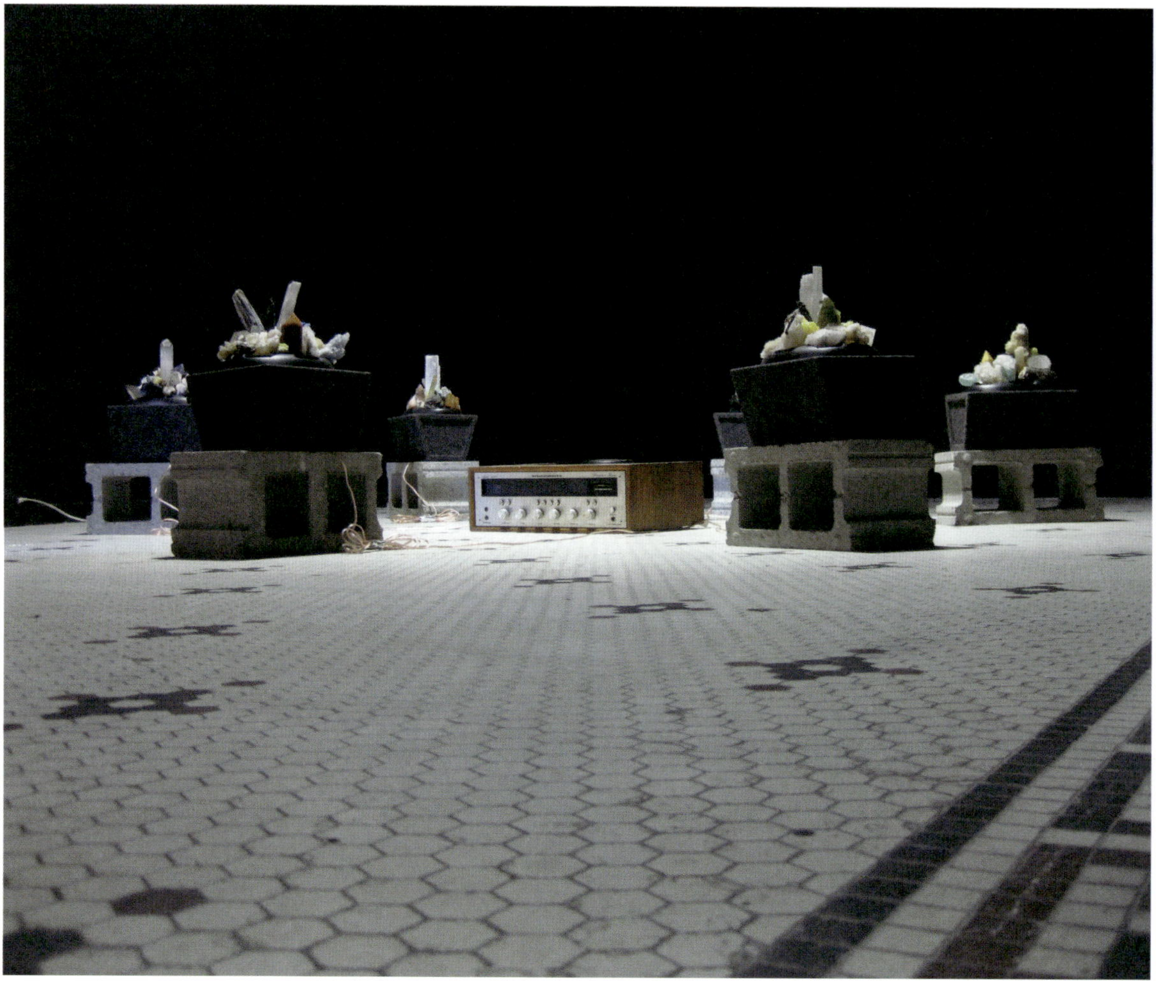

HOPE, LOVE, PEACE, GENEROSITY, PURPOSE, HARMONY

Practitioners of crystal healing therapy contend that specific crystals have the potential to heal and transform the body and spirit because of the respective frequencies at which they vibrate and that an individual crystal's vibrations directly correspond to certain metaphysical energies inherently present in all people. Through relaying a looped, oscillating frequency through a large collection of specimens (determined by their relative frequencies) *Hope, Love, Peace, Generosity, Purpose, Harmony* proposes, as a gesture of good will, the amplification of the collective qualities of the crystals within, as well as beyond, the exhibition space.

2008

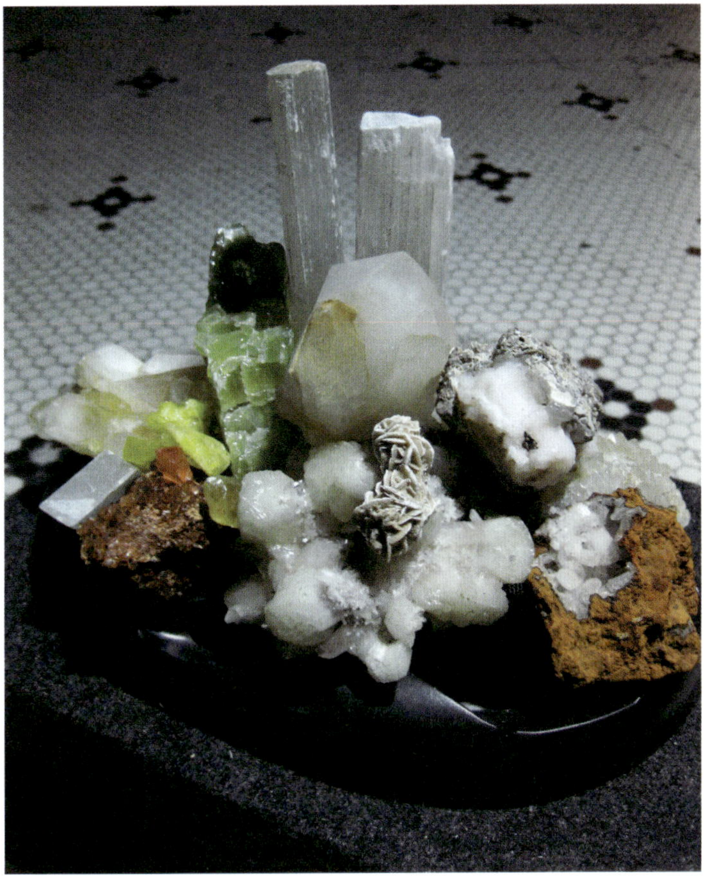

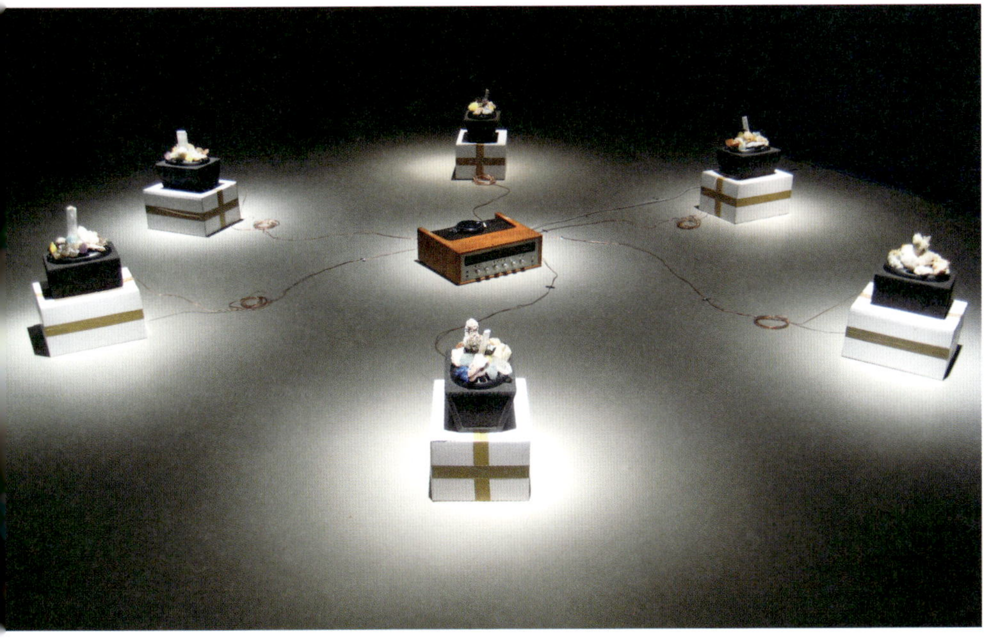

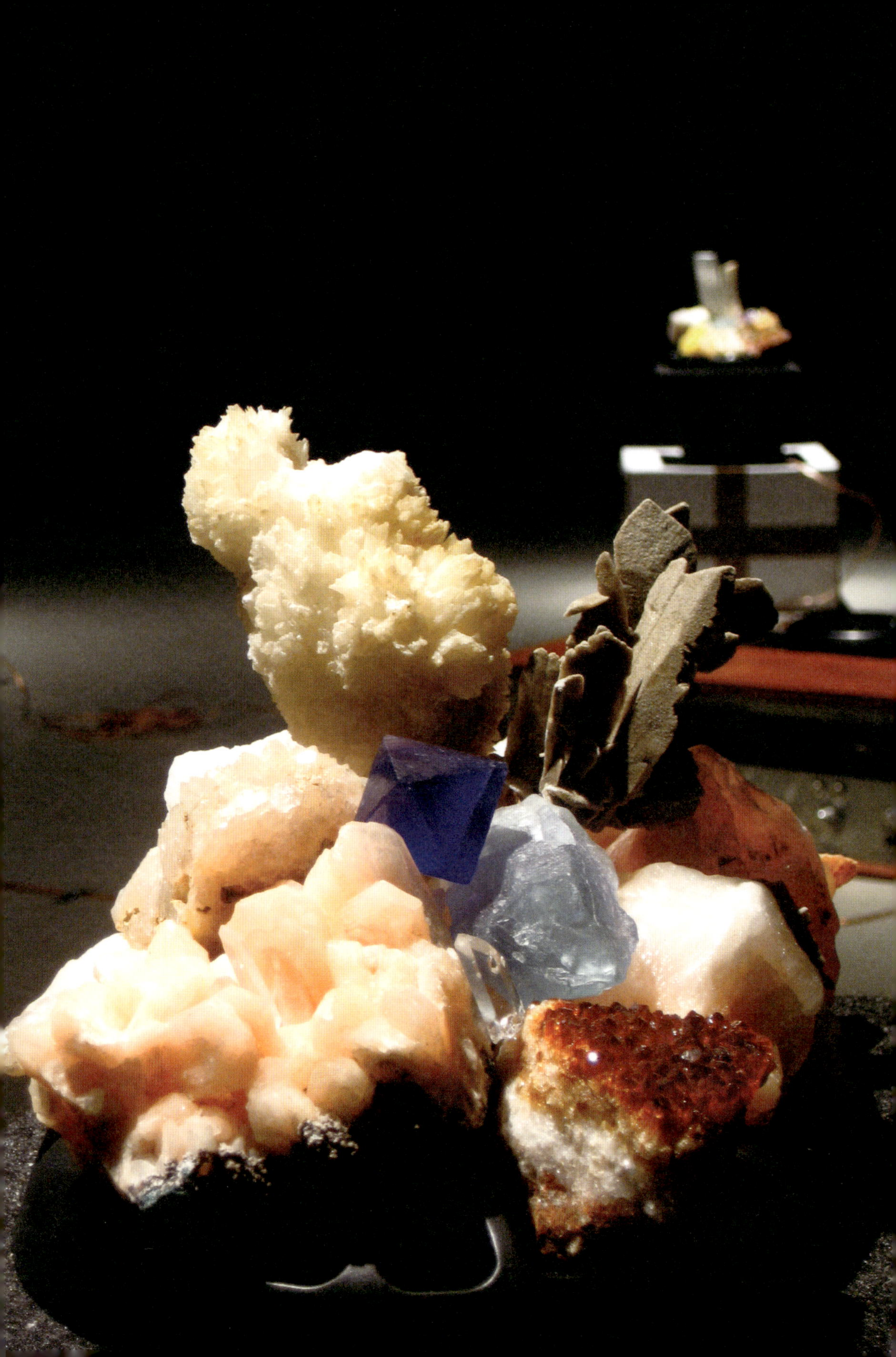

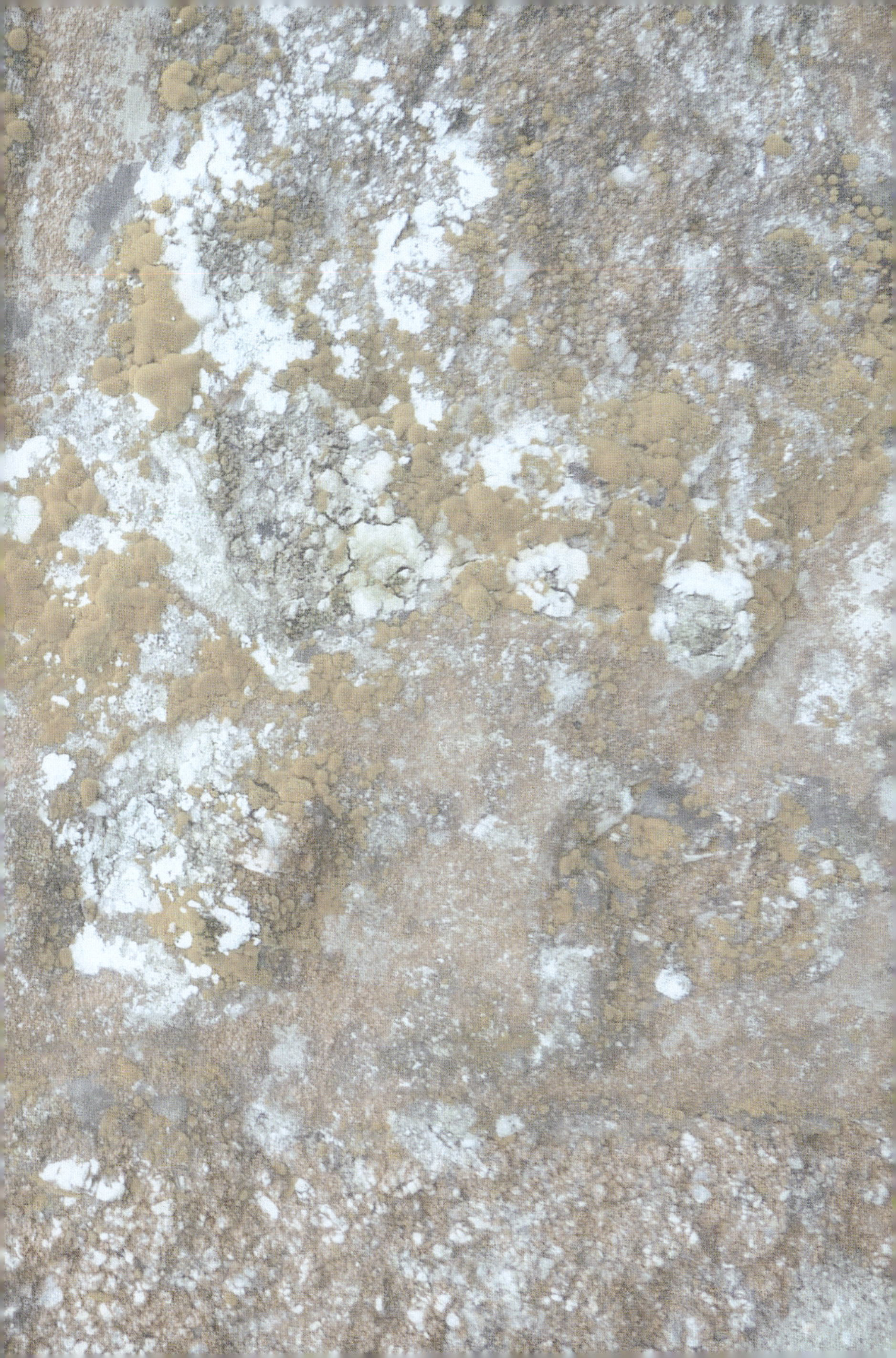

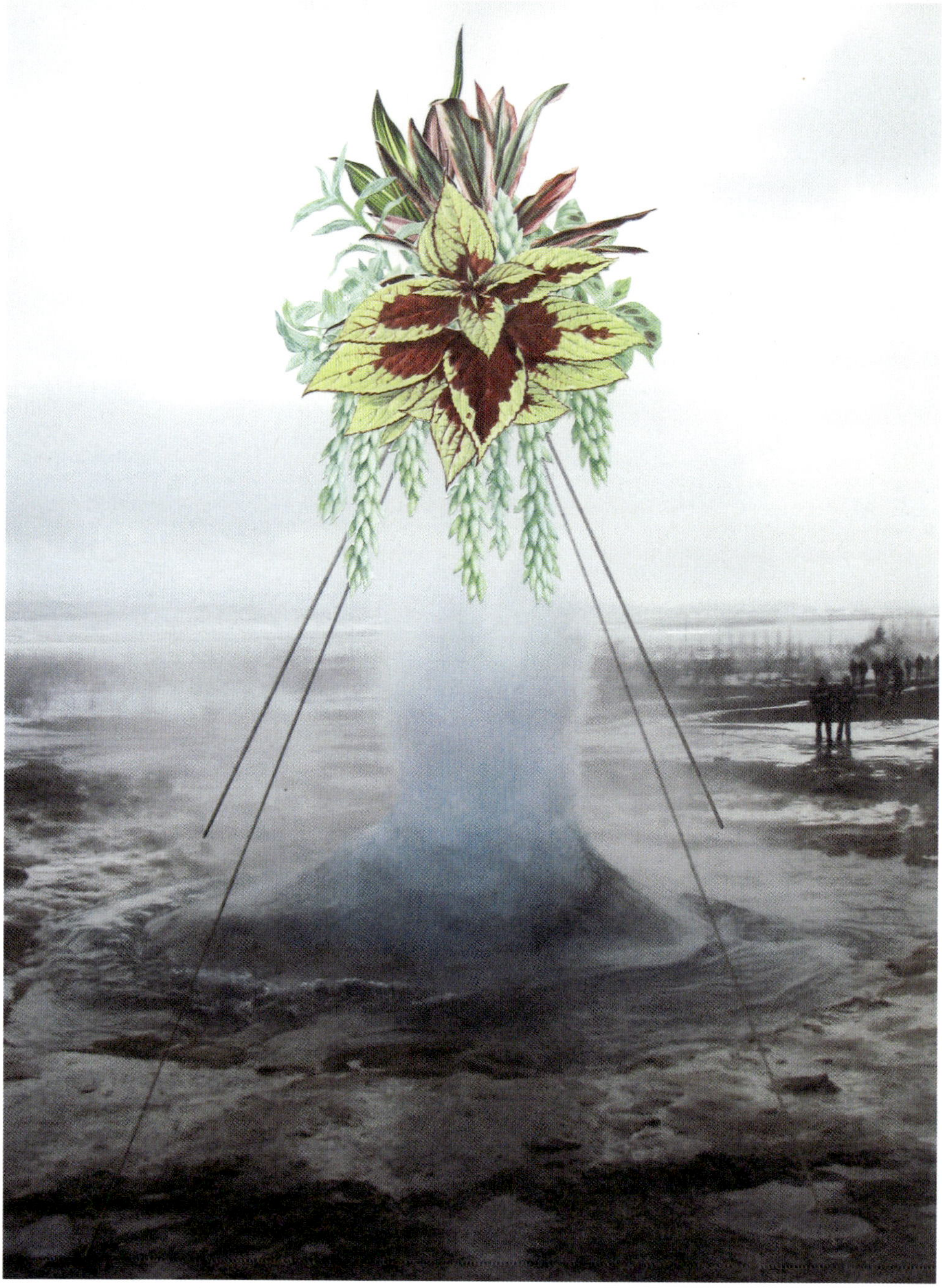

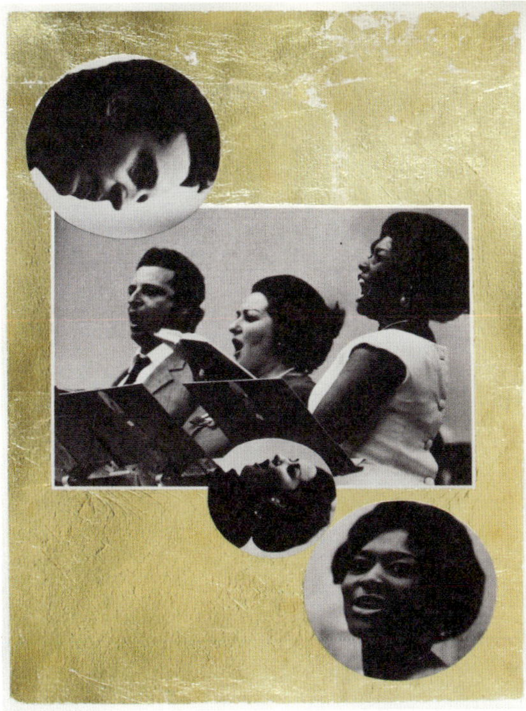

GEYSER SUSTAINING ALIEN TROPICALS
2012

SMALL CHOIR HAVING AN OUT-OF-BODY EXPERIENCE
2011

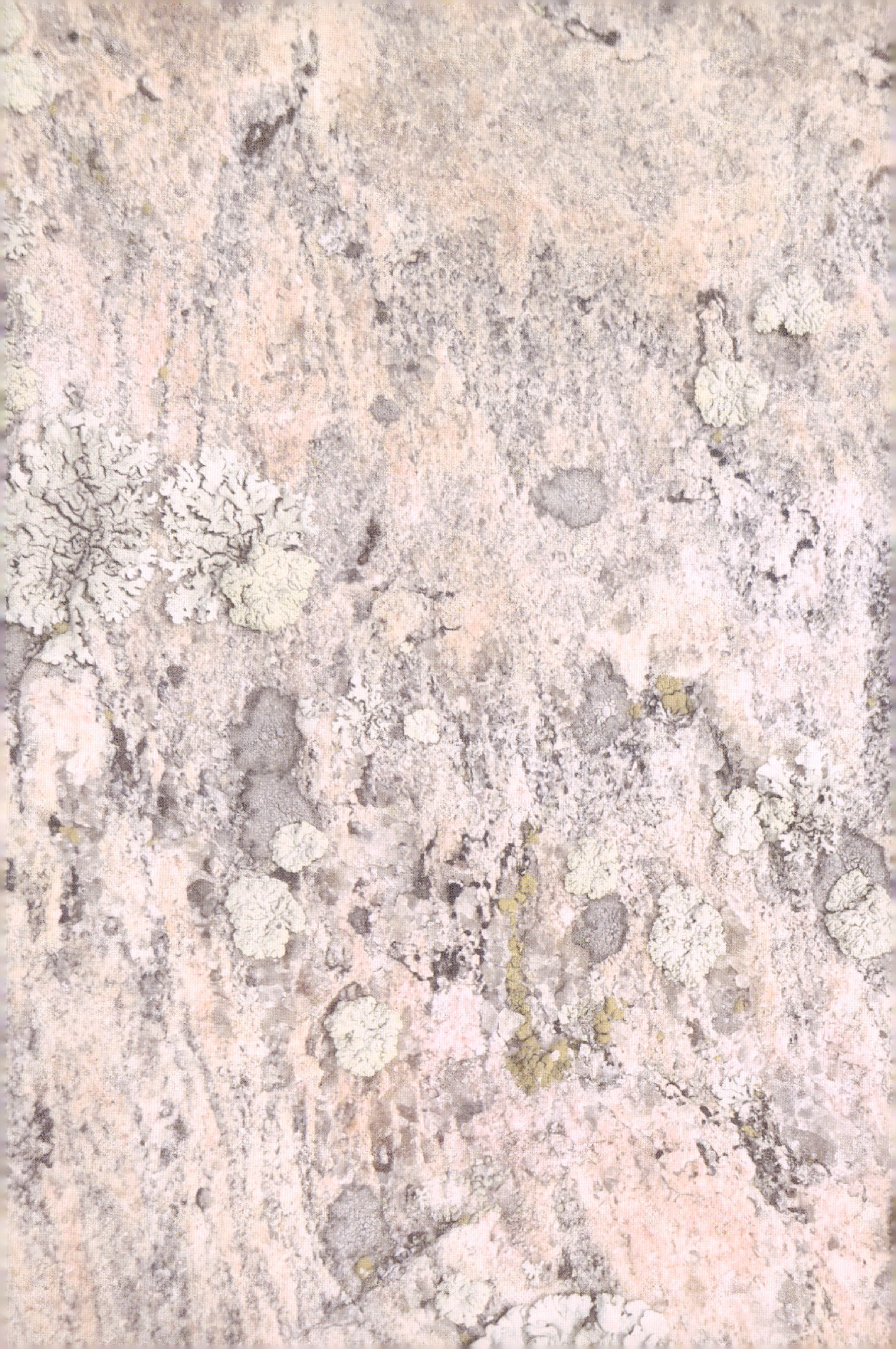

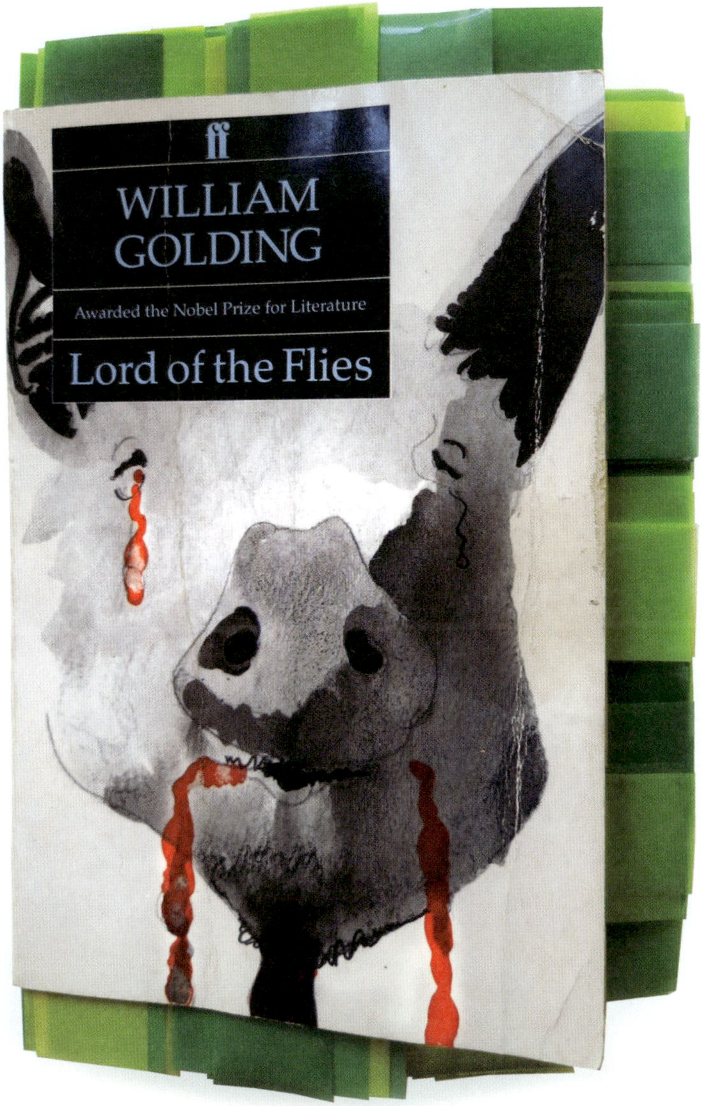
ff
WILLIAM
GOLDING
Awarded the Nobel Prize for Literature
Lord of the Flies

LORD OF THE FLIES

Used paperback copy of William Golding's *Lord of the Flies*.
Marked, through the course of reading, by Post-it Note tabs.

2008

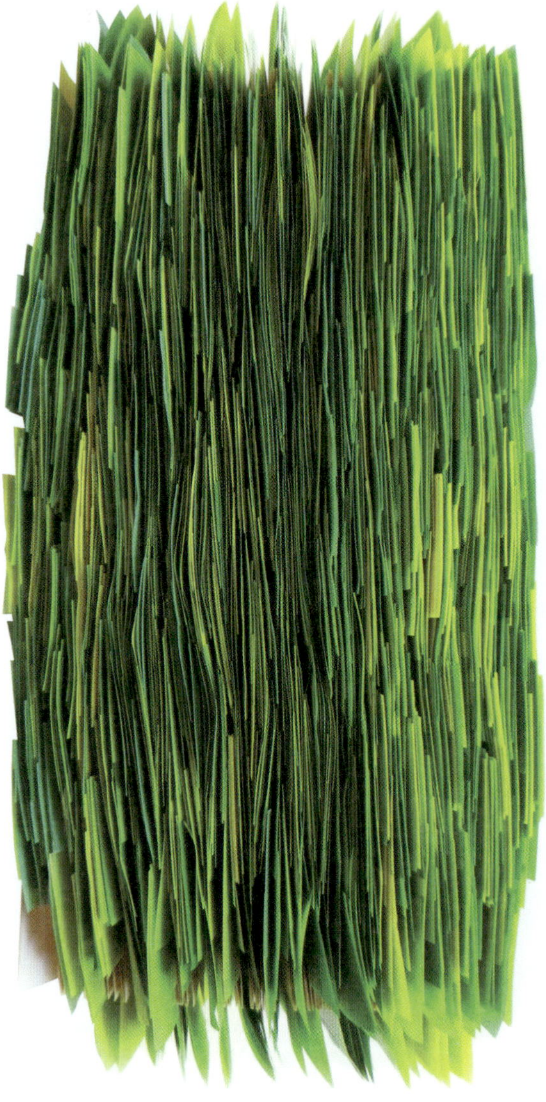

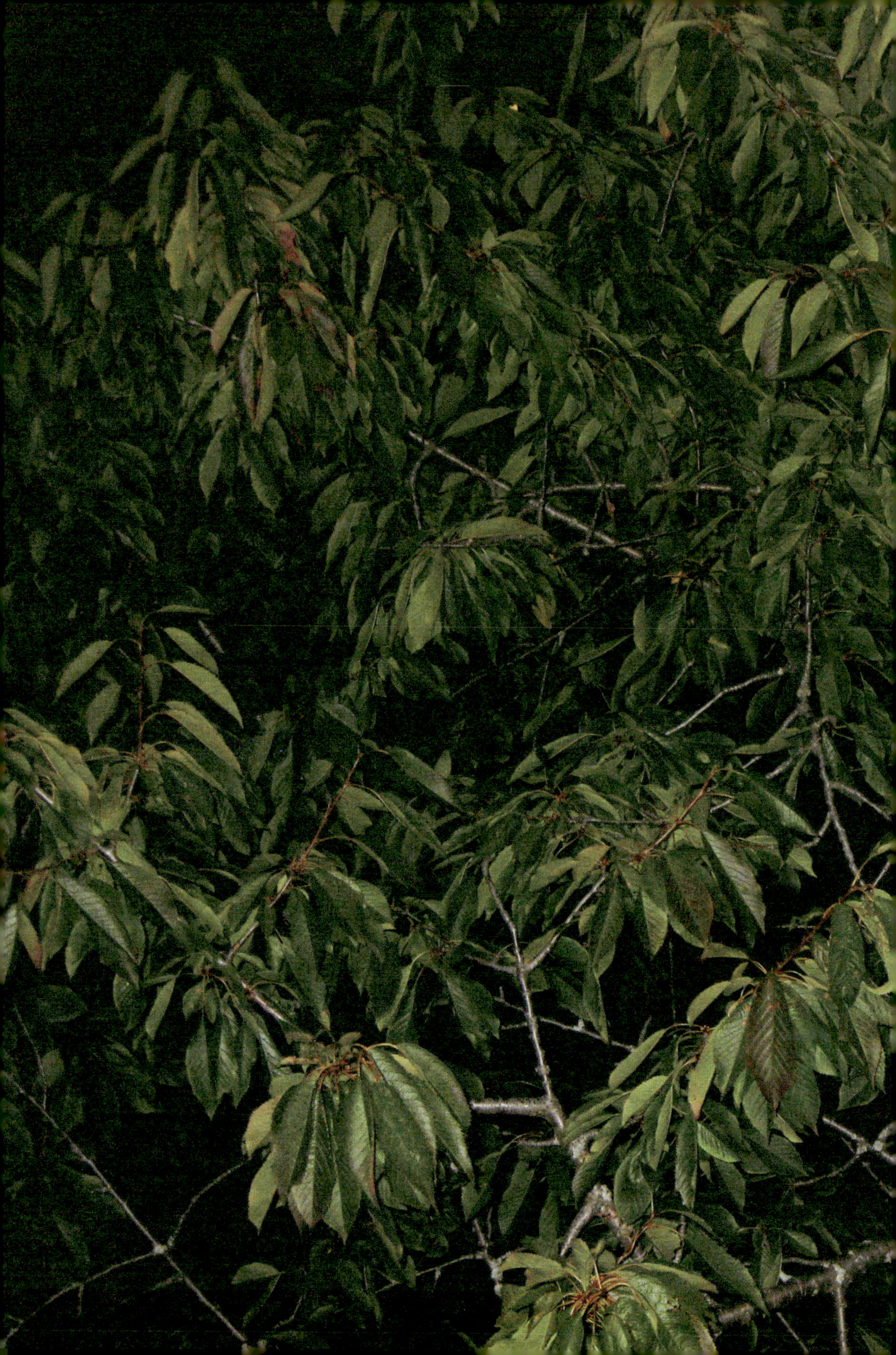

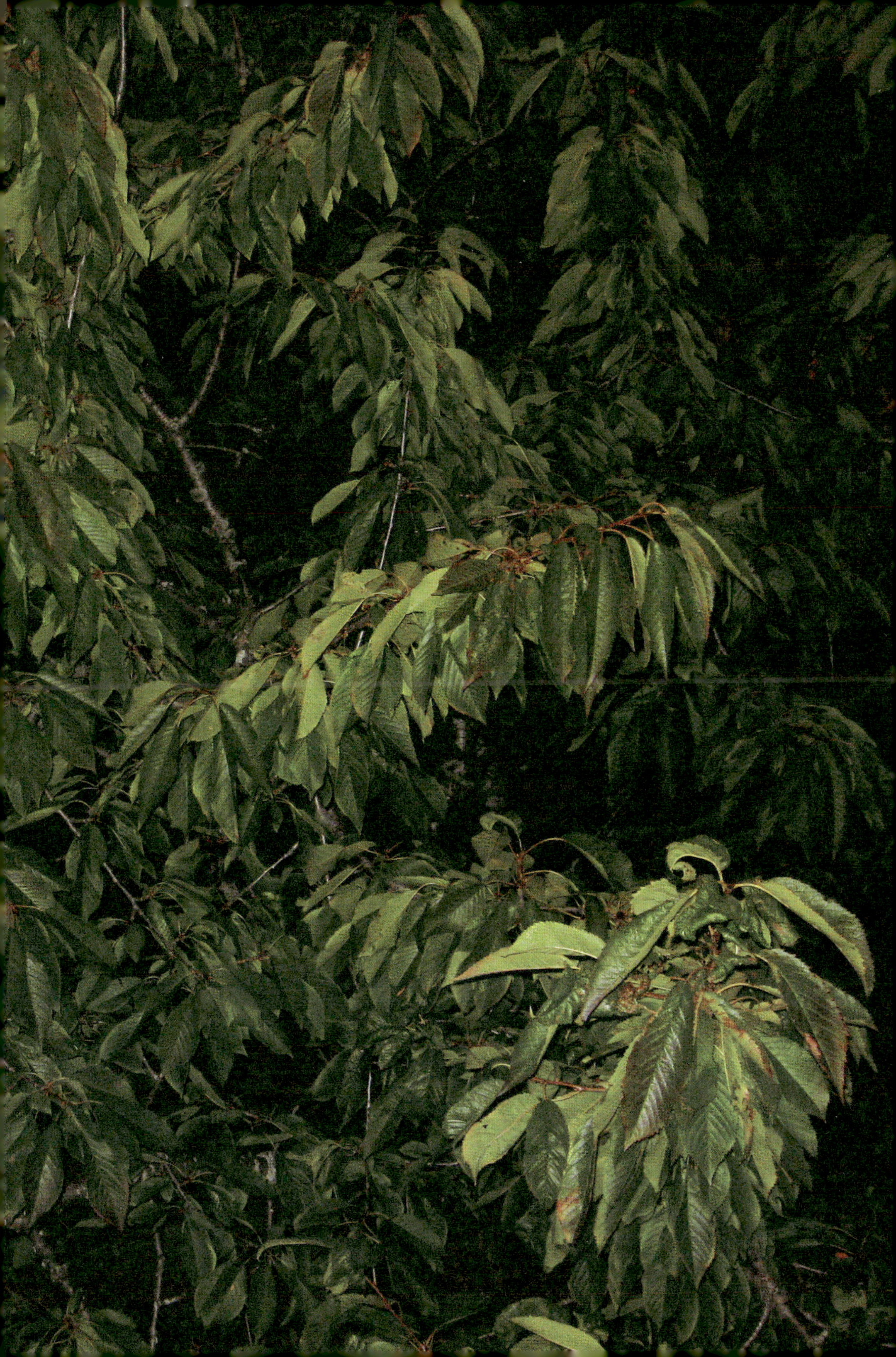

100 AGES

2011

FUTURE AGE

Gold rings placed onto the branches of potted saplings.

2011, 2012, 2013

FUTURE FUTURE AGE

Golds rings inlayed in driftwood and petrified wood.

2011, 2012, 2013

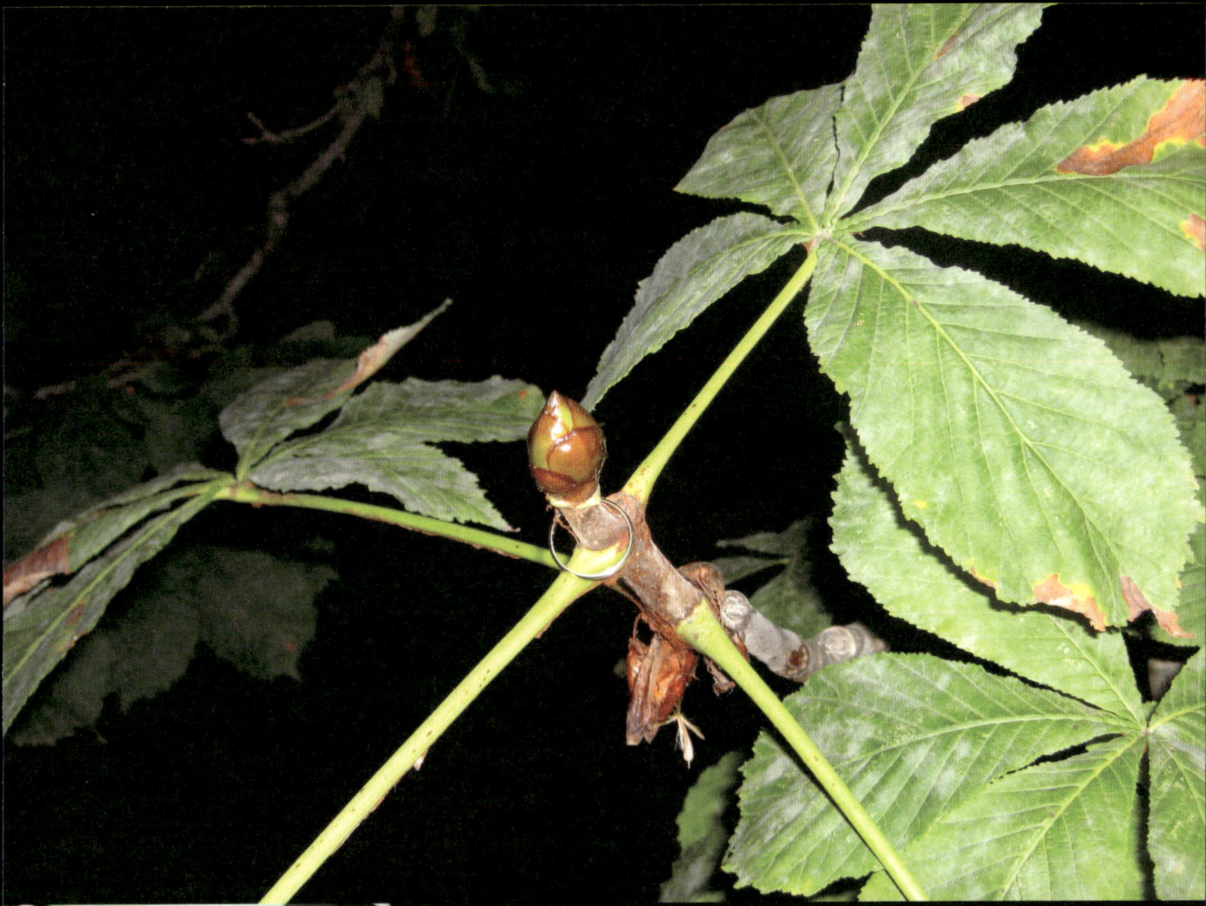

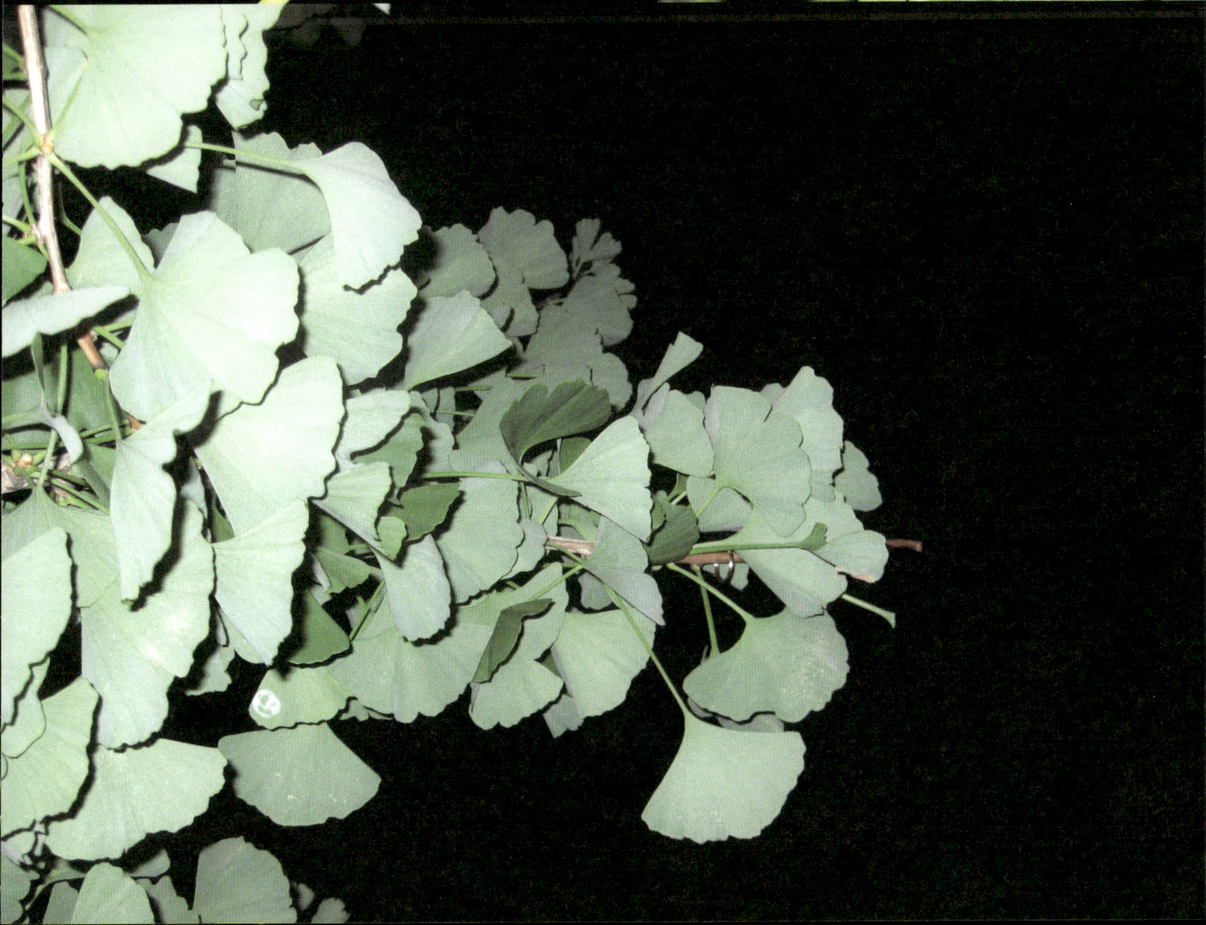

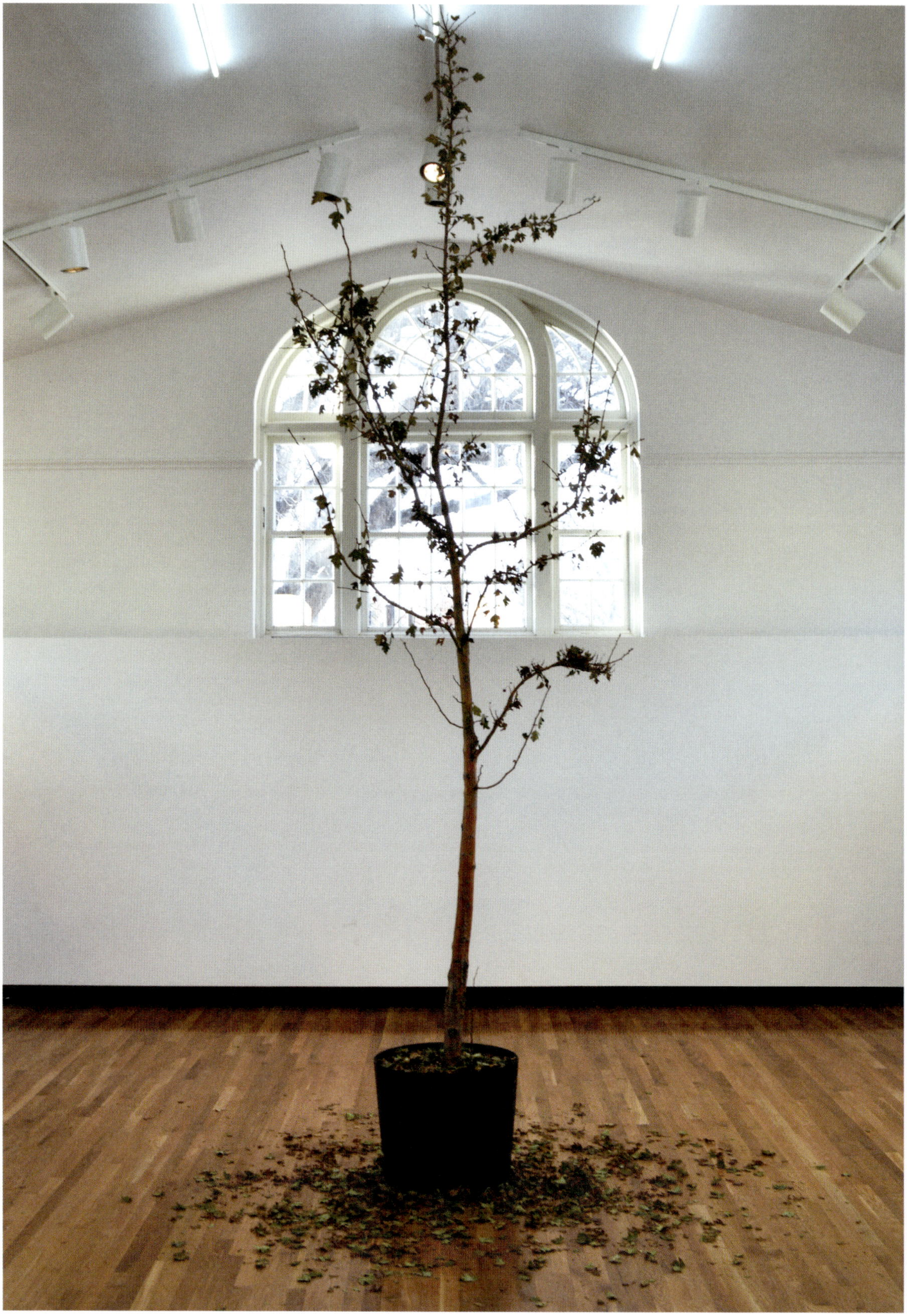

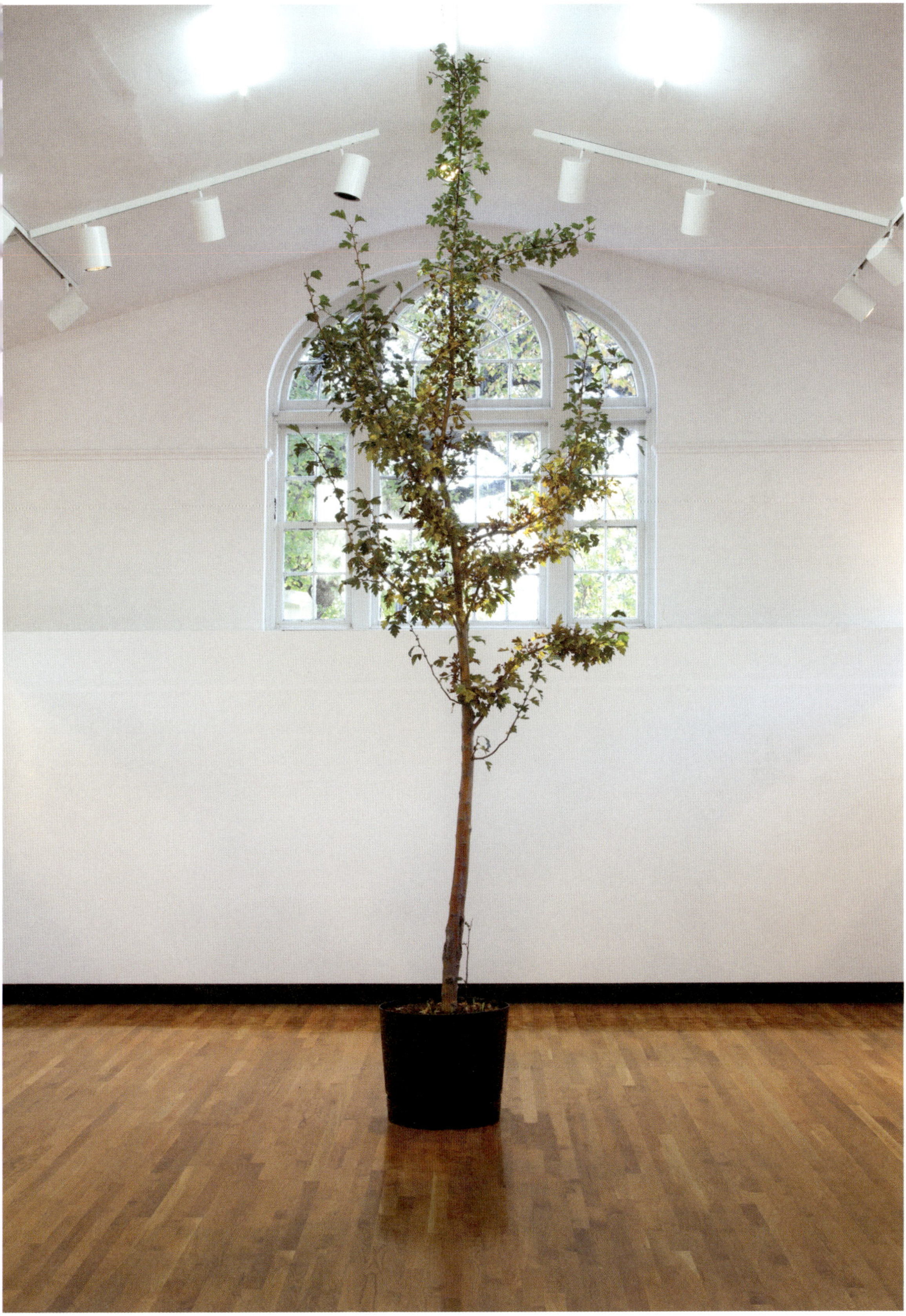

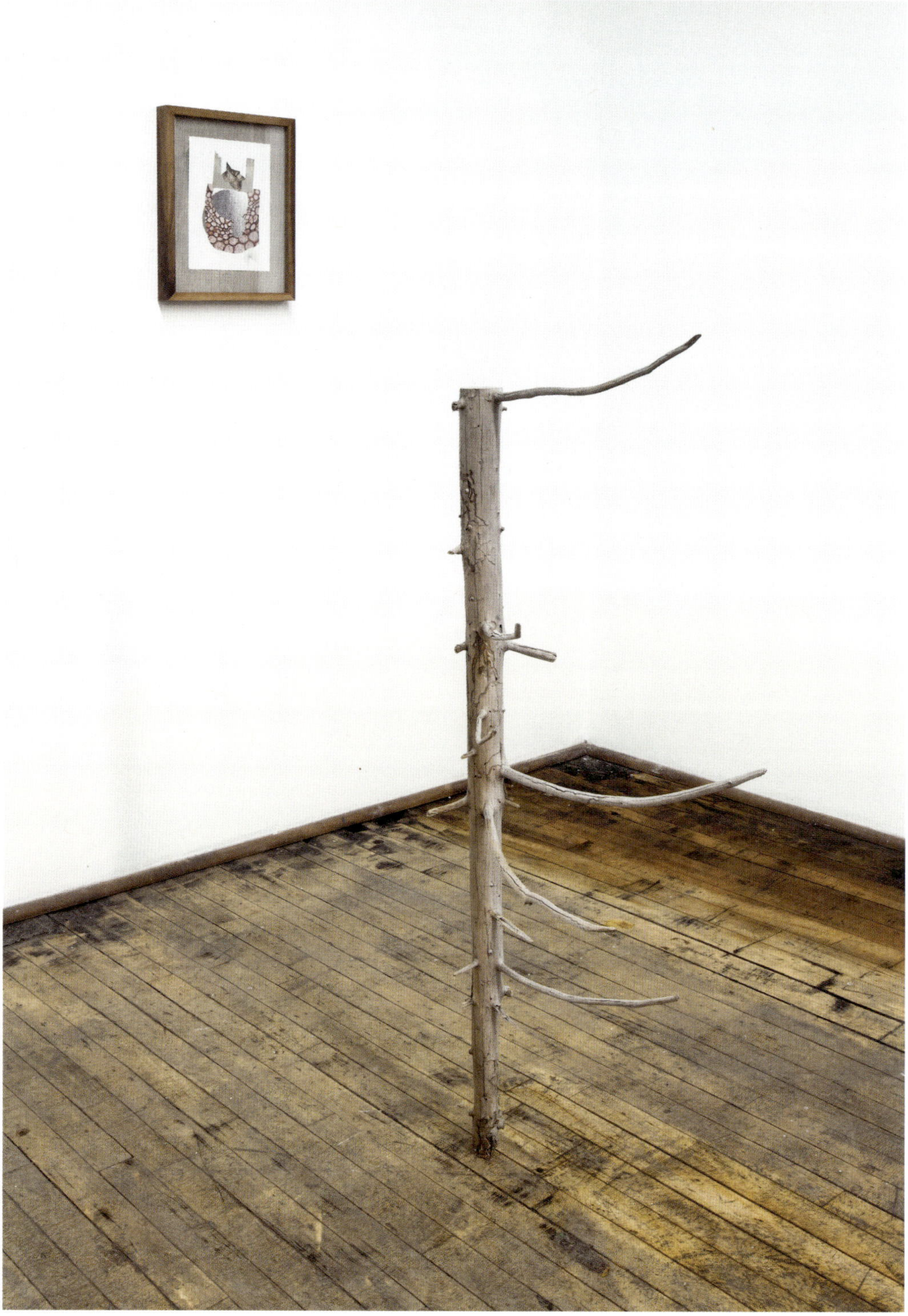

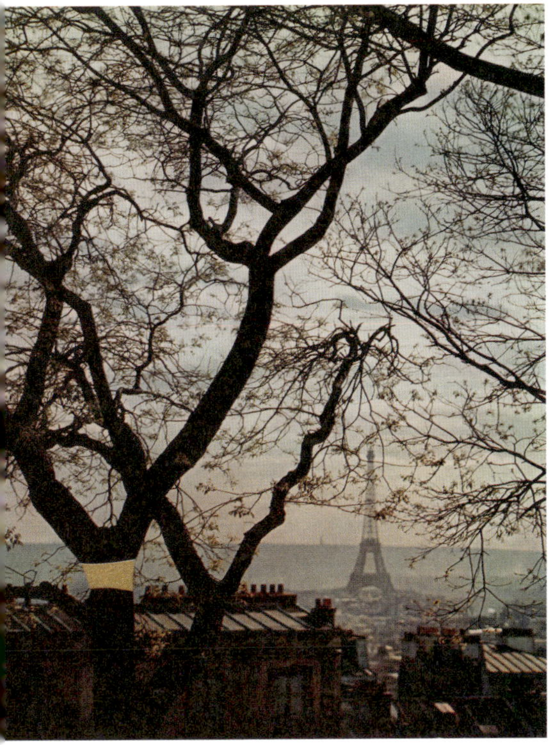
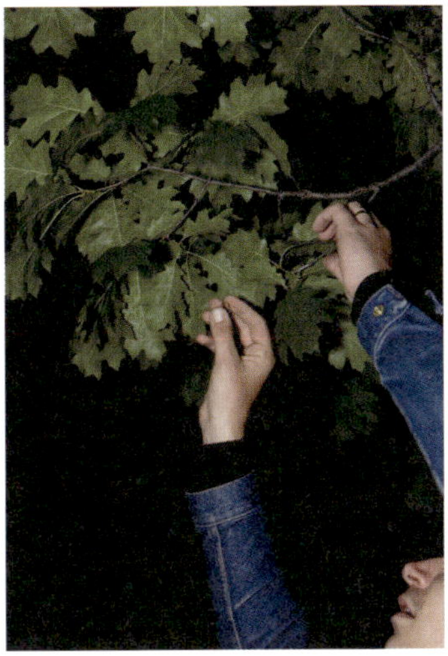
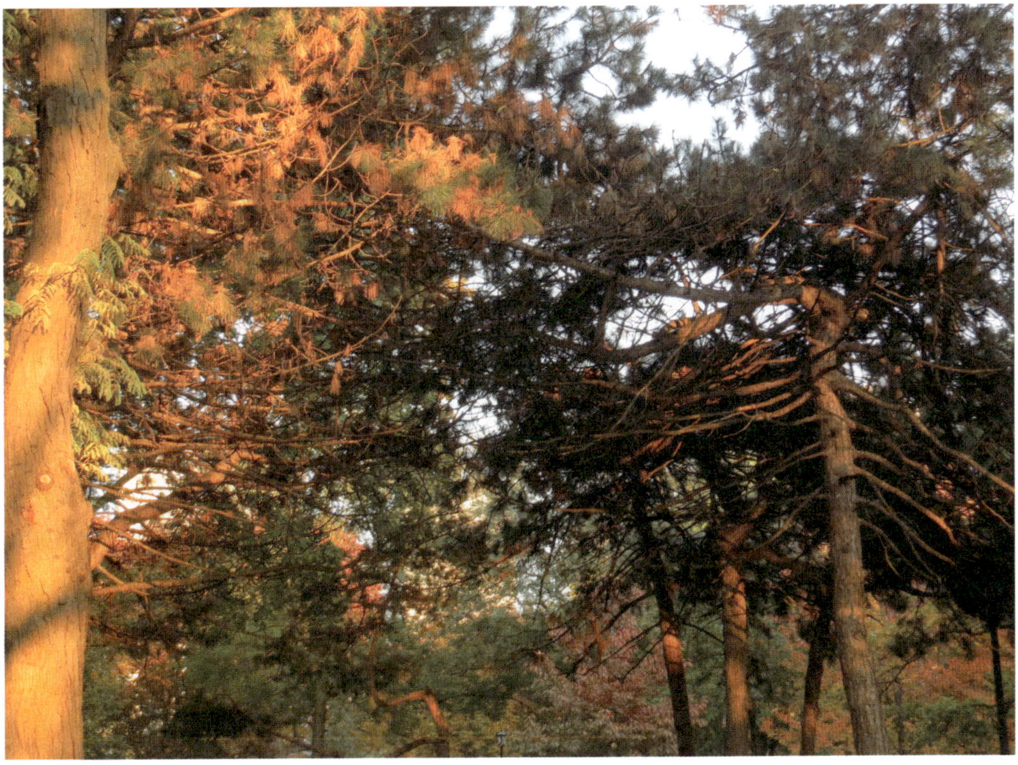

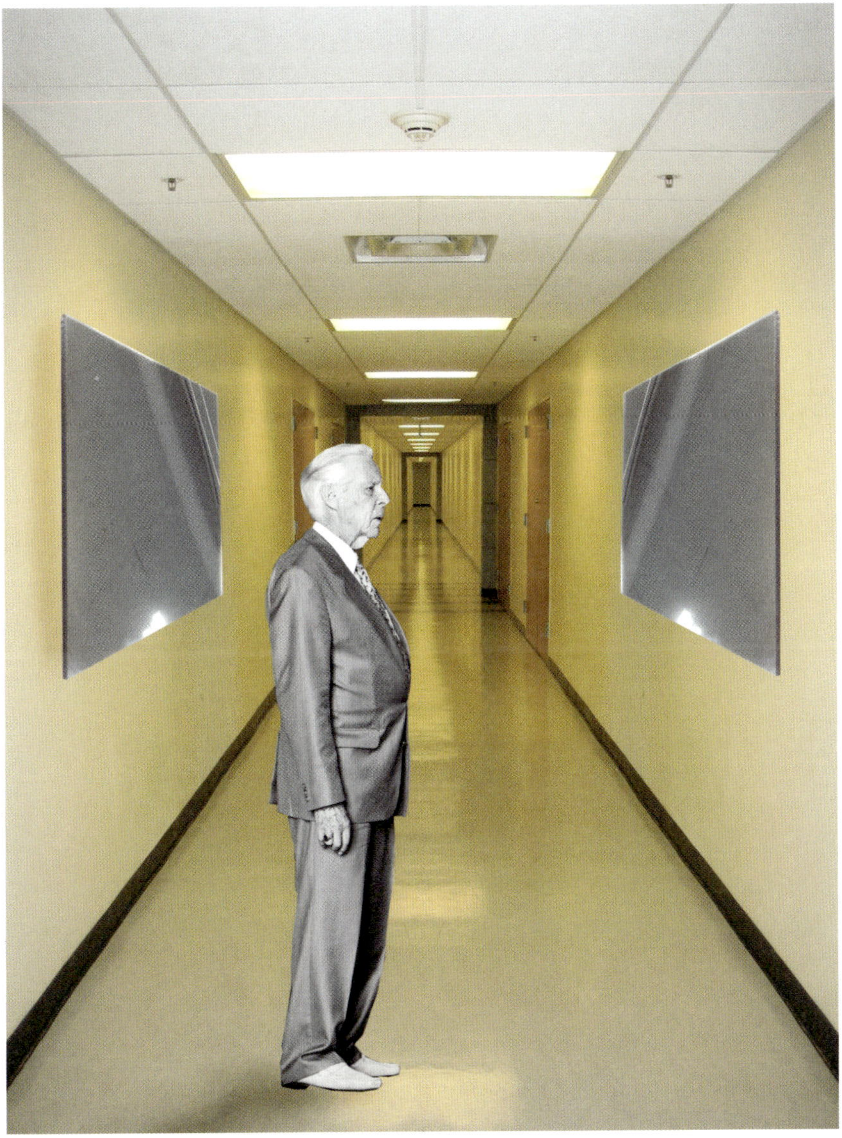

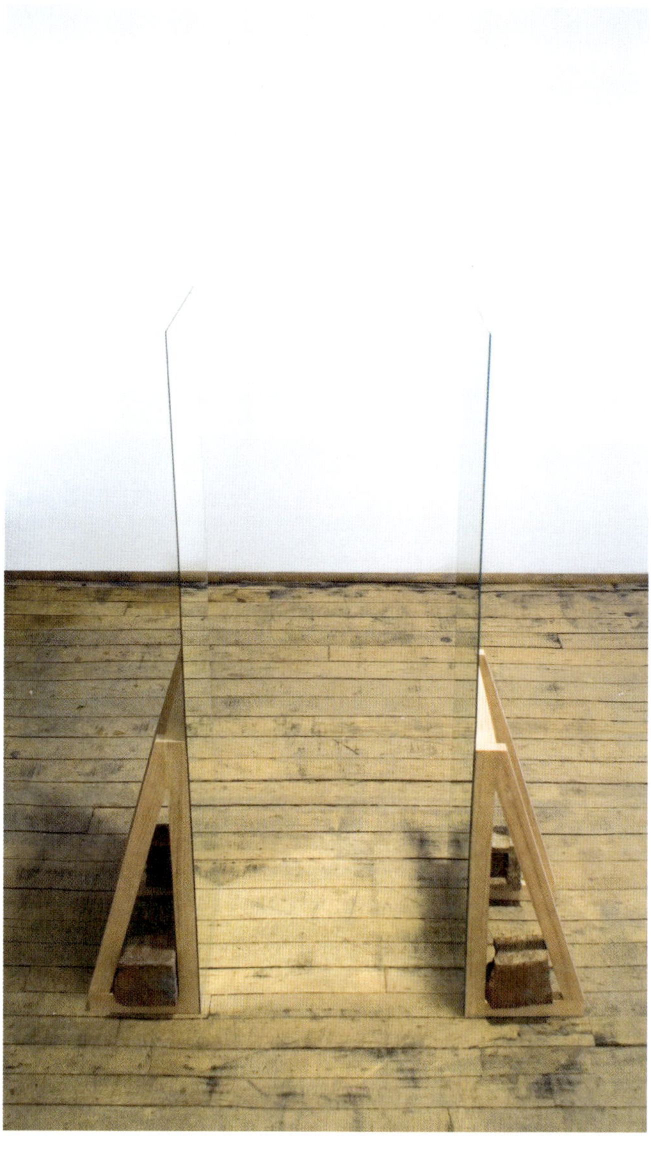

HAUNTED MIRROR CORRIDOR

2013

SPIRITS LOOKING AT THEMSELVES

A haunted mirror and mirror face each other, forming an endlessly reflecting corridor.

2010, 2013

SPIRITS LOOKING UP AT THEMSELVES

A mirror haunted by children, from the collection of the Museo de la Ciudad, Querétaro, with standing mirror.

2009

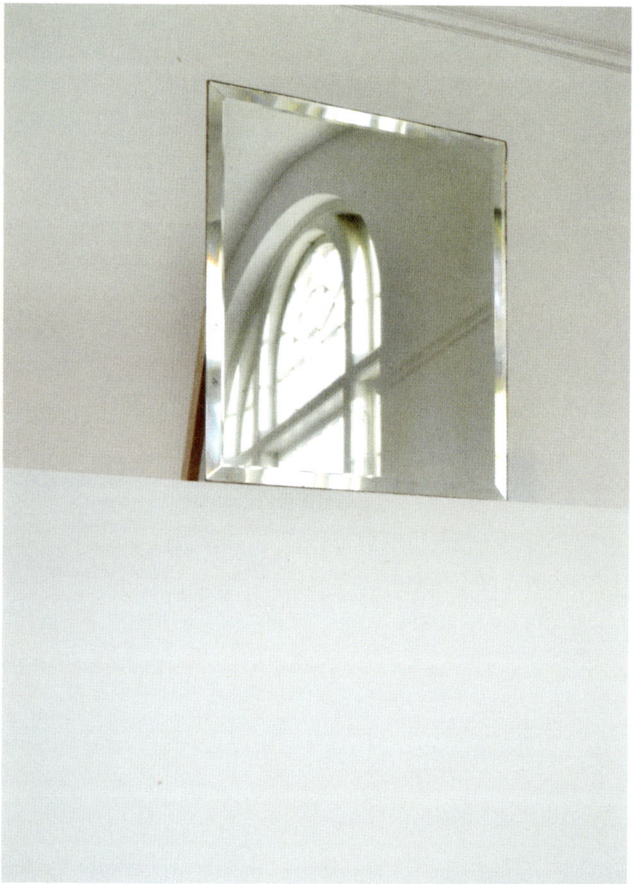

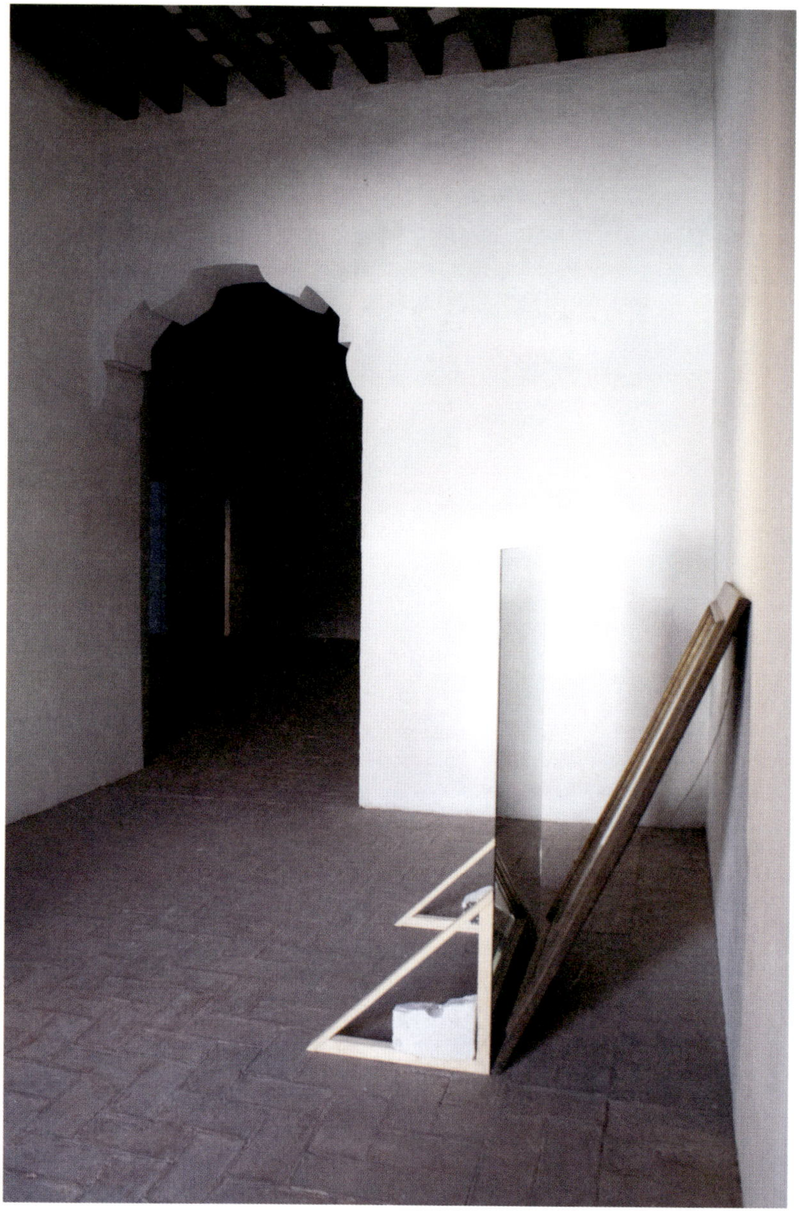

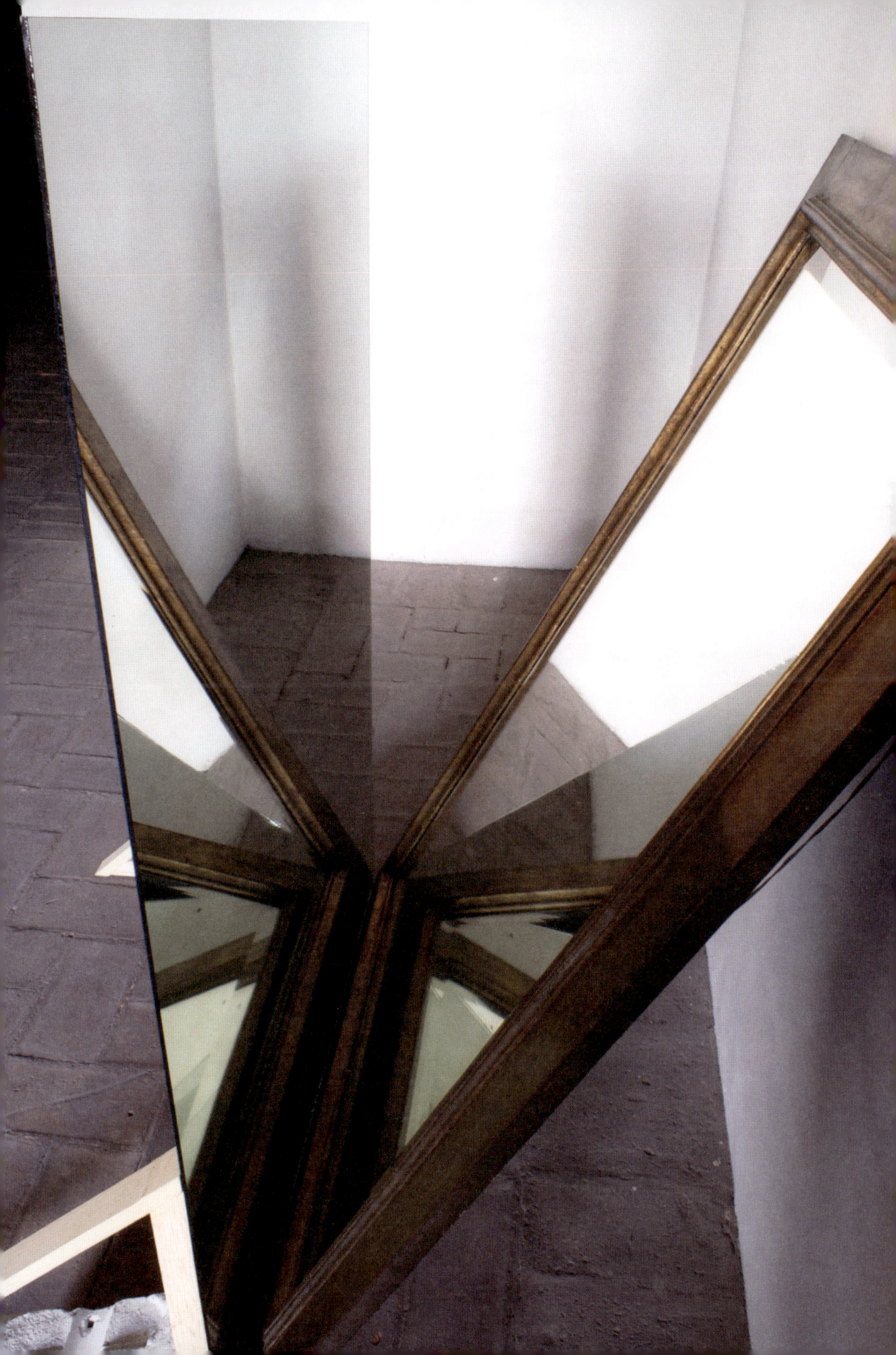

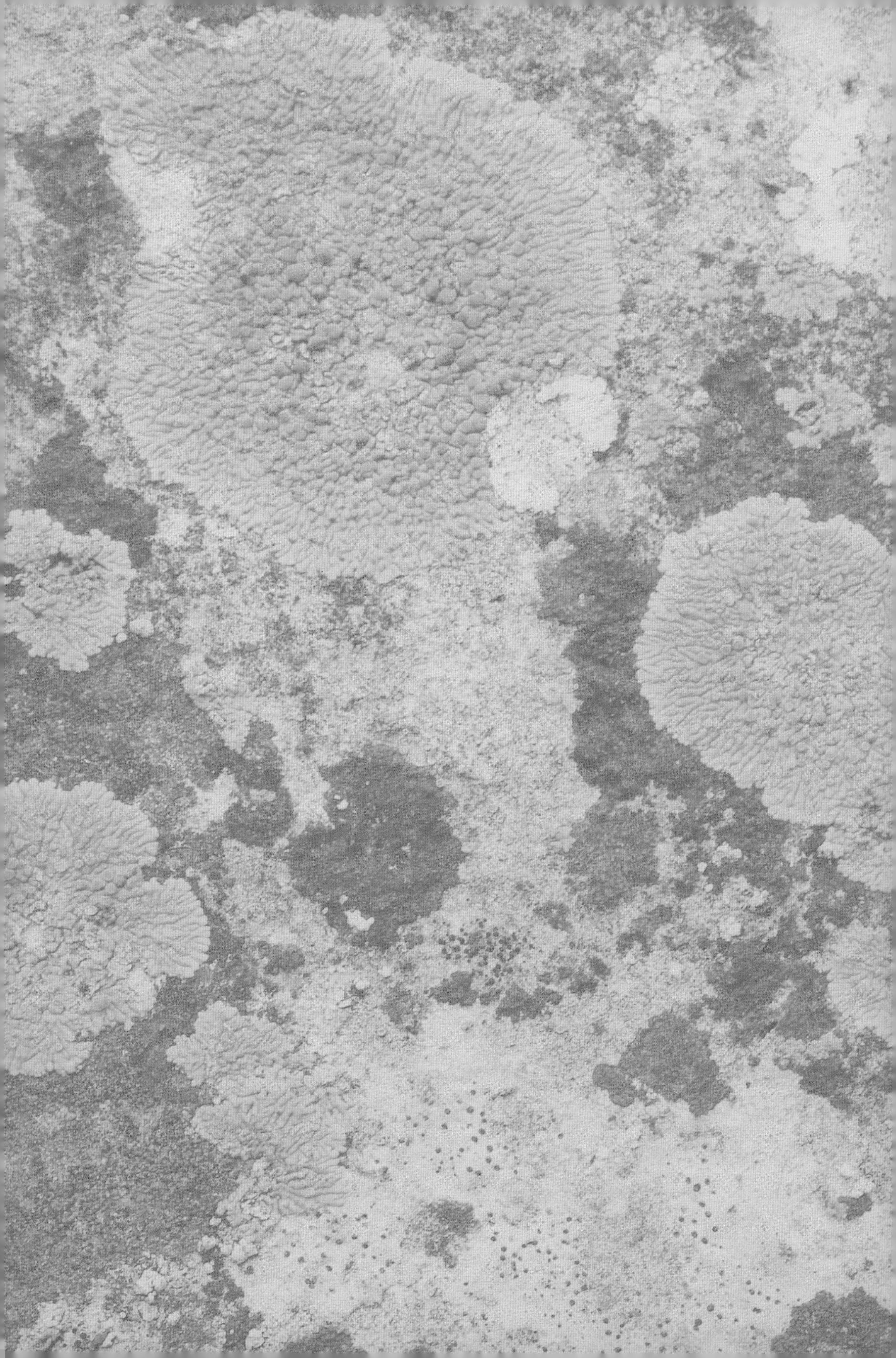

MOON

A cyanotype print produced by a coin placed on treated paper and exposed during the partial Lunar eclipse of the full Moon of:

June 26, 2010

DON'T GO

2013

CLAY STEALING CLAY
(POTS SEPARATED FROM THEIR SHADOW)

with Miruna Dragan

2013

EXTRAORDINARY TALENTS IN BALLET'S FUTURE

2013

DARKNESS CONQUERS DAY

2013

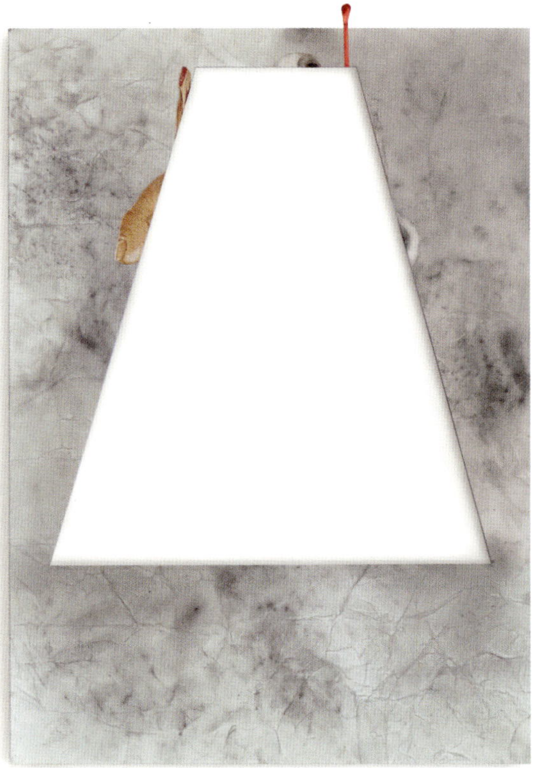

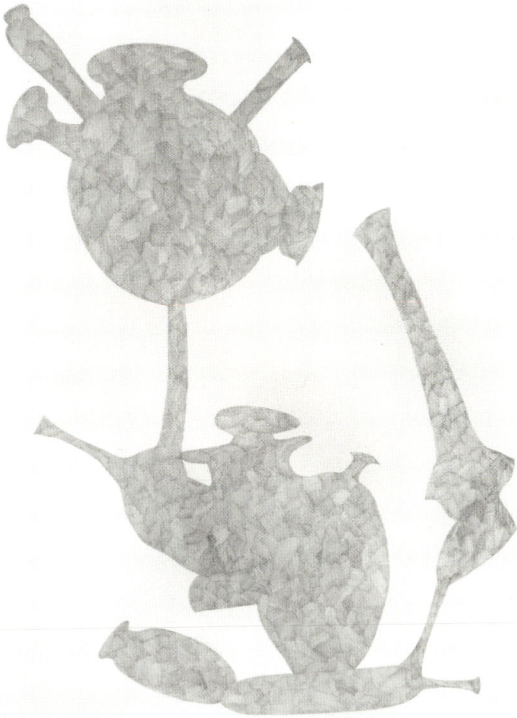

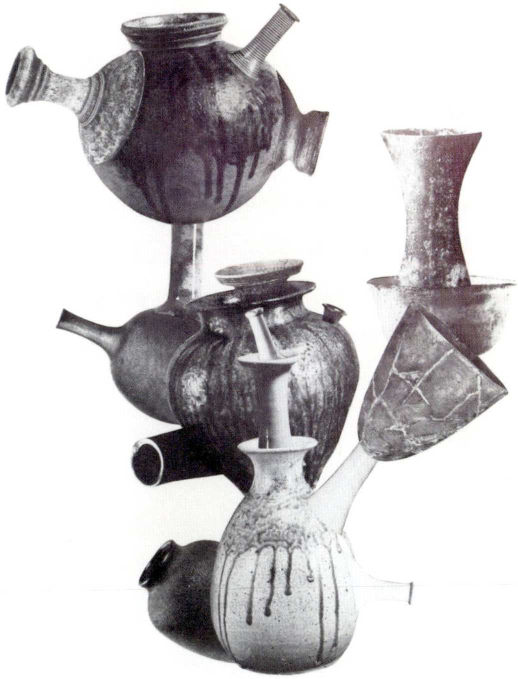

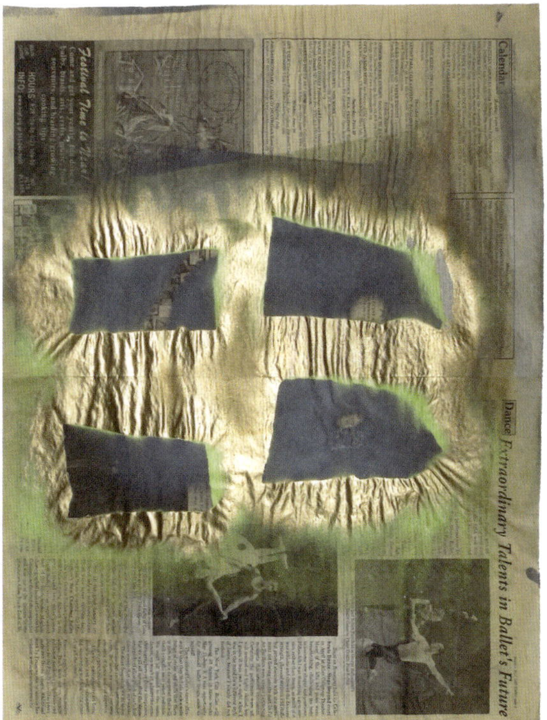
Calendar
Dance
Extraordinary Talents in Ballet's Future

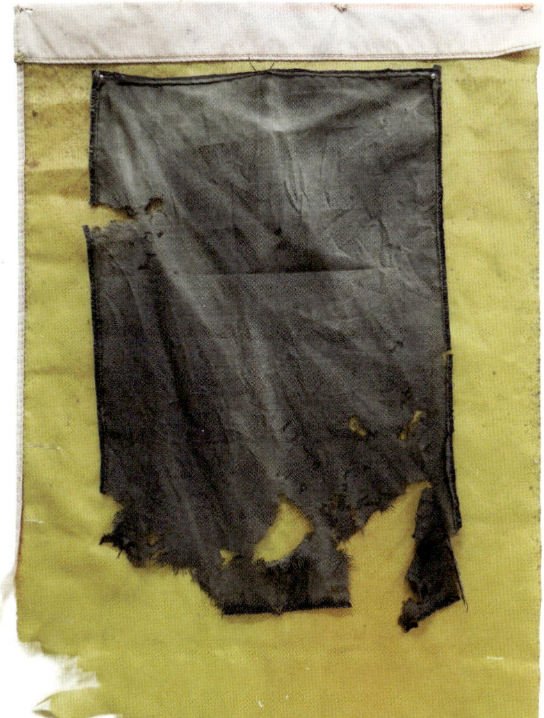

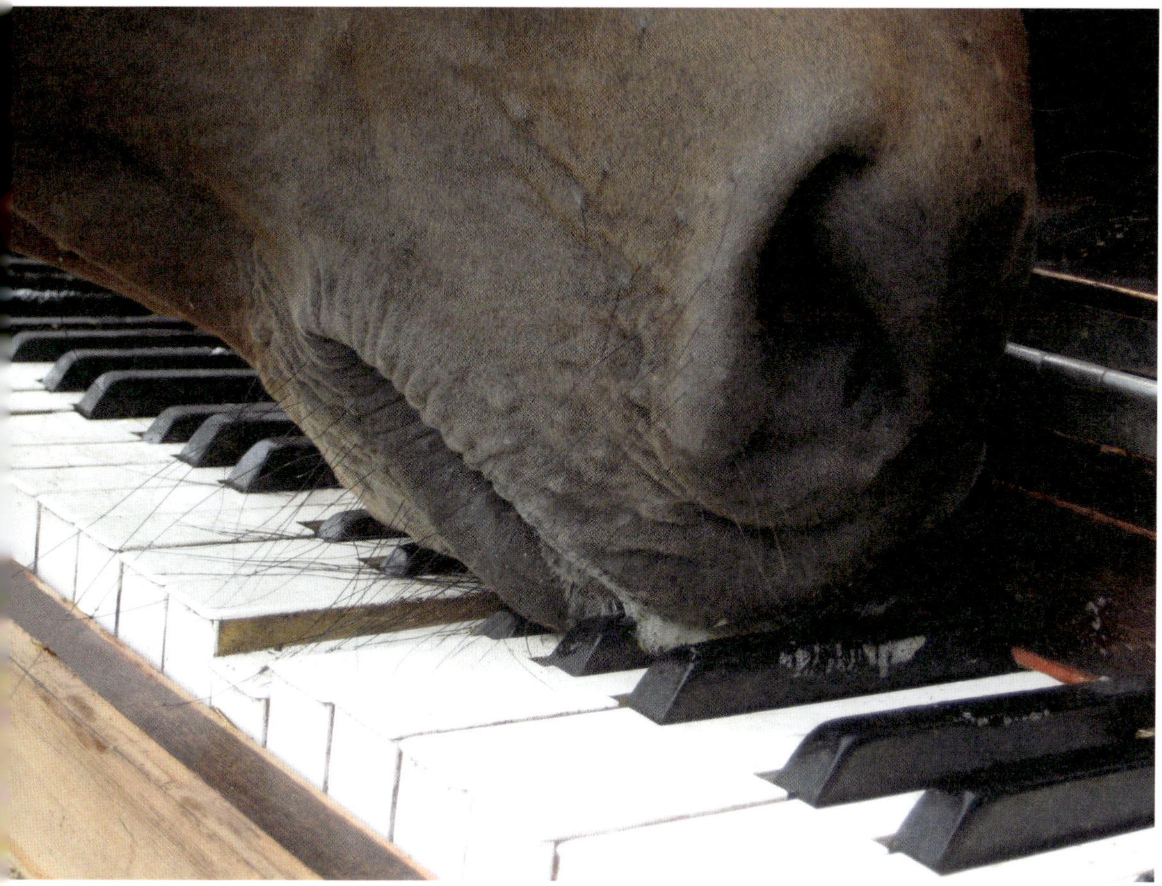

PIE POWDER

From a corruption of the French *Pied Poudre* (dusty feet), the term Pie Powder suggests a form of wandering. An upright piano was placed in a field with a number of horses for 763 days. The project became dependent upon the animals' curiosity to determine its course. The piano remains as evidence.

2010

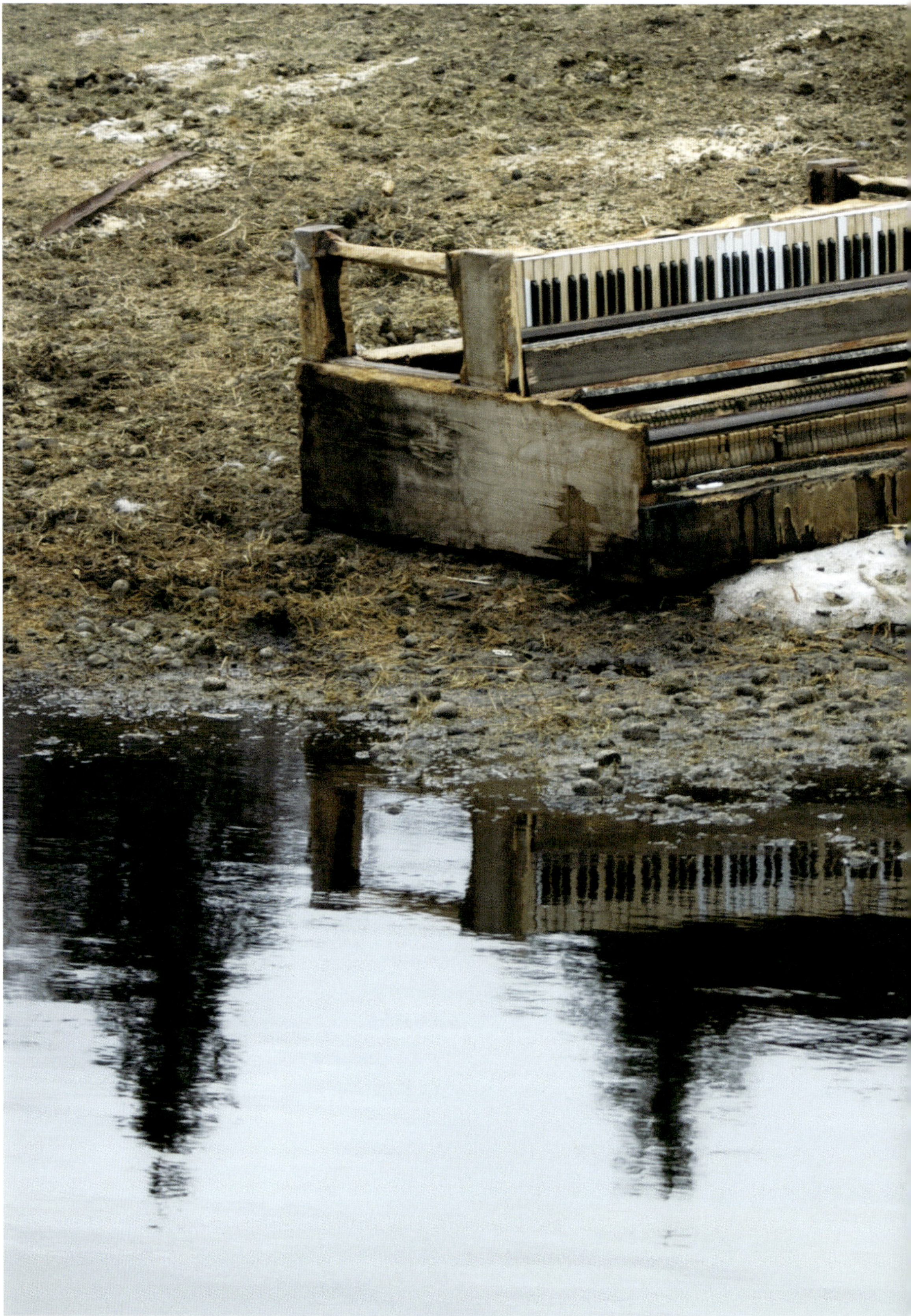

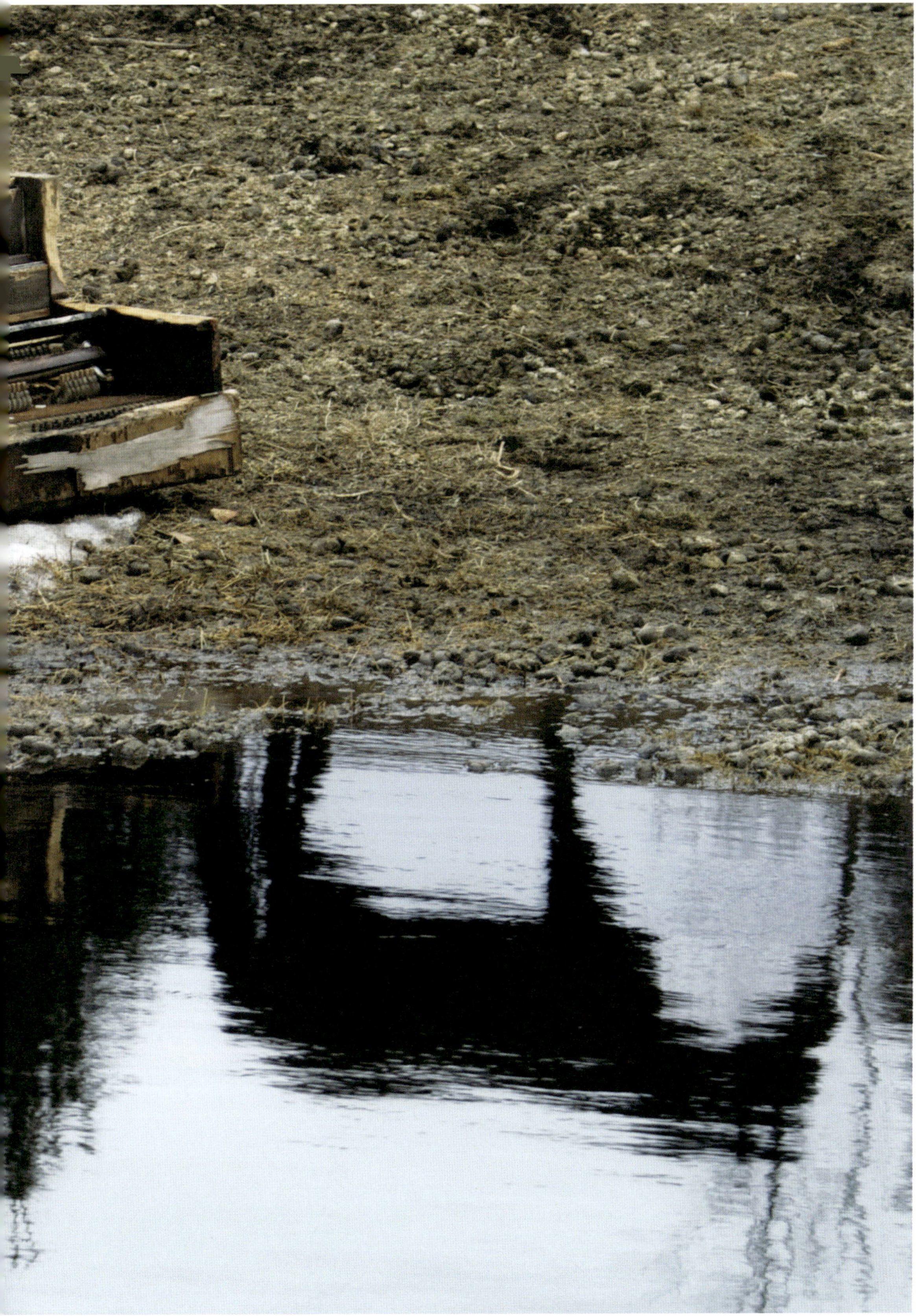

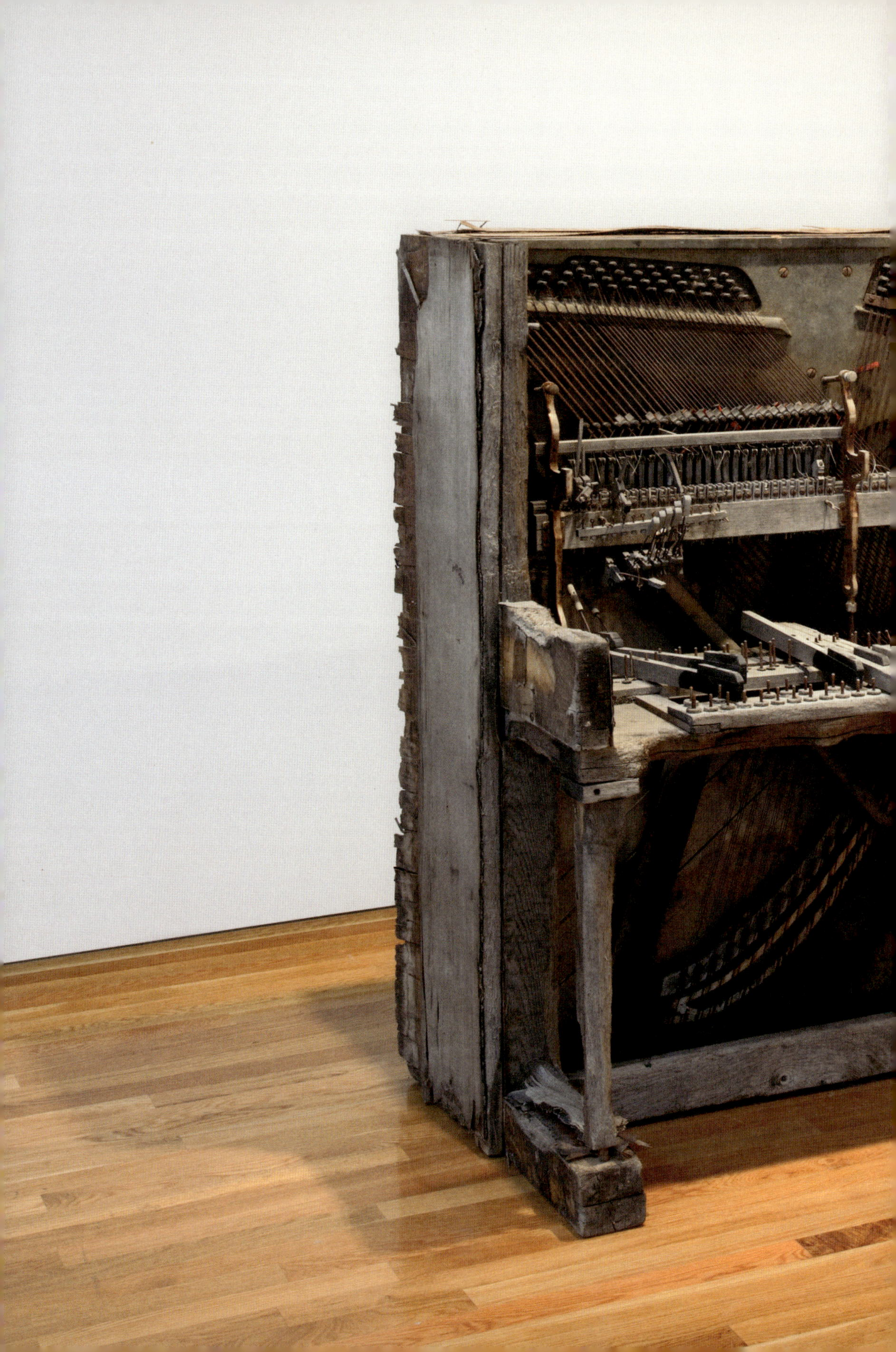

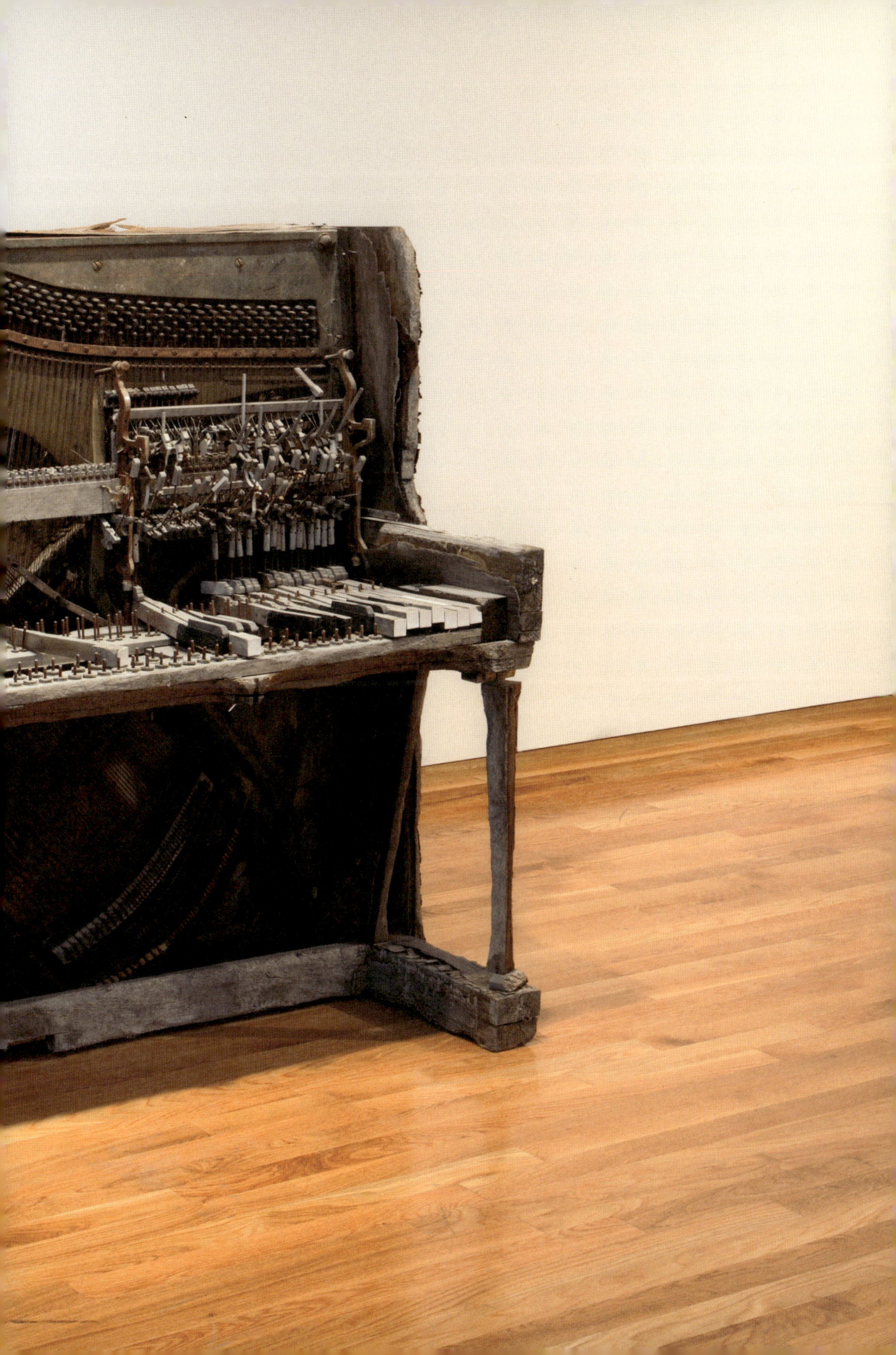

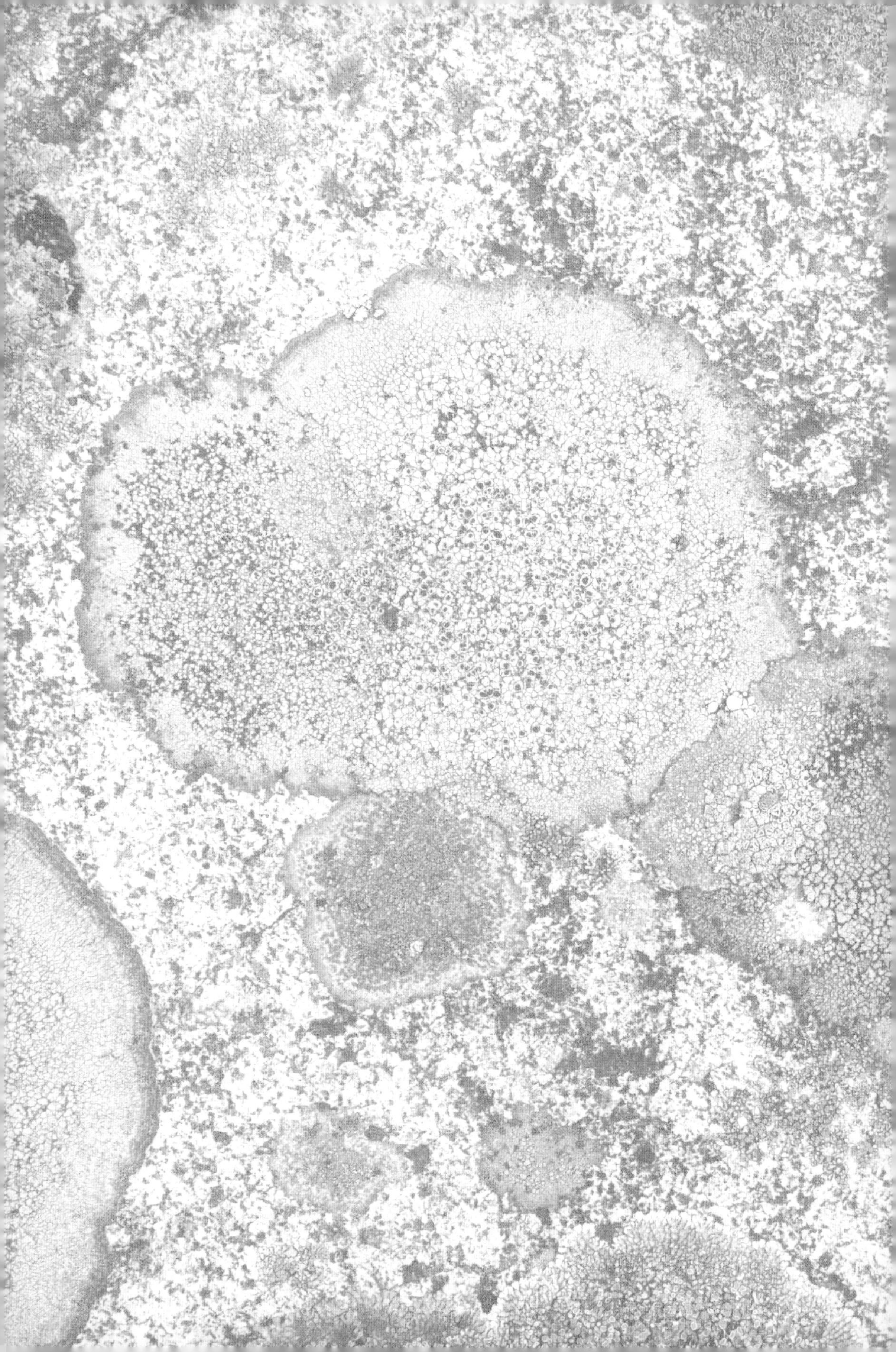

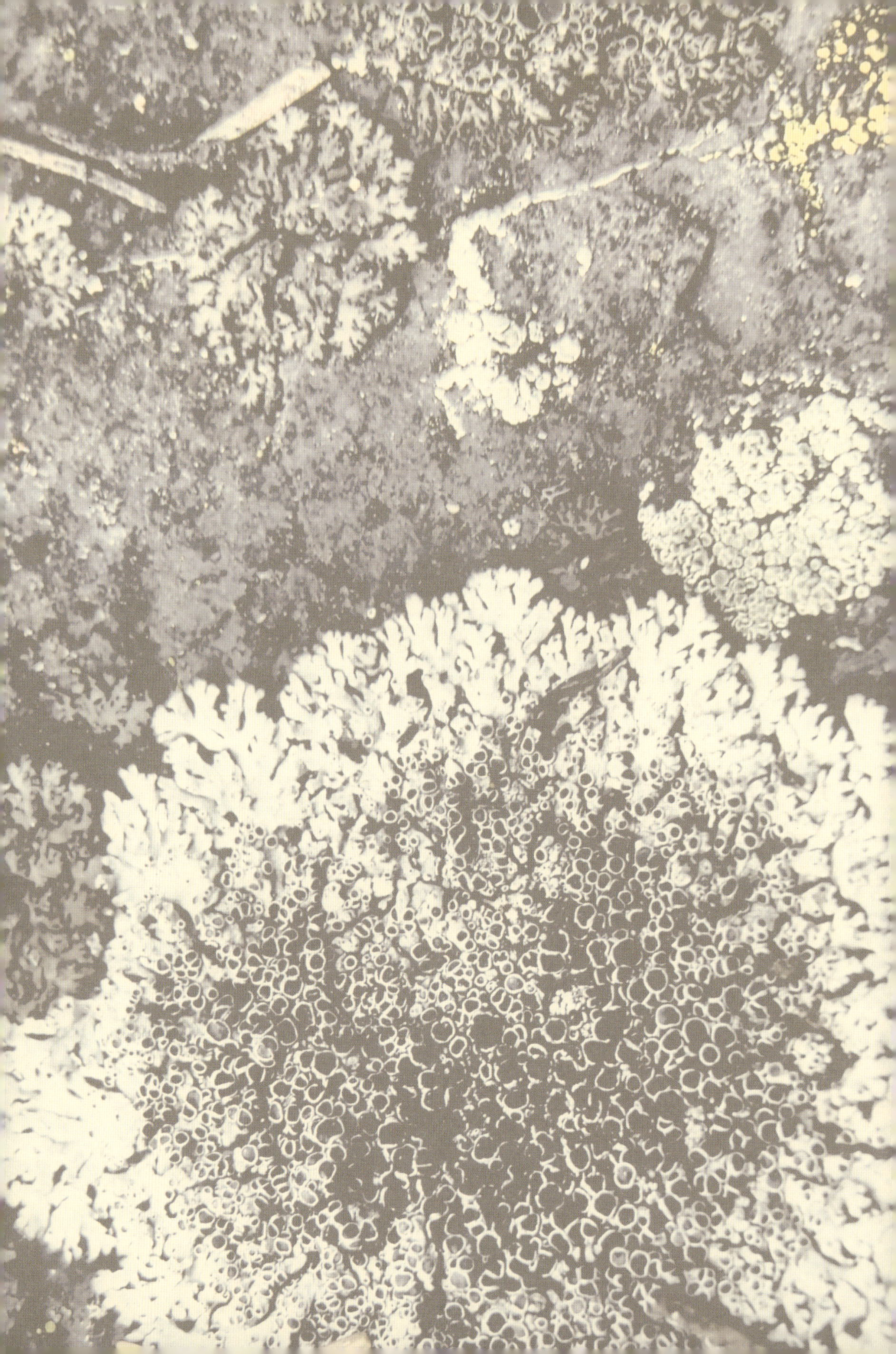

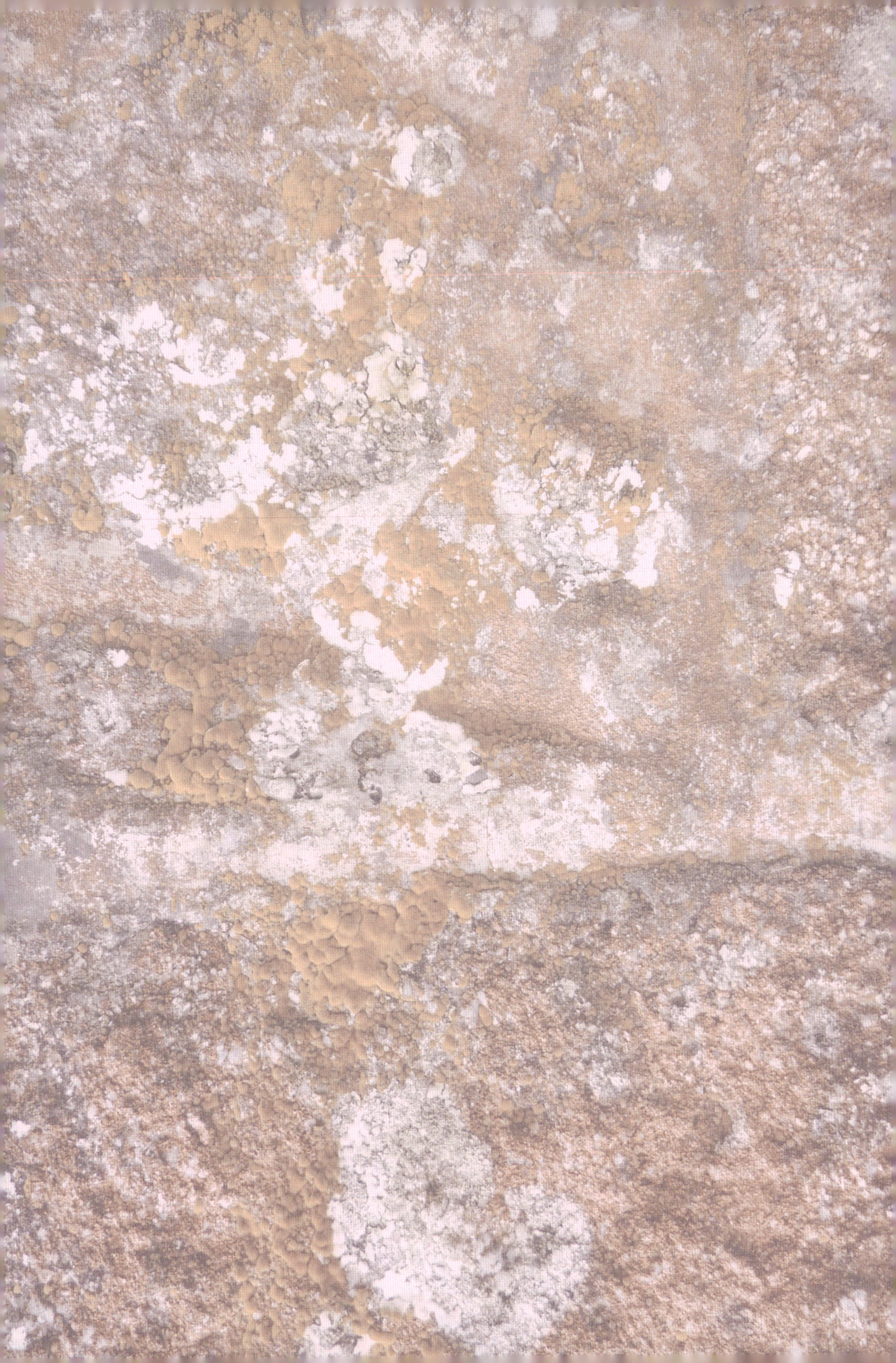

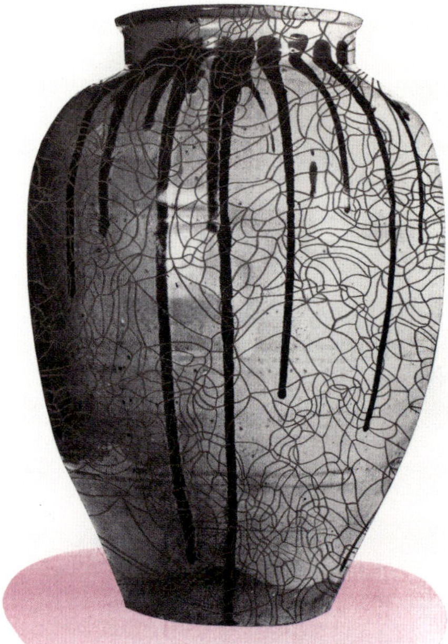

Time, Transformation, and the Social Life of Objects

Candice Hopkins

One of the first works of Jason de Haan's I encountered was *Pie Powder* (2008 – 2010). I learned about the work from a chance conversation with the artist, and later tracked the project's progress through its images. The sculpture consists of an upright black piano that the artist had placed in a field of horses for 763 days. Through their inherent curiosity, the horses interacted with the instrument: they chewed it, scratched their hides on it, they pawed it with their hooves. In time, the piano toppled to the ground, its legs gnawed raw, its inner workings broken and exposed. It later reemerged in the gallery space. Here, worn and weathered and placed upright again, it became a talisman of the ages.

The initial idea to bring the instrument to the North, to lay it in a field and let nature take its course, had circuitous beginnings in a pub in Dawson City, Yukon. Folks gather nightly at the pub to hear "Barnacle Bob" play shanties from the Klondike Gold Rush, songs of myth, heroism and strength of character, on a beautifully worn piano that has stood for well over 100 years.

While witnessing one such performance in the dead of winter 2008, de Haan noticed that, "most captivating [were the] chipped and yellowed ivory keys—which I began to associate with teeth (mostly horse's), which had worn themselves down, eating through songs and players, for over a century."[1]

The truth, as though stretched through time, takes on mythical proportions in the Yukon. It is a place most encounter only through story, where the line between fact and fiction is deliberately blurred. It is also a place that actively cultivates a suspension of belief—where anything, even the tallest of tales, likely had their beginnings with a small kernel of truth. With P*ie Powder*, de Haan has put his finger on something; the sculpture is an example of how time and shifting contexts can imbue objects with new meanings and with story. This is also how his piano becomes talisman of sorts—like the original, it too is now enveloped with narrative. Socio-cultural anthropologist Arjun Appadurai terms this quality "the social life of things."[2] Appadurai explains that, "even though from a theoretical point of view human actors encode things with significance, from a methodological point of view it is *the things-in-motion* that illuminate their human and social context."[3] The title of the piece is also a nod to how the understandings of things, but also words, shift over the centuries. "Pie Powder," for example, is a poor transliteration of the French term *Pied Poudre*, the dusty feet of a wanderer.[4]

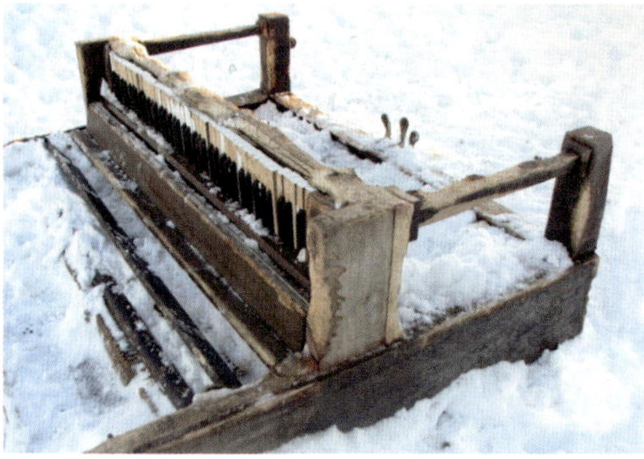

Mimicking how that pub's antique piano was doggedly trekked to the Klondike so many years before by river raft, de Haan transported his piano by truck on the same route overland between Edmonton and Dawson City. This is also the way that many of the first prospectors reached the Yukon gold fields in the late 1800s. Those who decided on the interior route arrived only to discover that the most valuable gold claims were staked long before. The quickest route to the Yukon involved taking an ocean steamer up the West Coast, with the final leg of the journey spent hauling the mandatory 1000 pounds of goods per person straight up and over the carved ice staircases of the Chilkoot or the White Pass. By taking great pains to reproduce this historic journey in the present, de Haan conflates personal with historical myth.

Pie Powder is but one example of how, in de Haan's hands, objects become markers of time. There are also his series of busts that mysteriously grow crystalline beards of salt (*Salt Beards*, 2009 – 2013); a set of 100 gold rings slipped over the finger-like branches of trees, the branches subsuming the rings as they grow (*100 Ages*, 2011); and a one-time collaboration with Scott Rogers, ominously marking the end of days (*The End Is Near Here Is Near The End*, 2009). In this last piece, a work installed in Toronto for an exhibition on the apocalypse, an illuminated sign atop an industrial building declares: "Theendisnearhereisneartheend." The text, installed upside down and backwards, becomes clear only when viewed as a reflection. Slowing down and working harder to decipher the sentence serves to have its portentous message resonate a little longer. Along with creating objects that act as documents of time, de Haan's sculptures bring about the conditions for what can

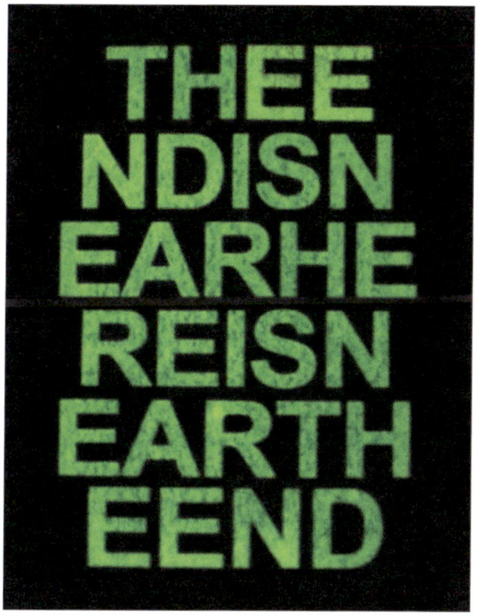

be considered a "generative excess," as they are encrusted with layers of signification. English professor and theorist Bill Brown also equates the "magic by which objects become values, fetishes, idols, and totems" to an excess.[5] For Brown, this surfeit is one of the qualities of the "thing-ness" of objects.

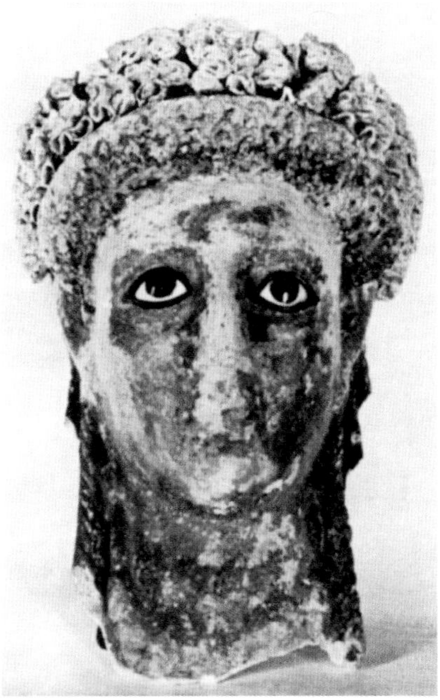

In *Salt Beards*, each of the eight pre-existing busts has a different origin—some are characters from myth, others modeled upon historical figures. The first of the series, *Salt Beards (Barba de sal)* (2009), relies on a bronze female bust borrowed from the regional museum in Querétaro, Mexico. After cultivating the salt crystals on the sculpture, which grew to subsume the lower half of the figure's face, de Haan re-exhibited the altered sculpture. This new form serves to destabilize the identity and the gender of the figure. This act of transformation is more than a deliberate obscurification. For the artist, it is a means "to reactivate (re-awaken) the figure, to unlock it from the moment of completion ... to imagine a continued growth and change that is potentially physical (biological/geological) and ideological."[6]

De Haan's intervention into the staid sculptures provides them with new life, and with this, new meaning. The desire to awaken the hidden life inside a sculpture is recurrent within art history. Jean-Léon Gérôme's *Pygmalion and Galatea* (ca. 1890), which hangs in the Metropolitan Museum of Art in New York, is perhaps the best-known example. The painting depicts the tale of

Ovid's *Metamorphoses* at the moment that the sculpture Galatea is awakened by Venus, fulfilling Pygmalion's rather fetishistic desire for a wife whose beauty is equal to that of his ivory sculpture. But contained within Ovid's myth is a darker storyline, one that warns of the dangers of worshipping false idols. Before his sculpture was magically roused, Pygmalion had fallen in love with his creation. This love all but consumed him.

An initial source for de Haan's series is Colombia's Salt Cathedral of Zipaquirá, thereby referencing another form of worship. The cathedral is otherworldly, made of caves carved out of salt some 200 metres below the surface of the earth, its crystalline walls glowing in the soft light. Despite being filled with religious icons, including a monumental cross, the Cathedral is not an official place of worship; it lacks a bishop and is not recognized by the Catholic Church. The original sanctuary was informal, carved by miners in the 1930s as a place for daily prayer. Official or not, Zipaquirá as a place of belief is irrefutable. The Salt Cathedral is an example of an ideological transformation of the material world. It is an enigma. Through their own material metamorphoses, *Salt Beards* occupy this same empyreal space, and like the Salt Cathedral, they point to how the accumulation of time can solidify belief.

The project, *100 Ages*, offers another material intervention. Over the course of twelve hours on a chilly night in October 2011, de Haan placed 100 small gold rings over 100 tree branches in Queen's Park, Toronto. Small markers with green lights illuminated a path to mark his progress. Each ring is small enough to slip over a human finger. In contrast to the other events that night, commissioned as part of Scotiabank Nuit Blanche, *100 Ages* is understated, slow and process-based. A beautifully typeset postcard—gold ink printed on matte black paper—inviting the public to come and witness the action, was distributed in the days prior. What de Haan set into motion that night will take decades to reveal itself; some tree branches will subtly alter their shape to accommodate the rings, others will subsume them altogether.

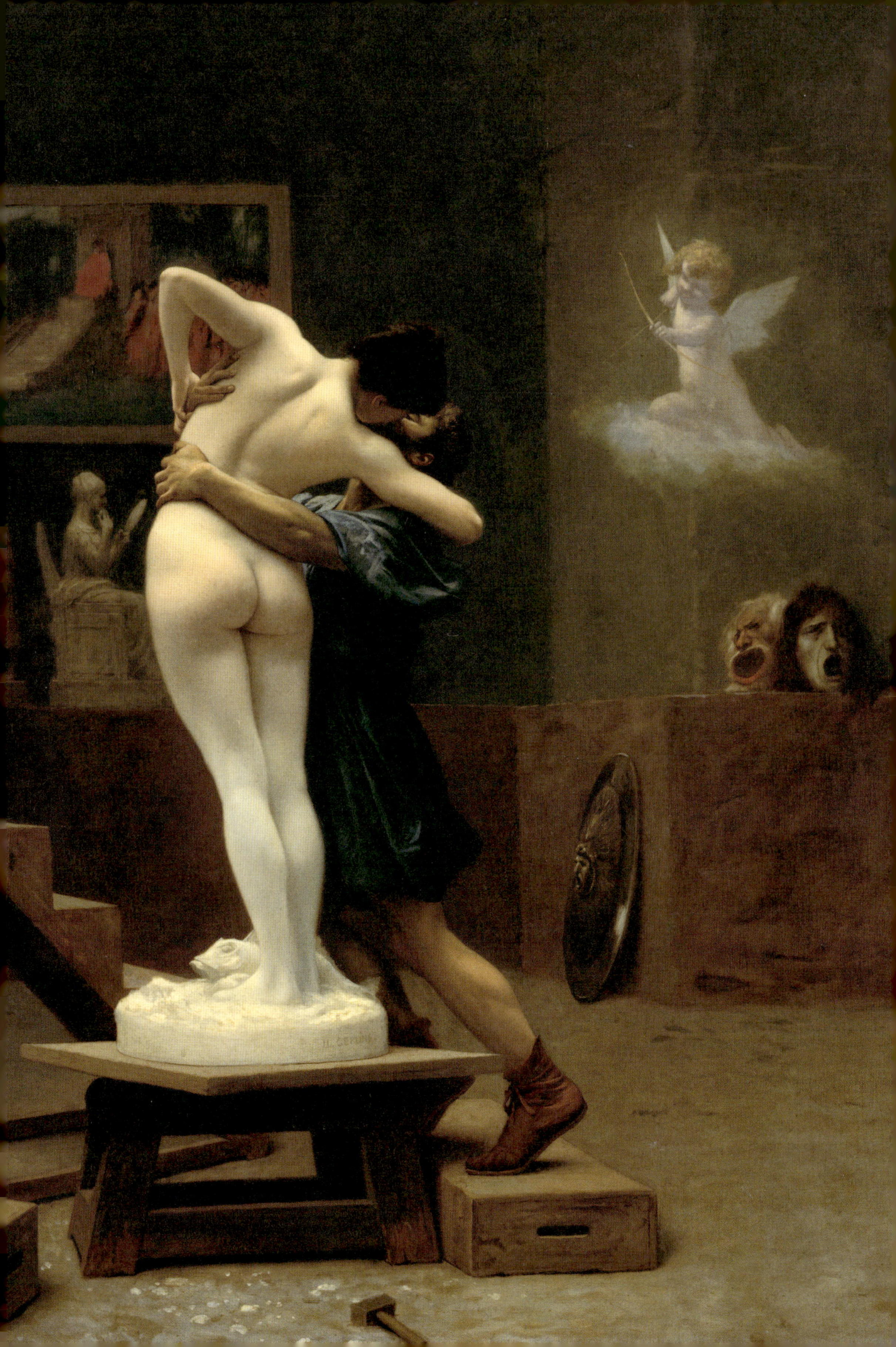

The rings in *100 Ages* will potentially outlast the trees. Gold is one of the most durable metals; it resists the signs of age. De Haan notes it is also an "inert, stable material [with] almost twice the weight of lead. No single acid dissolves it. It is unaffected by oxygen or hydrogen sulfide...gold does not rust, tarnish, corrode, crumble, decompose or decay, even after centuries on the sea floor or in a damp, dripping cavern."[7] It is coveted in almost every culture. In the Americas, the Aztec believed that gold came directly from heavens. For them, it was quite literally, "sun shit."[8] The desire for gold was also at the heart of alchemy, the ancient quest for material and spiritual transformation. Alchemists devoted their lives to the practice of converting base metals—such as lead and copper—into the "noble" metals, silver and gold. Many also sought to produce the "elixir of life," which promised everlasting youth. The pseudo-scientific experiments in alchemy are credited with the birth of chemistry. But unlike much of modern science, spirituality and science co-existed in alchemy; in this practice belief and magic were as much a "truth" as fact and reason. De Haan's projects, such as *100 Ages* and *Salt Beards*, recreate this sense of magic, cultivating the fertile space between truth and what is believed to be real.

De Haan's sculptures call attention to the slow process of transformation. These objects refocus our attention from a single moment to the expanse of time, to shifts that might be imperceptible if it wasn't for the evidence provided in the form of objects and actions. Critic David Levi Strauss characterizes the age we live in now as one of "Distraction Culture."[9] Since he first identified this condition in the late 90s, it has become more acute. We receive information at unprecedented speeds and in such great quantities that our ability to process this information all but breaks down. We perpetually skim the surface of things, never delving into the depths, never getting to the root of the matter. With his accumulative practice, one that cultivates slowness as an artistic strategy, de Haan goes against the hyperspeed of contemporary society. In the age of perpetual distraction, artworks that embody the potential to refocus our attention are all the more necessary.

In July 2013, physicists announced that they had captured a ray of light in a prism and held it there for a full minute. This wasn't the first time they have stopped light; previously, the longest that they had held it was for mere seconds. De Haan's print, *Moon* (2010), also concerns captured light. Using the available light from a lunar eclipse as the only method of exposure, he produced a print consisting of a small ghostly circle that floats on a background of inky blue paper. The circle *as moon* is in fact the trace of a coin. The print was exposed during the partial lunar eclipse on June 26, 2010. This date created a serendipitous alignment between the sun and the moon and with another important moment: June 26 is the artist's birthdate. The resultant print is then, "an overlap of the astral, the fleeting, and the personal."[10] Yet, *Moon*, which de Haan describes as "a true photograph of an event," offers another act of mimicry. For anthropologist Michael Taussig, mimetic acts are most generative when they offer the possibility to "live subjunctively as neither subject nor object of history but as both, at one and the same time."[11] The available light captured in *Moon* perhaps points to another understanding of illumination. For philosopher Walter Benjamin, illumination is equivalent to historical knowledge. "The true picture of the past flits by," he writes. "The past can be seized only as an image which flashes up at the instant when it can be recognized and is never seen again."[12] He also offers the following words of warning: "For every image of the past that is not recognized by the present as one of its own concerns threatens to disappear irretrievably."[13] In capturing light, de Haan is also arresting the past.

Perhaps as a way to dig deeper into this mimesis and to consider the past and future tenses of living works (including their multiple temporalities) de Haan has created the series, *Future Age* (2010). Each sculpture in the series consists of a piece of found wood (driftwood and a petrified tree) with a gold ring set within the sawn end of the former tree. Some of the pieces of found wood are placed as though they are freestanding, while others lean against the wall. These sculptures do something a bit different than *Pie Powder*, *Salt*

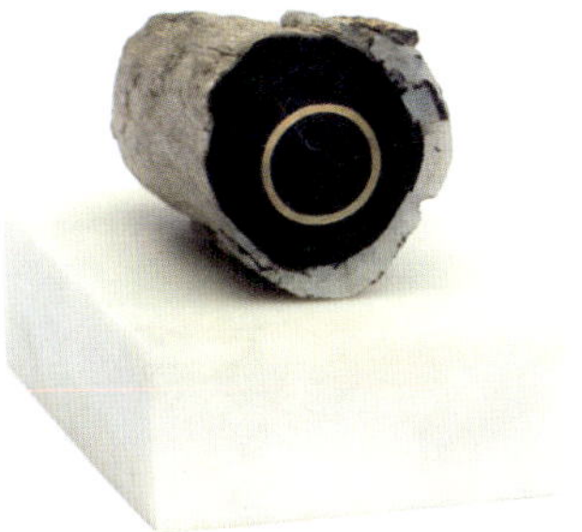

Beards and *Moon*, which each document the slow build-up of time. *Future Age* concerns a coming moment, and with this, the opportunity for reflection and to gaze back again at the past. With *Future Age*, one can imagine cutting into a tree at the end of its life only to discover that one of its growth rings was made entirely of metal. If each of the rings represents a year in the life of the sentinel, this one reveals a past golden age. De Haan's sculptures cultivate belief; in doing so they take on some of the qualities of talismans, objects that are so similarly charged with belief and narrative that they reverberate as though animated from within.

[1] Jason de Haan, email correspondence with the author, August 14, 2013.

[2] See Arjun Appadurai's edited volume, *The Social Life of Things: Commodities in Cultural Perspective* (London: Cambridge University Press, 1986).

[3] Arjun Appadurai, "Introduction: Commodities and the Politics of Value," *The Social Life of Things: Commodities in Cultural Perspective*, 5. Italics mine.

[4] In medieval England, Pie Powder Courts were held in public markets and fairs. These courts served to settle disputes within the grounds of the fairs and markets, particularly those between merchants and consumers.

[5] Bill Brown, "Thing Theory," in *Things* (Chicago: University of Chicago Press, 2004), 5.

[6] Jason de Haan, email correspondence with the author, August 14, 2013.

[7] Ibid.

[8] Jimmie Durham, *Jimmie Durham: Between the Furniture and the Building (Between a Rock and a Hard Place)* (Munich: Kunstverein München, 1998), 85.

[9] See David Levi Strauss's essay "Can You Hear Me Now?" in his book *Between the Eyes: Photography and Politics* (Aperture: New York, 2003).

[10] Jason de Haan, email correspondence with the author, August 14, 2013.

[11] Michael Taussig, *Mimesis and Alterity: A Particular History of the Senses* (New York: Routledge, 1993), 255.

[12] Walter Benjamin, "Theses on the Philosophy of History," in *Illuminations*, trans. Harry Zohn (New York: Schocken Books, 1969), 255.

[13] Ibid.

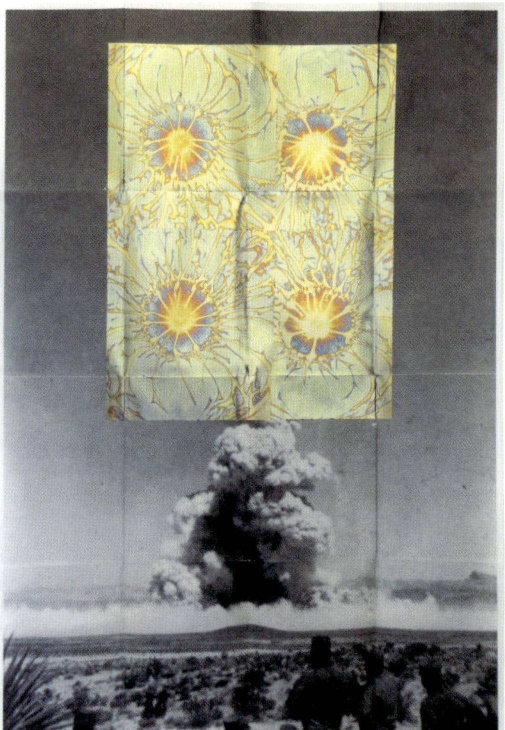

The Only True Alien Planet

Nicholas Brown

Already, too, the relic hunters were at Cape Kennedy, scouring the burning saw grass for instrument panels and flying suits and - most valuable of all - the mummified corpses of the dead astronauts.

These blackened fragments of collar-bone and shin, kneecap and rib, were the unique relics of the space age, as treasured as the saintly bones of medieval shrines.

The Dead Astronaut (1968) is one in a series of short stories by J.G. Ballard presaging the failure of human space exploration. Residing in an abandoned launch site, two former NASA employees await the return of a satellite containing their late colleague's remains. In the effort to locate and bury him the couple must enlist a gang of scavengers who traffic relics of a bygone space program.

This surrealistic elegy to space exploration is markedly terrestrial, and markedly prescient given our current condition in which the dream of deep space travel is all but forgotten. In Ballard's narrative, satellites return to a barren desert inhabited by mourners and opportunists. Astronauts are either long deceased or permanently earth-bound, their missions obsolete. Wonder has given way to nostalgia.

Living in the post-NASA era—inheritors of mankind's failure to dream—we find refuge in Jason de Haan's poetic forays into space and time. Like Ballard's characters scouring the landscape for vestiges of a future-perfect past, we encounter objects that serve as reliquaries, remainders, and records. They bear traces of gestures, alternately revealing and concealing vast temporal dimensions by way of humble means. Such explorations include *Untitled Cube* (2009), a diminutive black box whose mirrored interior, we are told, contains and recursively emits the Northern Lights. Reminiscent of the earliest experiments in celestial photography, *Moon* (2010) features a small circle at the center of a field of Prussian blue, which simultaneously stands in for and chemically registers the moon's activities. Its lunar impression was created by placing a coin on photosensitive paper under the light of a partial lunar eclipse. In a pair of works entitled *Future Age* and *Future Future Age* (both 2012), a gold ring encircles the trunk of a live ash sapling and the rings of a petrified wooden branch have been impregnated by a gold ring. These works superimpose outer and inner realms, as the object's surface—its enigmatic presence—stands in for the invisible processes and events that unfold over time.

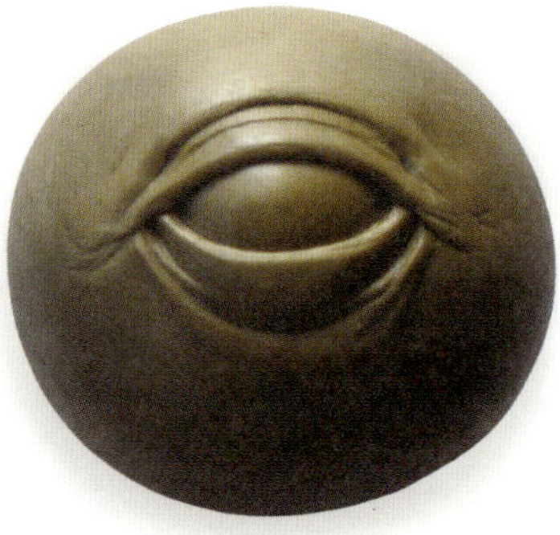

Through a remarkable economy of materials and gestures, de Haan establishes intersecting themes and topos that draw out the imaginary using a deft touch and the curiosity of a keen amateur inventor. The experience is spellbinding, and yet nagging questions arise. Can we allow ourselves to fully commit to the artist's mysticism and mythology? Inheritors of the dead astronaut's legacy, we live the contradiction of unfettered technology and waning curiosity. Our capacity for enchantment by these surfaces and their otherworldy narratives collides with skepticism and melancholia. But I would argue that as much as these objects register desire, they also engender ironic associations that disrupt the quest for transcendence. Navigating the absurd and the sublime, Jason de Haan's world resides in the realms of both science and fiction.

In fact, de Haan is a veteran of the sci-fi genre. His large-scale works *New Jerusalem* (2010) and *New Jerusalem Cloud-shrouded* (2012) bear testimony to an obsessive engagement with collecting, excising and repurposing the futuristic and surreal imagery that adorns the morass of mass marketed genre paperbacks. Portal-like and nearly identical from a distance, the large collages depict floating landscapes set against cosmic backdrops. Assembled with material cannibalized from over a thousand book covers, these topographies exhibit the visual language of genre fiction in imagery and palette.[1] Accretions of hyperrealistic images rendered in saturated (if faded) colour, they seem to inhabit multiple dimensions. Echoing the romantic poets, de Haan's titles evoke the post-apocalyptic City of God. Concatenations of imagery teeming from edge to edge depict this end-days metropolis as a cancerous amalgam. Forms repeat and reverberate — most notably an endless procession of spheres, be they glass domes, planetary orbs, or floating disembodied eyes — producing a widening gyre of centrifugal force that gives way to a hole at the planet's core: a centre that cannot hold.

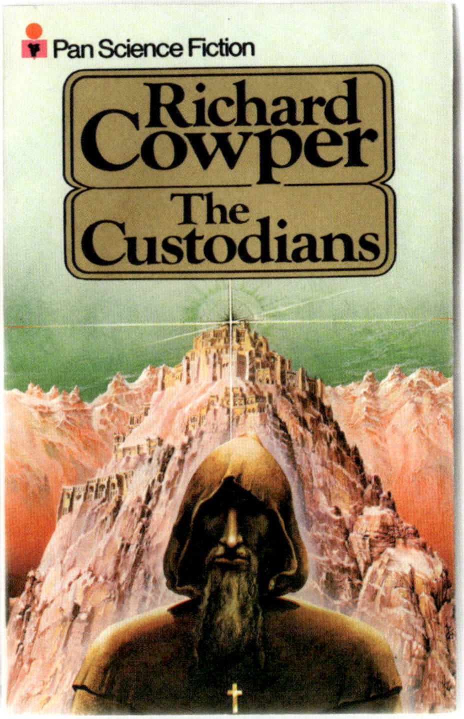

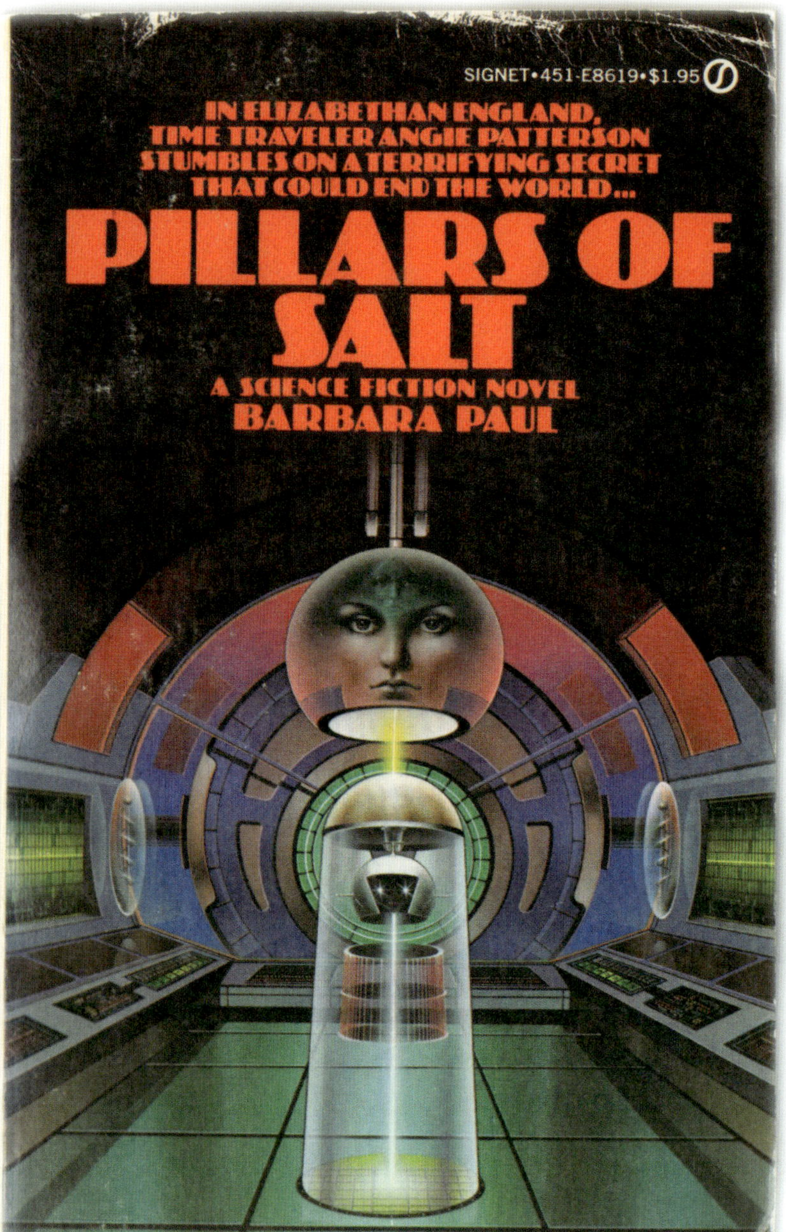
SIGNET•451-E8619•$1.95
IN ELIZABETHAN ENGLAND, TIME TRAVELER ANGIE PATTERSON STUMBLES ON A TERRIFYING SECRET THAT COULD END THE WORLD...
PILLARS OF SALT
A SCIENCE FICTION NOVEL
BARBARA PAUL

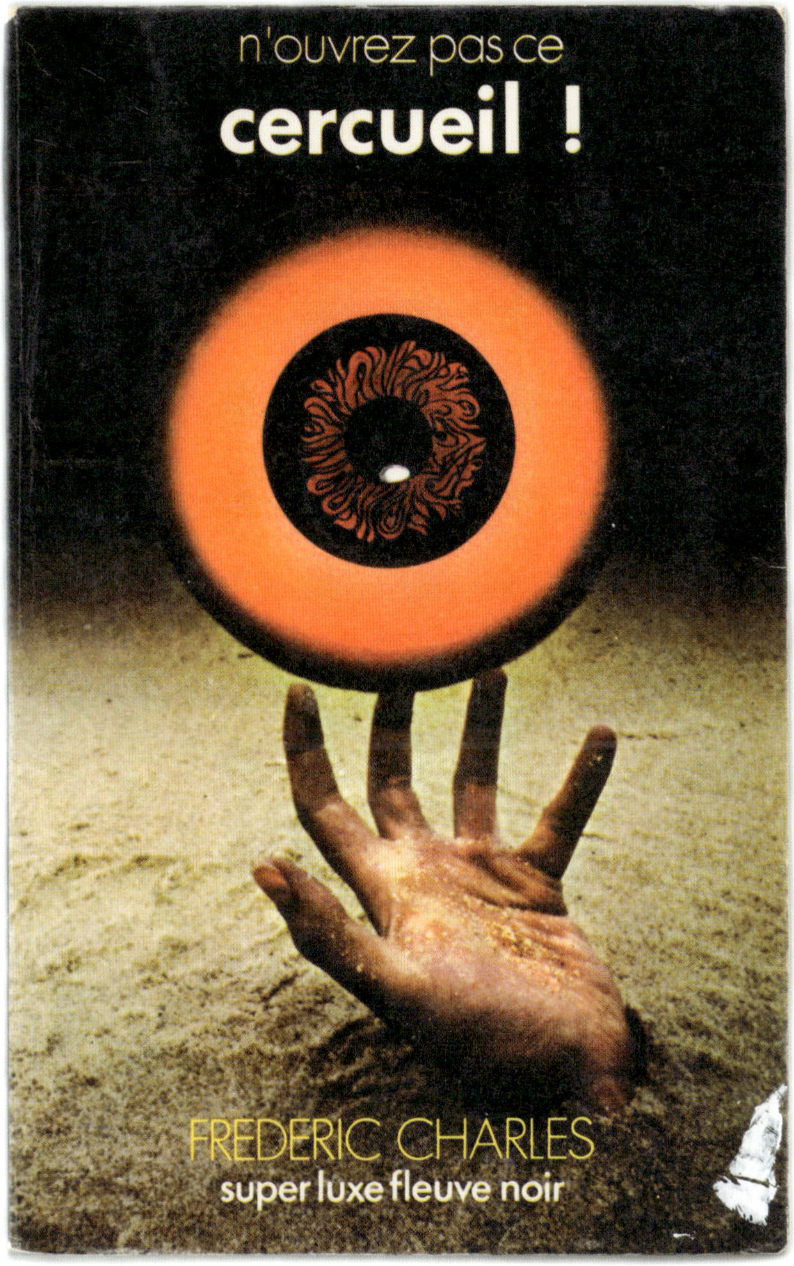
n'ouvrez pas ce
cercueil !
FREDERIC CHARLES
super luxe fleuve noir

New Jerusalem, Cloud-shrouded looks at first glance like a copy of the earlier work rendered out-of-focus; upon closer inspection, the entire landscape is shrouded in a canopy of polychromatic cuttings. Both sinister and absurd, the "cloud shroud" implies the spectre of death, or mourning, but the codes remain scrambled and the vast trajectory of human existence is invoked but never fully revealed.

New Jerusalem encompasses a spectacular array of science fiction tropes that comprise much more than the sum of its parts. Though disembodied from its source, each component nevertheless has its origin in eye-catching (if seemingly arbitrary) cover art.[2] *TIMESTOP, The Stealer of Souls, The Seed of the Earth, The Omega Point, The Destruction of the Temple, The Day After Doomsday, The Custodians, The Black Cloud*: these are just a sampling of the titles harvested to produce *New Jerusalem*.

The narratives of these and other novels allude to many recurring themes that locate the *New Jerusalem* series within de Haan's broader concerns. We encounter repetition and reenactment of historical events and processes ("The year is 2016, and President Kennedy is being murdered—again and again and again"); the rebirth of civilization ("What mysterious power chose this strange group of people to rebuild the shattered world?"); and time travel as a process that overlaps with the present ("In Elizabethan England, time traveler Angie Patterson stumbles on a terrifying secret that could end the world...").[3] The collages oscillate between iconographic representation in their current configurations and the residue of their source material; their surface thingness transubstantiates into a portal to other dimensions.

As source material, mass-marketed paperbacks are surely the antithesis of the Benjaminian aura. Though tantalizing, they possess no fetishistic allure. Seemingly interchangeable covers give form to an infinite archive of undifferentiated titles. Foregrounded as material, they set up an alternative relation to the singularity

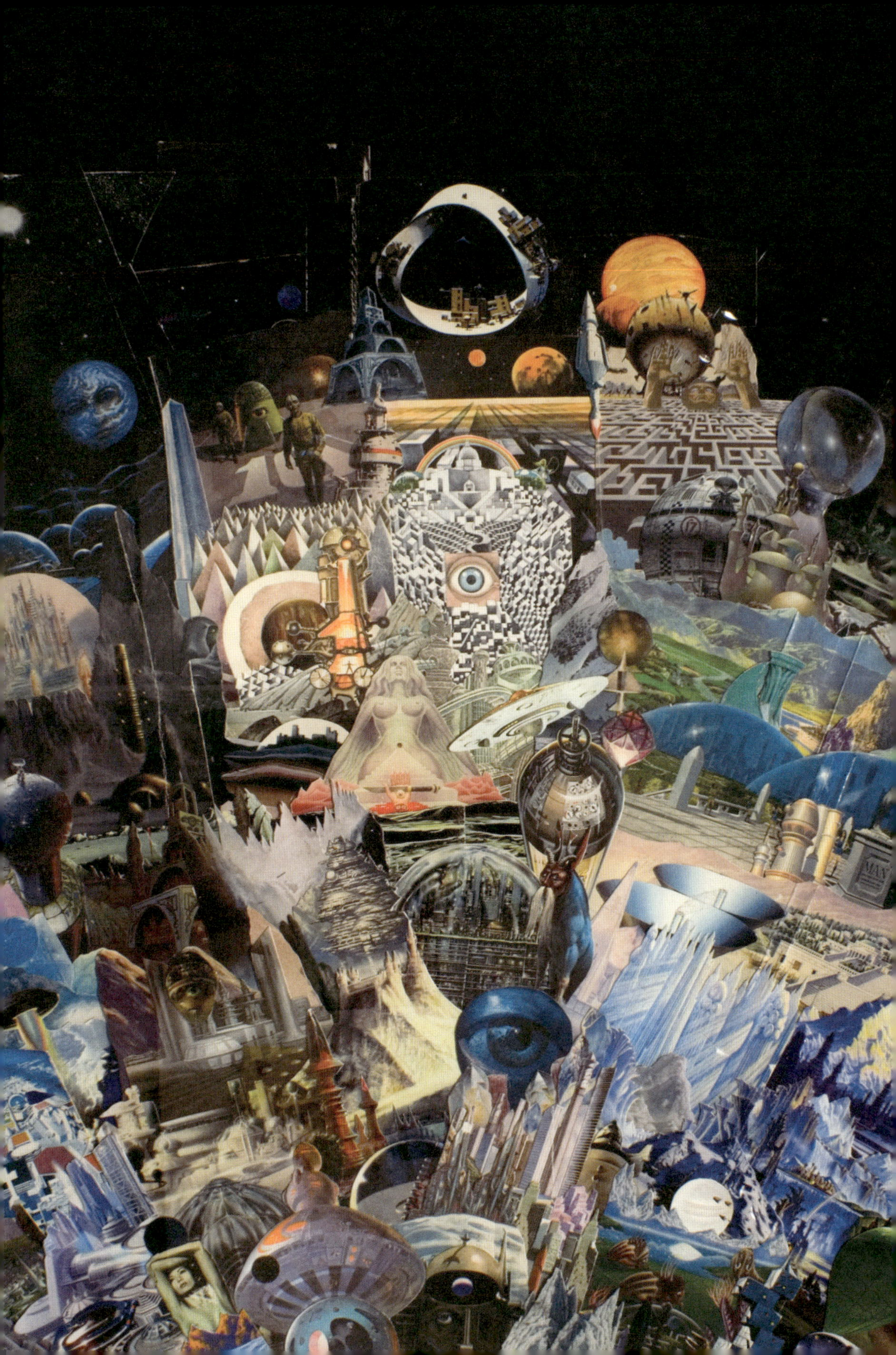

of the enshrined objects that populate much of de Haan's universe. This apparent tension also gives us a chance to reflect on the curious role that books and written narratives occupy in the artist's sculptural trajectory. In an earlier project entitled *Where the Ocean Meets this Guy* (2007), de Haan constructed a one-man sailboat over the course of a month-long exhibition. The project was generated from the artist's growing, specialized library on a range of nautical themes, which includes mariner's tales, instructional texts, and the Coles Notes edition of *Gulliver's Travels*. His library occupies a parallel sphere of performance and identification. As a product of the landlocked province of Alberta, de Haan found his communion with the water by bathtub reading: "it was not the first time I had fallen asleep reading in the tub, awakening in the then frigid waters to the mere singular version of Gulliver's little men."[4] Ultimately the boat would never see the ocean (or the sky), but acts as an index of the artist's occupations: bathtub bibliophile, amateur craftsman, and first-person storyteller.

Part of the thrill and the challenge of Jason de Haan's work lies in the gaps between what can be seen and what is to be believed — between the cover and the contents. We encounter objects and surfaces that radiate heavenly aura, or lock us outside of their supercharged cores. Beyond the allure of the present thing is the off-screen component: narrative, history, rumour and fact. The paradox is that while these things radiate otherworldly presence, they remain profoundly insufficient as vehicles for knowledge and understanding. Like the austronaut's remains, de Haan's works speak to a culture that is both alive and dead. They evoke wonder, but seem to refuse to fulfill the teleological dream of scientific progress.

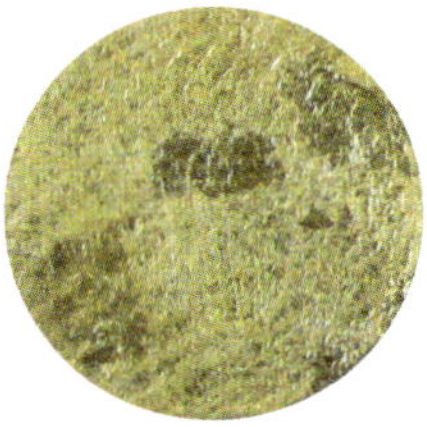

Circles, big and small, populate Jason de Haan's universe. Spheres, domes, wheels, and rings unite the body with the cosmos. They may act as surrogates, transporting the heavens into tangible material, or as containers, delineating space and establishing order. Ballard famously said, "the only true alien planet is Earth." Perhaps we no longer yearn to transcend the earth because we have seen it viewed from outer space, and in a way we are already there. The circle stands in for the infinite, but also circumscribes a limit of imagination, of the ability to know. We are enjoined to suspend disbelief, to behold that the Northern Lights of Dawson City are contained in the box, and that the opposing mirrors of *Spirits Facing Themselves* are truly haunted. But it's really more about the container than its contents. Endlessly looping back between the thing in our midst and the pursuit of a reality that is deferred, or permanently locked beneath surfaces, we behold the orbiting remains of a culture, of wonder.

[1] In a neat parallel to Ballard's fraught relationship with the space program, de Haan's selections range from the 1950s to the 1980s, effectively bracketing off the advent of NASA and its eventual retreat from the dream of interstellar travel into lower earth orbit.

[2] The process brings to mind that of "pulping," in which mass-marketed books that fail to sell are stripped of their covers and recycled.

[3] Quotations sourced from the covers of the following titles in order: Barry N. Malzberg, *The Destruction of the Temple*, (London: Paperback Library Original, 1975); Rena Vale, *The Day After Doomsday*, (New York: Signet, 1979); and Barbara Paul, *Pillars of Salt* (New York: Signet, 1979).

[4] Jason de Haan, *Where the Ocean Meets this Guy* (Calgary: Stride Gallery, 2007), exhibition catalogue.

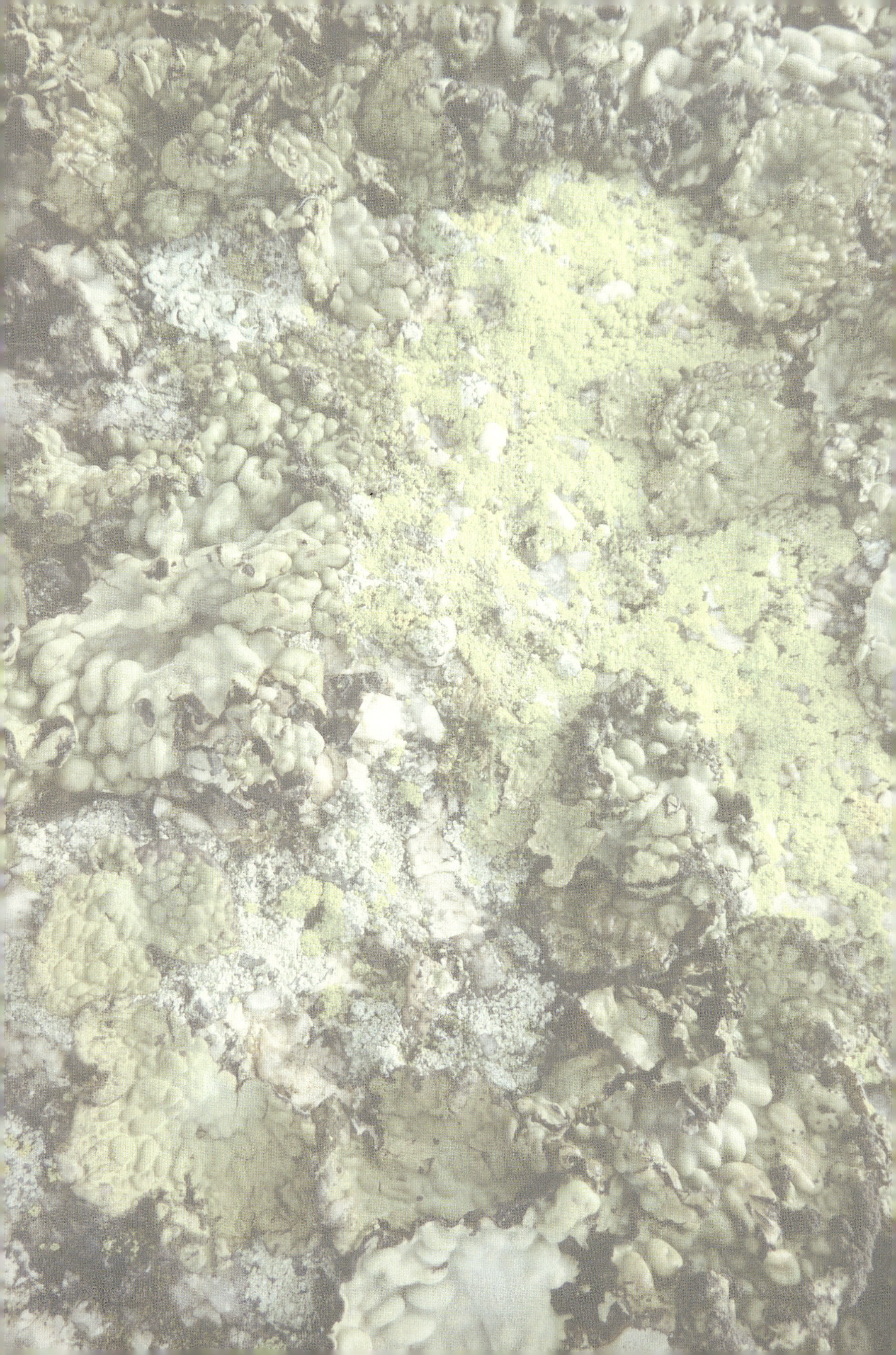

Image List

(inside front and back covers) Neolithic skull and its prosthetic seashell ear (detail), found at Roque d'Aille. Photo by Gustaf Sobin (1935-2005).

Pg. 1 *Untitled*, 2013. Carved Campo del Cielo meteorite. 7 x 3 x 3 cm. Collection of the artist.

Pg. 5 Neolithic skull and its prosthetic seashell ear. Photo by Gustaf Sobin.

Pg. 8 Unknown stairway architecture, photograph of a lost book page. Image from artist's archives. Source unknown.

Pg. 10 George Washington's dentures. Animal and human teeth, lead and ivory. Collection of the Mount Vernon Estate and Gardens. Image from artist's archives. Source unknown.

Pg. 11 *Untitled*, 2013. Carved Campo del Cielo meteorites. Dimensions variable. Collection of the artist.

Pg. 13 The artist's copy of Herman Melville's *Moby Dick*. Harmondsworth, Middlesex: Penguin English Library, 1976. (Cover, detail of J.M.W. Turner's *Whalers*).

Pg. 15 *The Great Stalacpipe Organ*, the world's largest musical instrument, Luray Caverns, Virginia. "Stalactites covering 3 1/2 acres of the surrounding caverns produce tones of symphonic quality when electronically tapped by rubber-tipped mallets. This one-of-a-kind instrument was conceived by Mr. Leland W. Sprinkle of Springfield, Virginia, a mathematician and electronics scientist at the Pentagon. After visiting the caverns with his son and experiencing the organ-like sounds of a stalactite being tapped, Mr. Sprinkle submitted a complex plan for a stalactite-tapping instrument. It took 36 years of frustrating research, design and experimentation to bring his dream to its present state of perfection. Three years alone were spent searching the vast chambers of the caverns to select and carefully sand stalactites to precisely match the musical scale." (Source: luraycaverns.com, accessed December 18, 2013).

Pg. 19 Man carved from salt, Wieliczka Salt Mine, Poland. "This deposit of rock salt in Wieliczka-Bochnia has been mined since the 13th century and is the oldest of its type in Europe. Spread over nine levels, it has 300 km of galleries with works of art, underground chapels and statues sculpted in the salt, making a fascinating pilgrimage into the past of a major industrial undertaking. The Wieliczka and Bochnia Royal Salt Mines illustrate the historic stages of the development of mining techniques in Europe, from the 13th to 20th centuries. Wieliczka Saltworks Castle, used for the management of the property, dates from the medieval period and has been rebuilt several times in the course of its history." (Source: http://whc.unesco.org/en/list/32, accessed December 18, 2013).

Pg. 20 The actor Joseph Jefferson as Rip Van Winkle in 1869. Photograph by Napoleon Sarony. Image from artist's archives. Source unknown.

Pg. 23 1 Botswanan Thebe.

Pg. 24 *Spirits Looking Up at Themselves*, 2009. Haunted mirror and mirror. Dimensions variable. Installation view of the exhibition Nowhere Bodily is Everywhere Ghostly at Museo de la Ciudad, Querétaro, Mexico. Curated by Gabriel Hörner. Collection of the Museo de la Ciudad.

Pg. 27 Pieter Bruegel the Elder, *Big Fishes Eat Little Fishes*, 1556 (detail). Ink on paper. 21.6 x 30.7 cm. Graphische Sammlung Albertina, Vienna.

Pg. 33 *Salt Beard (Old Whalesback)*, 2012. Salt on borrowed ceramic bust. 125 x 92 x 60 cm. The Banff Centre graciously loaned this sculpture, its maker unknown, for the exhibition Nowhere Bodily is Everywhere Ghostly at the Southern Alberta Art Gallery, Lethbridge, 2012. Curated by Ryan Doherty. No longer exists.

Pg. 34 *Salt Beard (Mercury)*, 2010. Salt on found marble bust, steel and rust. 180 x 67 x 52 cm. Private collection.

Pg. 35 & 36 *Barba de sel,* 2009. Salt on borrowed bronze bust. 82 x 55 x 32 cm. Sculpture of Doña Josefa Ortiz de Domínguez, or *La Corregidora*, borrowed from the collection of Museo Regional, Querétaro, Mexico. Destroyed.

Pg. 37 *Salt Skegg*, 2009. Salt on borrowed plaster bust, plywood and stone. 172 x 77 x 58 cm. Likeness of Kristjan Daviðson loaned by Helgi Gislason, for the exhibition Sleepless Nights at Galleri Kling & Bang, Reykjavik. Curated by David Diviney. Private Collection.

Pg. 38 (upper) *Salt Beard proposal*, 2010. Mica flakes on found book page. 30 x 20 cm. Collection of the artist. (lower) *Salt Beard (Byblos)*, 2011. Salt on fired clay from the collection of the Department of Fine Art, American University of Beirut. 88 x 38 x 27 cm. Private collection. Produced for the exhibition Geyser Sustaining Alien Tropicals at Mar Agat, Beirut. Curated by Cecilia Andersson.

Pg. 39 (fore) *Salt Beard (Mercury)*. (mid) *Salt Beard (Newton)*, 2012. Salt on found plaster bust, walnut. 185 x 90 x 35 cm. (back) *Death Threats*, 2012. Graphite rubbings on black paper of found sites inscribed with death threats. 130 x 90 cm each. Installation view of the Sobey Art Award Exhibition, Museum of Contemporary Canadian Art, Toronto, 2012. Curated by Sarah Fillmore.

Pg. 41 *Eternal Note of Sadness*, 2013. Archival inkjet print of a digital collage, letterpress. 51 x 31.5 cm. Edition of 5. Private collection.

Pg. 43 (upper left) *Set of ten books, each containing notation of each second of each minute of each hour of each day of each week of each month of each year, for the next century, the countdown begins when you read this*, 2010. Acrylic ink and variegated gold foil. 75 x 50 cm. Private collection. (upper right) *Proposal for the casting of a Gothic Cathedral in a cement cube, the structure is removed and the form is enterable*, 2010. Acrylic ink, gold foil and collage. 75 x 50 cm. Collection of the artist. (lower left) *Preparing to release a device that will instantly freeze a thunderhead, bringing it crashing to Earth*, 2010. Graphite and collage. 75 x 50 cm. Collection of the artist. (lower right) *Object to send into orbit, two mirrored surveillance domes attached to form a sphere*, 2010. Acrylic ink, silver foil and collage. 75 x 50 cm. Collection of the artist.

Pg. 45 *Petrify Me*, 2013 (detail). Embossed text gathered from various headstones in the Wall, SD graveyard: the Badlands. 125 x 85 cm. Private collection.

Pg. 46 & 47 *Petrify Me*, 2013 (detail). Embossed texts gathered from various headstones in the Bon Accord, AB graveyard. 92 x 64 cm. Collection of the artist.

Pg. 48 *Petrify Me* (detail).

Pg. 50 *New Jerusalem*, 2010. 1500+ collaged science fiction paperback book covers, mounted on black linen. 210 x 210 cm. Private collection.

Pg. 51 *New Jerusalem, Cloud-shrouded*, 2012. 1500+ collaged science fiction paperback book covers, mounted on black linen. 210 x 210 cm. Collection of the Toronto Dominion Bank.

Pg. 52 & 53 *New Jerusalem* (detail).

Pg. 54 *New Jerusalem* and *New Jerusalem, Cloud-shrouded*. Installation view of the exhibition Year Zero at Clint Roenisch Gallery, Toronto, 2012.

Pg. 55 *New Jerusalem, Cloud-shrouded* (detail).

Pg. 57 *Untitled Cube* (detail), 2009. Mirrored tiles, foil tape and Aurora Borealis. 30 x 30 x 30 cm. Edition of 3. Collection of the artist.

Pg. 58 *Untitled Cube*. Installation view with *Future Age* (fore) and *Spirits Looking at Themselves* (back) at the Southern Alberta Art Gallery, Lethbridge, 2012. Curated by Ryan Doherty.

Pg. 60 (left to right, from top): 10 Krona, Iceland; 10 Bututs, Gambia; 5 Cents, Barbados; 1 Peso, Chile; 5 Kroner, Norway; 1 Tolar, Slovenia; 1 Ruble, Russia; 20 Drachmas, Greece; 1 Kwacha, Malawi; 5 Kopeks, Ukraine; 10 Cents, Australia; 2 Euro, France; 50 Centimes, Haiti; 2 Pence, Guernsey; 10 Senti, Tanzania; 2 Shillings, Uganda: 10 Fils, Bahrain; 5 Laari, Maldives; 50 Senti Tanzania; 10 Pence, Guernsey; 20 Pence, England; 100 Pounds Lebanon; 1 Qepik, Azerbaijan; 1 Centavo, Argentina; 20 Pence, England; 50 Shillings, Somolia; 50 Sucres, Equador; 10 Cents, Seychelles.

Pg. 61 *Cannon Ball*, 2012. One coin from each of the world's active currencies. 9 cm sphere. Edition of 3. Collection of the Royal Bank of Canada and private collections.

Pg. 63 *Life After Doomsday*, 2008. In situ.

Pg. 64 *Life After Doomsday*. Open edition drink coaster. Dimensions variable. Produced for the 2008 Artcity Festival, Calgary. Collection of the intermedia artists books and multiples study collection at the University of Maine and multiple private collections.

Pg. 65 *Life After Doomsday*. Open edition drink coaster. Dimensions variable. Produced for the exhibition Life After Doomsday as part of the 2010 Cultural Olympiad at Access Gallery, Vancouver. Curated by Jesse Birch and Liz Park.

Pg. 67 *The Wood and Wave Each Other Know*, with Miruna Dragan, 2011. HD Video, 38 min. (looping). Installation view, the Khyber ICA, Halifax. Collection of the artists.

Pg. 68 & 69 *The Wood and Wave Each Other Know*, 2011. 24 page bookwork, full colour. 43 x 28 cm. Edition of 500.

Pg. 70 & 71 *The Wood and Wave Each Other Know* (production still).

Pg. 72, 73, 74 & 75 *The Wood and Wave Each Other Know* (film stills).

Pg. 77 *There's Still Nothing New Under The Sun* (detail), 2011. 32 page bookwork, laser-jet on Canary yellow paper. 28 x 21.5 cm. Published by youandmebaby. Edition of 50.

Pg. 78 *There's Still Nothing New Under The Sun*.

Pg. 80 *Moby Dick* (Reykjavik), 2009. Archival inkjet print, documentation of an ongoing activity. 30 x 23 cm. Edition of 3. Collection of the artist.

Pg. 81 *Moby Dick* (Beirut), 2011. Archival inkjet print, documentation of an ongoing activity. 30 x 23 cm. Edition of 3. Collection of the artist.

Pg. 82 & 83 *Moby Dick* (Michigan), 2013. Archival inkjet print, documentation of an ongoing activity. 30 x 23 cm. Edition of 3. Collection of the artist.

Pg. 84 *Moby Dick* (South Shore, Nova Scotia), 2011. Archival inkjet print, documentation of an ongoing activity. 30 x 23 cm. Edition of 3. Collection of the artist.

Pg. 85 *Moby Dick* (Vancouver), 2010. Archival inkjet print, documentation of an ongoing activity. 30 x 23 cm. Edition of 3. Collection of the artist.

Pg. 87 (upper) *Hope, Love, Peace, Healing, Generosity, Purpose, Harmony*, 2008. Crystal specimens, speaker, amplifier and audio component. Dimensions variable. Detail view, Access Gallery, Vancouver, 2010. Collection of the artist.

Pg. 87 (lower) *Hope, Love, Peace, Healing, Generosity, Purpose, Harmony*. Detail view, Access Gallery, Vancouver, 2010.

Pg. 88 *Hope, Love, Peace, Healing, Generosity, Purpose, Harmony*. Installation view, Access Gallery, Vancouver, 2010.

Pg. 89 (upper) *Hope, Love, Peace, Healing, Generosity, Purpose, Harmony*. Detail view, Access Gallery, Vancouver, 2010.
(lower) *Hope, Love, Peace, Healing, Generosity, Purpose, Harmony*. Installation view, Galerie Sans Nom, Moncton, 2008.

Pg. 90 *Hope, Love, Peace, Healing, Generosity, Purpose, Harmony*. Detail view, Galerie Sans Nom, Moncton, 2008.

Pg. 92 *Geyser Sustaining Alien Tropicals*, 2012. Collage on archival inkjet print. 76 x 56 cm. Collection of the artist.

Pg. 93 *Small Choir Having a Collective Out-of-Body Experience*, 2011. Collage and gold leaf on paper in handmade artist's frame. 38 x 28 cm. Private Collection.

Pg. 95 *Lord of Flies*, 2008. Paperback and post-it note tabs. 18 x 13 x 13 cm. Collection of the artist.

Pg. 96 *Lord of Flies*.

Pg. 98 & 99 *100 Ages*, 2011. Installation of 100 gold rings on 100 trees and accompanying announcement card, Queen's Park, Toronto, 2011. Curated by Candice Hopkins. Permanent installation.

Pg. 100 *100 Ages*.

Pg. 101 (upper) *100 Ages*. (lower) *100 Ages*.

Pg. 102 *Future Age*, 2012. Gold ring on Hawthorne tree. Installation view, the last day of the exhibition Nowhere Bodily is Everywhere Ghostly at the Southern Alberta Art Gallery, Lethbridge, 2012. Curated by Ryan Doherty. Private Collection.

Pg. 103 *Future Age*. Gold ring on Hawthorne tree. Installation view, the first day of the exhibition Nowhere Bodily is Everywhere Ghostly at the Southern Alberta Art Gallery, Lethbridge, 2012.

Pg. 104 *Future Future Age*, 2012. Gold ring inlaid in found driftwood. 167 x 29 x 7 cm. Installation view of the exhibition Year Zero at Clint Roenisch Gallery, Toronto, 2012. (background) *Out-of-Body*, 2011. Collage and foil on paper in handmade artist's frame. 38 x 28 cm. Collection of the artist.

Pg. 105 (upper left) *Future Age*, 2011. Gold leaf on found book page, 38 x 28 cm. Collection of the artist. (upper right) *100 Ages*. (lower) *100 Ages*.

Pg. 107 *Haunted Mirror Corridor*, 2012. Digital collage. Dimensions variable. Collection of the artist.

Pg. 108 *Spirits Looking at Themselves*, 2010. Haunted mirror and mirror. Dimensions variable. Installation view of the exhibition Like Dust at Clint Roenisch Gallery, Toronto, 2010. Private Collection.

Pg. 110 & 111 *Spirits Looking at Themselves*. Installation view, Nowhere Bodily is Everywhere Ghostly at the Southern Alberta Art Gallery, Lethbridge, 2012. Curated by Ryan Doherty. Collection of the artist.

Pg. 112 *Spirits Looking Up at Themselves*, 2009. Haunted mirror and mirror. Dimensions variable. Installation view, Nowhere Bodily is Everywhere Ghostly at Museo de la Ciudad, Querétaro, Mexico. Curated by Gabriel Hörner. Collection of the Museo de la Ciudad.

Pg. 113 *Spirits Looking Up at Themselves* (detail).

Pg. 115 *Moon*, 2010. Detail view of cyanotype print. 127 x 76 cm. Edition of 3. Private collection.

Pg. 116 *Moon*.

Pg. 118 *Don't Go*, 2013. Collage on rubbing taken from Byblos Harbour. 61 x 42 cm. Collection of the artist.

Pg. 119 (upper) *Clay Stealing Clay (pots separated from their shadow)*, with Miruna Dragan, 2013. One collage and one drawing. 59 x 42 cm each. Collection of the artists. (lower left) *Extraordinary Talents in Ballet's Future*, 2013. Found sheet of newsprint. 57 x 38 cm. Collection of the artist. (lower right) *Darkness Conquers Day*, 2013. Two flags found on the shore of Longyearbyen Harbour, Spitsbergen. 54.5 x 44 cm. Collection of the artist.

Pg. 121 *Pie Powder*, 2010. Piano gnawed by horses for 763 days. Dimensions variable. Collection of the artist.

Pg.122 & 123 *Pie Powder*.

Pg. 124 & 125 *Pie Powder*. Installation view of the exhibition Nowhere Bodily is Everywhere Ghostly at the Southern Alberta Art Gallery, Lethbridge, 2012. Curated by Ryan Doherty.

Pg. 130 *Repaired Pot*, 2012. Collage. 38 x 28 cm. Collection of the artist.

Pg. 132 *Pie Powder*.

Pg. 133 *THEENDISNEARHEREIS-NEARTHEEND*, with Scott Rogers, 2010. Open edition poster, glow-in-the-dark silkscreened text on tar paper. 61 x 46 cm. Produced for the exhibition Life After Doomsday as part of the 2010 Cultural Olympiad at Access Gallery, Vancouver. Curated by Jesse Birch and Liz Park. Numerous private collections.

Pg. 134 Woman's Head, Ancient Egyptian statuary. Herzog Collection, Budapest. Image from artist's archives. Source unknown.

Pg. 136 Jean-Léon Gérôme (1824–1904), *Pygmalion and Galatea*, ca. 1890. Oil on canvas. 88.9 x 68.6 cm. Gift of Louis C. Raegner, 1927 (27.200). Image copyright © The Metropolitan Museum of Art. Image source: Art Resource, NY

Pg. 139 *Future Future Age*, 2011. Gold ring inlaid in petrified wood. 15 x 9 x 7 cm. Collection of the Museum of Longing and Failure, Bergen.

Pg. 140 *Untitled (bomb)*, 2013. Variegated gold leaf on poster. 55 x 37 cm. Collection of the artist.

Pg. 142 *Zeus at Olympus*, 2011. Carved Lebanese beach stone. 6 x 6 x 5 cm. Collection of the artist.

Pg. 143 The artist's copy of Richard Cowper's *The Custodians* (cover art by Geoff Taylor). New York: Pan Science Fiction, 1978.

Pg. 144 The artist's copy of Barbara Paul's *Pillars of Salt* (cover art by Paul Stinson). New York: A Signet Book / New American Library, 1979.

Pg. 145 The artist's copy of Frederic Charles' *N'ouvrez pas ce Cercueil!*. Paris: Editions Fleuve Noir, 1974.

Pg. 147 *New Jerusalem* (detail).

Pg. 149 *Proposal for the casting of a Gothic Cathedral in a cement cube, the structure is removed and the form is enterable* (detail).

Pg. 164 *Monument to the Burden of the Future* (detail), 2012. Carved alabaster, bronze, black granite. 180 x 30 x 30 cm. Private collection.

Projects photographed by Jason de Haan except: Pg. 41 by Clint Roenisch; Pgs. 42,43, 74, 77 & 78, 88, 89 & 90, 91, 118, 119, 128 & 129, 153 by Miruna Dragan; Pgs. 57, 58, 59 & 60, 62, 64 by David M. C. Miller and Petra Mala Miller; Pg. 61, 164 by Toni Hafkenscheid; Pg. 87 by Kris Lindskoog; Pg. 92 by Paul Morstad and Dean Long; Pg. 112 by Jason Ebanks; Pg. 145 by Andrew Taggart and Chloe Lewis (MOLAF).

Images courtesy of Jason de Haan, Clint Roenisch Gallery and Art Resource, NY.

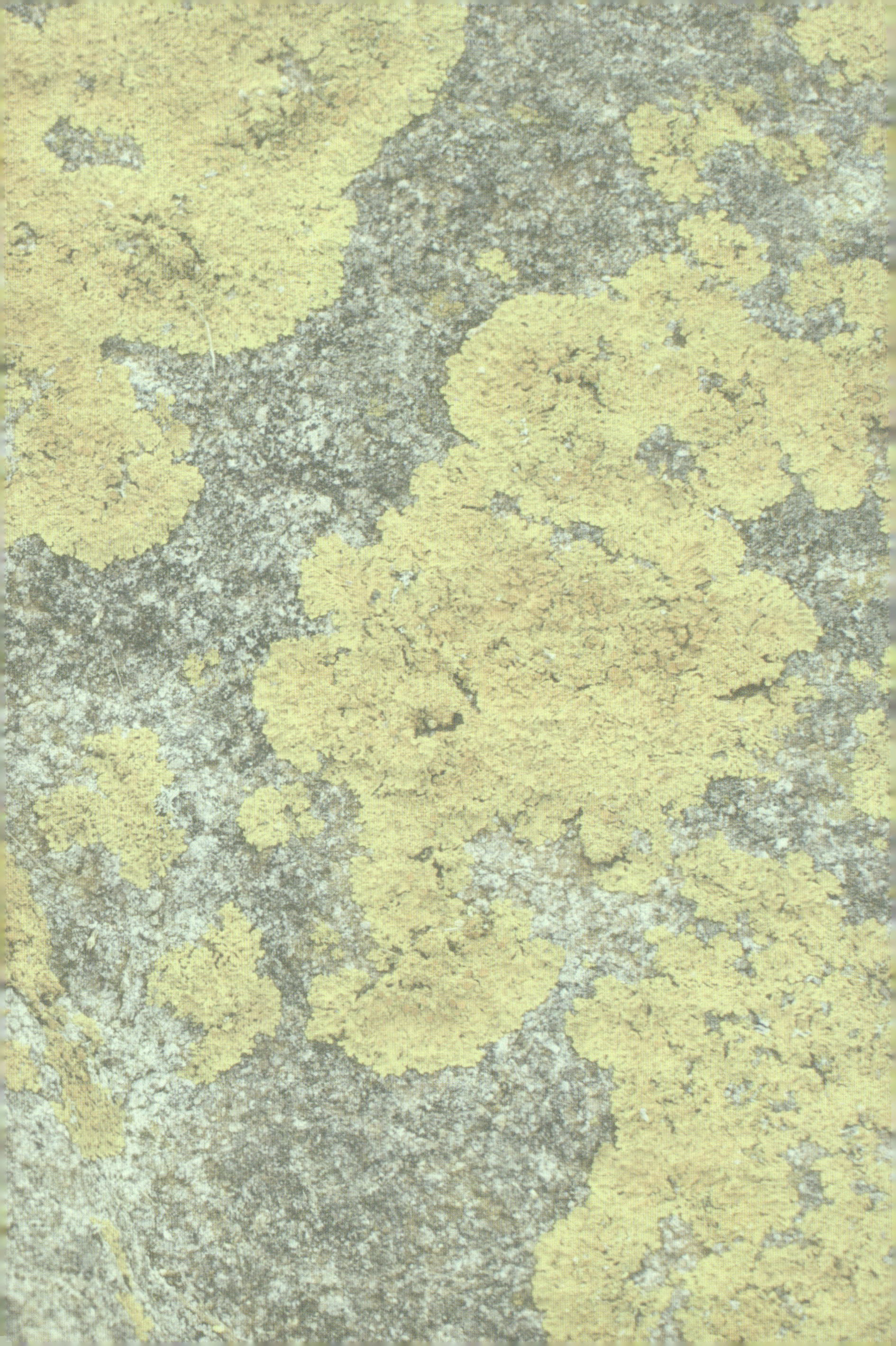

Biographies

Gustaf Sobin

Gustaf Sobin (1935–2005) was a U.S.-born poet and author who spent most of his adult life in France. Originally from Boston, Sobin attended the Choate School, Brown University, and moved to Paris in 1962. Eventually he settled in the village of Goult, Provence, where he remained for over forty years, publishing more than a dozen books of poetry, four novels, a children's story and two compilations of essays. These include: *Breath's Burials* (poetry, New Directions, 1995), *Luminous Debris* (1999) and *Ladder of Shadows* (2008) (essays, University of California Press), and *Collected Poetry* (Talisman House, 2010).

David Diviney

David Diviney is Curator of Exhibitions at the Art Gallery of Nova Scotia (AGNS). He obtained his BFA degree in 1995 from the Tyler School of Art at Temple University (Philadelphia) and graduated in 1998 from the MFA program of Nova Scotia College of Art and Design (Halifax). He was the Director of Eye Level Gallery (Halifax) until 2002 when he moved to Lethbridge, Alberta, then Kamloops, British Columbia, to pursue curatorial and teaching positions. He held the position of Assistant Curator, Southern Alberta Art Gallery (Lethbridge) and has taught courses in the areas of sculpture, drawing and gallery studies at Alberta College of Art and Design (Calgary), University of Lethbridge, Thompson Rivers University (Kamloops), and Sheridan College Institute of Technology and Advanced Learning (Oakville). In 2009, Diviney returned to Nova Scotia to work as Curator of Programs for the Art Gallery of Nova Scotia Western Branch in Yarmouth and, as of 2010, as the Curator of Exhibitions at the AGNS's main gallery in Halifax.

Ryan Doherty

Ryan Doherty joined the staff of the Southern Alberta Art Gallery (SAAG) as Curator in 2008 and as Director/Curator in mid-2013. He received his Master of Arts degree from the Centre for Curatorial Studies at Bard College in New York (2007). Doherty completed his undergraduate degree with a focus on curatorial studies at the University of Lethbridge in 1997, and continued working at the U of L Art Gallery curating exhibitions from their extensive collections. In 2000 he was awarded an International Residency Fellowship from the Department of Foreign

Affairs and International Trade which provided the opportunity to help produce a major travelling exhibition and visit a large number of American museums. At SAAG, his curatorial practice has explored the construction of meaning in our information age, variations in the use of the persona, and notions of maintenance, adaptability and institutional reflection. Recently, Doherty has served as a juror for two of Canada's most important awards for contemporary art, the Sobey Art Award in 2011 and 2012, and the 2013 RBC Canadian Painting Competition.

Crystal Mowry

Crystal Mowry is Senior Curator at the Kitchener-Waterloo Art Gallery (KW|AG). She earned her MFA from the Nova Scotia College of Art & Design University and an AOCAD from the Ontario College of Art & Design. Prior to her current appointment, Mowry was Assistant Curator at KW|AG and Programming Associate at YYZ Artists' Outlet.

During her time at KW|AG she has curated and organized numerous exhibitions including The Limits (2011) and solo projects with artists such as David Hoffos, John Kissick, Kelly Richardson and Jon Sasaki. Mowry's independent curatorial ventures include The Terrarium Project, an interdisciplinary collaborative project combining the efforts of artists, historians, a filmmaker, a horticulturalist and a landscape architect. The Terrarium Project was one of the recipients of the Harbourfront Centre's inaugural Fresh Grounds Commissions. In 2011 she received an OAAG Exhibition Award for Ernest Daetwyler: Barn Raising [Reality in Reverse]. Together with Ivan Jurakic, Mowry curated the Romancing the Anthropocene portion of Scotiabank Nuit Blanche in Toronto, 2013.

Richard Rhodes

Richard Rhodes is Editor of *Canadian Art* and author of *A First Book of Canadian Art*. Since 1979 he has written for numerous art publications in Canada and abroad and lectures frequently on art. Founder, with Dyan Marie, of C Magazine in 1983 he ran it as Editor and Publisher until 1990. As a curator, he organized Canadian participation at the 1985 São Paulo Biennale and curated more than a dozen exhibitions at The Power Plant in Toronto from 1990 through 1993. Subsequently as an independent curator, he has worked with Oakville Galleries and organized in 2000 a five-venue exhibition in Toronto of emerging art from The Netherlands. Between 2002 and 2012, he developed an ongoing series of one-day exhibitions staged over the course of the annual Toronto International Art Fair. In 2010 he was curator of Timeland, the Alberta Biennial of Contemporary Art. He has freelanced as a photographer of urban space for the Globe and Mail and taught the history and contemporary practice of photography at Ryerson University. His paintings of urban and rural sky space have been included in the nationally touring exhibition Weathervane and the project exhibition Grand River at the Kitchener-Waterloo Art Gallery in 2008. In 2003 received the Toronto Friends of the Visual Arts Achievement Award.

Candice Hopkins

Candice Hopkins (born 1977, Whitehorse, Yukon) is an independent curator and writer based in Albuquerque, New Mexico. Her writings on history, art and vernacular architecture are published widely, and she has lectured at such venues as Witte de With, Netherlands; the Dakar Biennale; and Tate Modern, London. In 2012 Hopkins presented a keynote lecture on the topic of the "sovereign imagination" for dOCUMENTA 13. Her recent curatorial projects include: Close Encounters: The Next 500 Years, a multi-site exhibition in Winnipeg co-curated with Steve Loft, Jenny Western and Lee-Ann Martin; and Sakahàn: International Indigenous Art co-curated with Greg Hill and Christine Lalonde, the National Gallery of Canada's largest survey of recent Indigenous art. Along with Lucia Sanroman, Irene Hoffmann and Janet Dees, Hopkins is a curator of the 2014 SITE Santa Fe biennial exhibition, Unsettled Landscapes.

Nicholas Brown

Nicholas Brown is a Canadian curator based in New Haven, Connecticut. In the fall of 2012 he was one of the curators of Shaping Community, a multi-site exhibition at Yale University. In late 2012 Nicholas contributed to *One for you and one for me*, an anthology of artist multiples edited by Dave Dyment and Gregory Elgstrand, published by YYZ Books. In 2012 he was curator in residence at Darling Foundry's Residence of the Americas in Montreal. Brown curated You had to go Looking for it, the exhibition in Toronto's financial district for Scotiabank Nuit Blanche, 2011. He was the founding Director/Curator of Red Bull 381 Projects, a unique non-profit exhibition space. From 2008–2010 he organized exhibitions and projects by contemporary artists including Cedric Bomford, Jessica Eaton, Niall McClelland, Christine Swintak and Jon Sasaki, among others. He was an organizer of Reverse Pedagogy II, a nomadic art school that took place during the 53rd Annual Venice Biennale in 2009. Brown has contributed essays and reviews to Fillip, Hunter and Cook, and C Magazine.

Jason de Haan

Jason de Haan's recent solo exhibitions include Clint Roenisch Gallery, Toronto (2012); Museo de la Ciudad, Querétaro (2012); with Miruna Dragan at The Khyber, Halifax (2011); ODD Gallery, Dawson City (2010) and Access Gallery, Vancouver (2010). His work has been presented in group exhibitions at Oakville Galleries (2012); with Miruna Dragan at 98 Weeks Research Project at the Thessaloniki Biennale (2011); Scotiabank Nuit Blanche, Toronto (2011); MOLAF, Bergen (2011); Art Gallery of Alberta (2010 & 2013); OK Quoi?, Sackville (2010) and Galleri Kling og Bang, Reykjavik (2009). De Haan participated in the Arctic Circle 2012 residency and the residency "The Soiree Retreat: A bit of a Chekhovian Situation" at The Banff Centre (2011). His work will be presented in exhibitions at the Dunlop Art Gallery, Regina in 2014; and at MASS, MoCA, North Adams in 2015. In 2012 de Haan was shortlisted for the Sobey Art Award representing the Prairies and the North and is currently a Master's candidate at Bard College, Annandale-on-Hudson, New York. He is represented in Canada by Clint Roenisch Gallery.

Acknowledgements

Oh man! There is no planet, sun, or star could hold you if you but knew what you are.
- Ralph Waldo Emerson

The work of Jason de Haan exists at the collision of precarity and unpredictability, approached with a sense of time wrapped in memory, mythology, fantasy and romance. His works seem as though they were rediscovered in some dusty attic or arcane museum collection—quiet gestures forgotten long ago—yet from a past that dreamed of a distant future still unrealized. De Haan is an artist who appeals to a person's heart as much as their intellect, garnering praise from high-ranking academics to six-year-old gallery visitors. It is a privilege to encounter his work, and equally so, to see his practice put to print and distributed widely.

This book is the most comprehensive and significant monograph on the work of Jason de Haan to date and is to be celebrated for its collection of insightful essays, exquisite photographs, and in particular, its thoughtful design, the result of countless hours by the artist himself. On behalf of our partnering institutions, our appreciation to Jason de Haan cannot be underestimated. He has worked tirelessly to create new work, to develop exhibitions across the country and now to publish this extraordinary new book, and most remarkably, he has done so with enthusiasm, patience and generosity.

Our sincere thanks to Nicholas Brown, Candice Hopkins and Richard Rhodes for their considered essays. Their contributions are varied in their approach, but uniform in their thoughtful and inquisitive analysis of de Haan's practice. Thanks as well to David Diviney, Curator of Exhibitions at the Art Gallery of Nova Scotia; Crystal Mowry, Senior Curator at the Kitchener-Waterloo Art Gallery; and Ryan Doherty, Director/Curator at the Southern Alberta Art Gallery for their round table discussion with de Haan, providing a valuable opportunity for the artist's own voice. These individuals should also be acknowledged for their efforts in bringing Jason de Haan's work to their respective organizations and enabling this remarkable publication to be co-produced. Moreover, the exhibitions could not have happened without the generosity of those willing to let work from their collection live elsewhere, if only temporarily: thanks to Clint Roenisch Gallery, Royal Bank of Canada, TD Canada Trust, The Banff Centre, Murray and Christine Quinn and the collections that wish to remain private.

We extend our gratitude to Shannon Anderson who edited the contents of this publication with a watchful and discerning eye. And to Dana Woodward, of Three Legged Dog Design, whose expertise was greatly valued while working carefully with de Haan in the final stages of this monograph.

On behalf of the Southern Alberta Art Gallery, Kitchener-Waterloo Art Gallery and Art Gallery of Nova Scotia, we express our deepest appreciation to our major funders: the Canada Council for the Arts, the Alberta Foundation for the Arts, the Ontario Arts Council, the Nova Scotia Department of Communities, Culture and Heritage and the City of Lethbridge.

Special acknowledgement must be given to the RBC Emerging Artists Project and in particular to Robin Anthony, Art Curator with the Royal Bank of Canada, who was instrumental in advocating on behalf of de Haan and the Southern Alberta Art Gallery to secure a large part of the funding for this endeavour. This program provided significant support, financially and otherwise, to foster the career of Jason de Haan, without which a book of this stature would not have been possible.

Ray Cronin, *Director & CEO, Art Gallery of Nova Scotia*
Ryan Doherty, *Director/Curator, Southern Alberta Art Gallery*
Shirley Madill, *Executive Director, Kitchener-Waterloo Art Gallery*

Art Gallery *of* Nova Scotia

SAAG SOUTHERN ALBERTA ART GALLERY

KITCHENER-WATERLOO ART GALLERY

Investing in the arts has been a longstanding priority of the Royal Bank of Canada and for many years, we have focused our attention on helping the next generation of Canadian talent achieve their potential and follow their dreams.

We recognize the challenges promising new artists face and are always looking for ways to assist – from mentorships and internships through our RBC Emerging Artists Project to funding and support through competitions like the RBC Canadian Painting Competition and the production of exhibitions and catalogues such as this monograph.

We are pleased to work with the Southern Alberta Art Gallery to support the practice of Jason de Haan through the production of this impressive book, *Noghwhere Bodili is Everywhere Goostly*.

As the curator for RBC's corporate art collection, I have focused on diversification by acquiring works by living artists who are considered the leading visionaries of our time. One of the key areas of expansion has been to collect artwork from emerging artists whose practices challenge our notion of what art is. There has been tremendous growth in the visual arts community, and for it to continue to prosper, we need to ensure that our artists have the support, funding and opportunities to develop their practice and achieve success.

On behalf of RBC, we hope you enjoy this special monograph of Jason de Haan's work.

Robin Anthony, *Art Curator, Royal Bank of Canada*

RBC® RBC Emerging Artists Project

This book would not have been possible without the affection and patience of Miruna Dragan, you have my heart. My thanks also to John and Brenda de Haan, for their unfaltering love and support.

My deepest gratitude goes to Ryan Doherty, David Diviney and Crystal Mowry, for their ongoing enthusiasm and trust, and to Nicholas Brown, Candice Hopkins and Richard Rhodes for the generous and thoughtful texts that they contributed to this publication. Thanks also to Shannon Anderson, for her keen eyes and clear thoughts during the editing process.

Thank you to those who helped to make the projects within these pages possible: Sid and Alice de Haan, Ryan de Haan and Guus van Laar, Alisha de Haan, Winni de Haan, Dan Bosch, Christina Cuthbertson, Rico Francis and Nawal Akl, Ed Bamling, Jesse McKee, Kitty Scott, Gabriel Hörner, Rafael Rodriguez, Charles Stankievech, Kris Lindskoog and Doha Chebib, Mike Bacon, Jeff Homme and Lindsay Sutton, Brian Ferguson, Scott Rogers, Dean Long and Julie Morstad, Paul Morstad, Wednesday Lupypciw, Jesse Birch, Liz Park, Lea Najjar, Cecelia Andersson, Erin MacMillan, Piet Langeveld, Daniel Wong, Erling Klingenberg, Hekla Dögg Jónsdóttir, Kyle Beal and Kaylin Pearce, Halsey Rodman, Pam Lins, Ohad Meromi, Harry Dodge, Aaron O'Connor, Taylor Davis, Kenji Fujita, Dmitri Hertz, Matthew Schrader, Rochelle Goldberg, Krista Peters, Sarah Fillmore, Warren McLachlan, Dan Joyce, Lance Blomgren, Mike Yuhaz, Andrew Taggart and Chloe Lewis, Jodie Statler, Neville Assad-Salha, Sarah Fuller, Wendy Tokaryk, Sean Procyk, Jeremy Pavka, Matthew Bourree, Brian MacNevin, Noel Begin and Kimberley Cooper, Kyle Whitehead, Matt Crookshank, Erika Kierulf, Meghann Riepenhoff, Leopold Kowolik and Bronwyn Martin, Bill and Gwen Bosch, Dorian Fitzgerald, and David Young. I also wish to extend warm thanks to Clint Roenisch for his steadfast belief in my work and to Toby Reid and Dana Woodward for their exceptional assistance in the preparation of this publication.

Thank you also to the generous lenders to this suite of exhibitions. I would like to acknowledge that many of the projects herein have been supported by a number of organizations: the Calgary 2012 Cultural Capital Program, the Vancouver 2010 Cultural Olympiad, Scotiabank Nuit Blanche, the Alberta Foundation for the Arts and the Canada Council for the Arts.

Lastly, my appreciation goes to the Royal Bank of Canada's Emerging Artists Project for its extraordinary support of this publication.

Jason de Haan

RBC Emerging Artists Project

Canada Council for the Arts / Conseil des Arts du Canada

Alberta Foundation for the Arts

Art Gallery of Nova Scotia

NOVA SCOTIA

SAAG Southern Alberta Art Gallery

City of Lethbridge

KITCHENER-WATERLOO ART GALLERY

Ontario Arts Council / Conseil des Arts de l'Ontario

This book is designed by Jason de Haan, with Toby Reid and Dana Woodward, and is published on the occasion of the following exhibitions:

Nowhere Bodily is Everywhere Ghostly
Curated by Ryan Doherty
Southern Alberta Art Gallery
September 29 - November 25, 2012

Noghwhere Bodili is Everywhere Goostly
Curated by David Diviney
Art Gallery of Nova Scotia
January 31 - April 16, 2014

Everywhere Ghostly is Nowhere Bodily
Curated by Crystal Mowry
Kitchener-Waterloo Art Gallery
September 26 - November 30, 2014

Published by:
Southern Alberta Art Gallery
601 Third Avenue South
Lethbridge, Alberta
T1J 0H4
www.saag.ca

Art Gallery of Nova Scotia
1723 Hollis Street
Halifax, Nova Scotia
B3J 1V9
www.artgalleryofnovascotia.ca

Kitchener-Waterloo Art Gallery
101 Queen Street North
Kitchener, ON
N2H 6P7
www.kwag.ca

Distributed by: ABC Art Books Canada
229-372, rue Sainte Catherine ouest
Montréal, QC H3B 1A2
www.ABCartbookscanada.com

Printed by: Shapco Printing Inc.
Printed in an edition of 1250 in the USA

Essays: Nicholas Brown, Candice Hopkins, Richard Rhodes

**The Skull With the Seashell Ear* is excerpted from *Luminous Debris: Reflecting on Vestige in Provence and Languedoc* by Gustaf Sobin and reprinted with the kind permission of the University of California Press.

Sobin, Gustaf. *Luminous Debris: Reflecting on Vestige in Provence and Languedoc.* Berkeley: University of California Press, 1999. http://ark.cdlib.org/ark:/13030/ft5j49p06s/.

Contributors: Jason de Haan, David Diviney, Ryan Doherty, Crystal Mowry

Editors: Shannon Anderson, David Diviney, Ryan Doherty, Crystal Mowry

Design: Jason de Haan with Toby Reid and Dana Woodward

Photography: Jason de Haan, Miruna Dragan, Jason Ebanks, Toni Hafkenscheid, Kris Lindskoog, David M. C. Miller and Petra Mala Miller, Paul Morstad and Dean Long, Clint Roenisch, Andrew Taggart and Chloe Lewis (MOLAF).

Library and Archives Canada Cataloguing in Publication
Everywhere goostly is noghwhere bodili : Jason de Haan / contributors, Nicholas Brown, David Diviney, Ryan Doherty, Candice Hopkins, Crystal Mowry, Richard Rhodes, Gustaf Sobin.

Published on the occasion of a travelling exhibition held September 29 - November 25, 2012 at the Southern Alberta Art Gallery; January 31 - April 16, 2014 at the Art Gallery of Nova Scotia; and September 26 - November 30, 2014 at the Kitchener-Waterloo Art Gallery.
ISBN 978-1-894699-61-7 (bound)

1. De Haan, Jason, 1981- --Exhibitions. I. Brown, Nicholas, 1982-, writer of added commentary II. Southern Alberta Art Gallery, issuing body, host institution III. Title: Jason de Haan.

N6549.D4257A4 2014 709.2 C2014-900024-3

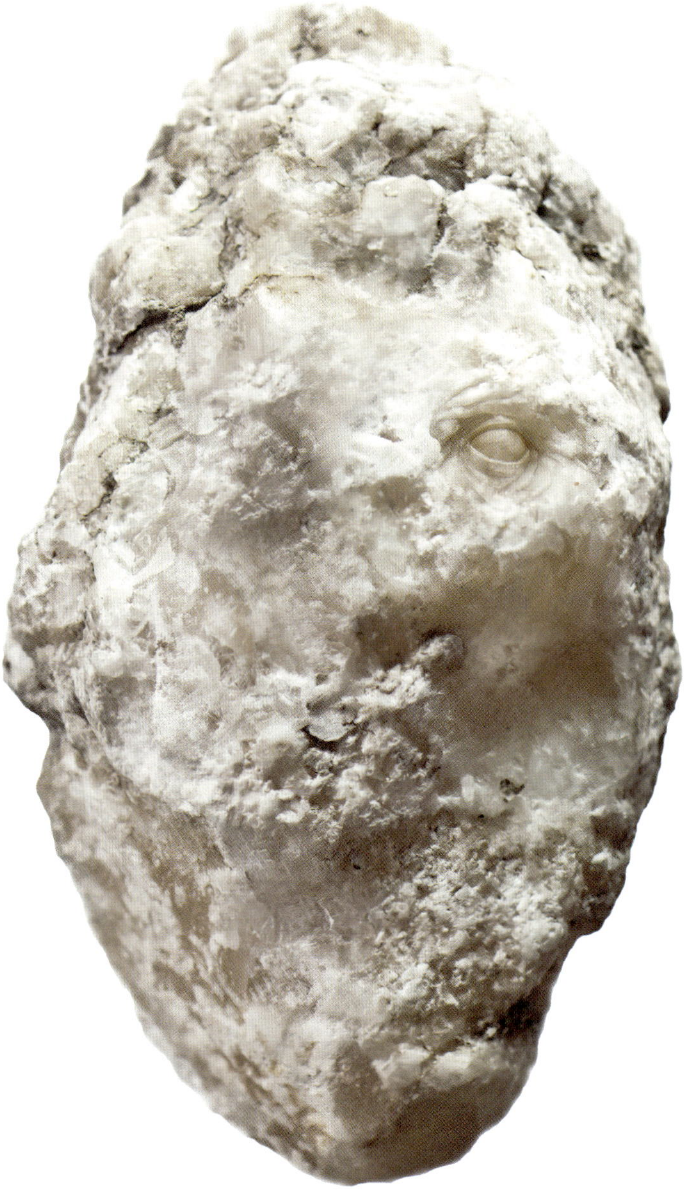

Noghwhere Bodili is Everywhere Goostly

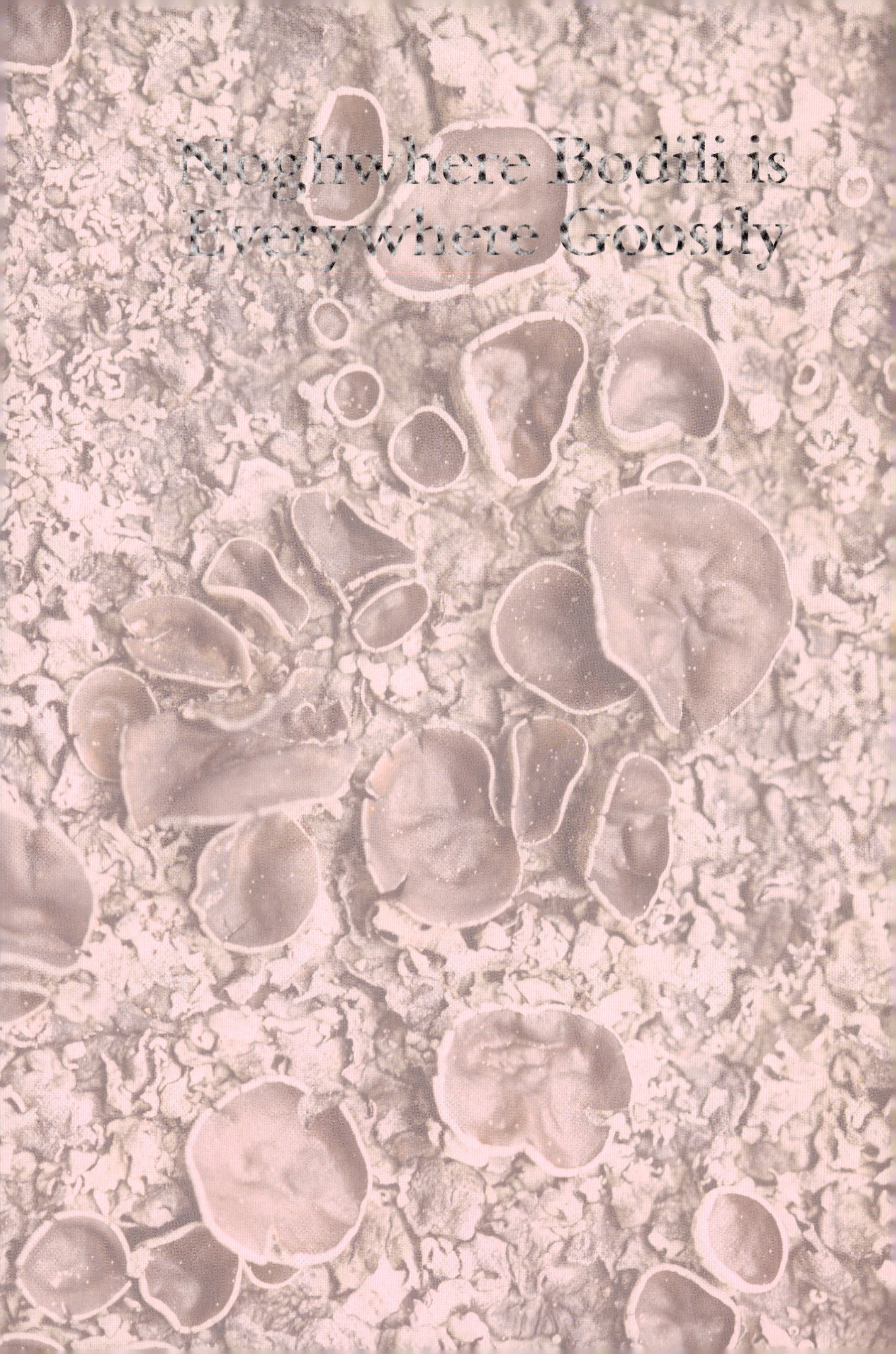

MMXIV